Plays of the 50s

VOLUME 2

edited by Katharine Brisbane

Currency Press • Sydney

CURRENCY PLAYS
General Editor: Katharine Brisbane

First published 2004
Currency Press Ltd,
PO Box 2287, Strawberry Hills, NSW, 2012, Australia.
enquiries@currency.com.au
www.currency.com.au

The Multi-Coloured Umbrella was first published in *Theatregoer*, Sydney, February/April 1961; *The Slaughter of St Teresa's Day* by Currency Press, Sydney, 1972; *Image in the Clay* by The University of Queensland Press, St Lucia, 1964.

Introduction © Katharine Brisbane, 2004; *The Multi-Coloured Umbrella* © Barbara Vernon, 1961; *The Slaughter of St Teresa's Day* © Peter Kenna, 1971; *Image in the Clay* © David Ireland, 1964; *The Life of the Party* © Ray Mathew, 2001.

NATIONAL LIBRARY OF AUSTRALIA CIP
DATA

Plays of the 50s.

ISBN 0 86819 695 9 (v.2).

1. Australian drama – 20th century.
I. Brisbane, Katharine.
(Series: Currency modern drama.)

A822.308

Set by Dean Nottle.
Printed by Ligare Book Printery.
Original cover design by Mango Design.

Australian Government

This project has been assisted by the Australian Government through the Australia Council, its arts funding and advisory body.

Contents

Introduction

Katharine Brisbane

Two events were of immediate significance in the emergence of these four plays. They are post the establishment of the Australian Elizabethan Theatre Trust (AETT) in 1954 and they are post-*Doll* (1955). They fill the space between the rush of exhilaration that followed the debut in Melbourne of *Summer of the Seventeenth Doll* in 1955 and the premiere of the much-vilified *The Ham Funeral* in Adelaide in 1961. They do more than that: they track the subterranean exploration that came to the surface with the hope these two events engendered and set the direction away from European realism towards a recognisably Australian rhythmic form.

Ray Lawler's *Summer of the Seventeenth Doll* was seen at the time (and for a good time after) as the spring—one of the many rebirths—of an Australia drama. From the distance of half a century we now see it as the consummate achievement of our realist domestic drama, the existence of which allowed the form to be questioned and, in a few years, discarded. Barbara Vernon's *The Multi-Coloured Umbrella* (1957) followed hard on its tail and was at once aligned with the *Doll* genre. But the play also has models in the author's keen observation of Australian manners and the American dramas of William Inge, William Gibson and Tennessee Williams. Peter Kenna's *The Slaughter of St Teresa's Day* (1959) shares the vernacular wit, the comedy turned to drama, the resolution by violence to be found in the *Doll* and other plays, but it is heightened in its language and more personal in its origins. David Ireland's *Image in the Clay* is a transitional piece, Chekhovian in form, moving further away from realism expressed by action towards a theatre of 'being'. And Ray Mathew's *The Life of the Party,* most radical of all, achieves the feat of being both a poet's critique of a rootless and damaged post-war urban Australia and a work that brings the Cold War down into the centre of the most remote Western nation in the world.

The reviewers and entrepreneurs of the time understandably did not know what to make of this new drama. What they had to compare it with were the British and American plays being presented by the commercial theatre and the 'world's best drama' offered by the amateur and semi-professional theatre.

Hugh Hunt, first director of the AETT—an Englishman with roots in the Dublin Abbey Theatre and Old Vic traditions—expressed the view that:

> Whilst it is too early to judge contemporary Australian dramatic literature, there is about the plays that have so far been performed a depressing similarity. From *Rusty Bugles* [1948] onwards these plays have belonged to 'the slice of life' school. Now, whilst the realistic play with its accurate observation of character, language and atmosphere has a rightful place in literature, it has obvious limitation and the limitations of backyard realism are considerable. Conflict and emotions are at the heart of all drama, but conflict can only be expressed by articulate people. When realism descends to the inhabitants of the backyard, conflict has to be couched in monosyllables and emotions have to take the form of physical violence. It is difficult to think of any Australian play which does not end up with a 'blue'. Passionate expression almost inevitably takes the form of fists and boots in a drama which cannot make full use of language.[1]

Hunt had clearly acquired no ear for the Australian language, but in 1958 it is certainly true that the *Doll*, Richard Beynon's *The Shifting Heart* (1957), Anthony Coburn's *The Bastard Country* (1959), *The Slaughter of St Teresa's Day* and *The Multi-Coloured Umbrella* were all superficially 'slice of life' and all ended in a 'blue'. In a country dubbed that year as suffering a 'cultural cringe'[2] the more colourful aspects of the working man and woman had defiantly become a preoccupation.

The AETT was not, however, directly responsible for the brief insurgence of these four plays and only one was found suitable for staging by the Trust management. All four were finalists in a variety of competitions offered in Australia by the Journalists' Club and General Motors' Holden and in London (for the Commonwealth) by the *Observer* newspaper. It was a flowering of the rising post-war appeal of the arts as a healing and friendship-gaining means towards achieving world peace and gave rise to the British Council and arts councils throughout Europe and the Commonwealth. *The Multi-Coloured Umbrella* found a path into the commercial theatre from Inverell, in northern New South Wales, where Barbara Vernon was a radio announcer and amateur actor and director. *The Slaughter of St Teresa's Day* became the first play presented by the AETT's short-lived national touring company, the Trust Players. *Image in the Clay* received its first performance at the tiny suburban Pocket Playhouse in Sydney; and *The Life of the Party* took the author to London,

---

[1] The second Kathleen Robinson Lecture at Sydney University, 1958, published in Hugh Hunt, *The Making of Australian Theatre*. Melbourne: Cheshire, 1960.

[2] A.A. Phillips, 'The Cultural Cringe' in *The Australian Tradition, Studies in a Colonial Culture*. Melbourne: F.W. Cheshire, 1958.

where it had its premiere at the Lyric Opera House, Hammersmith.

The Multi-Coloured Umbrella, after its first performance at the Inverell Town Hall, was given a thorough rewrite and taken up first by Melbourne's Little Theatre (later St Martin's Theatre) and then by Sir Frank Tait who mounted a two-week season for J.C. Williamson's at Sydney's Theatre Royal. The season was a mixed success. JCW's patronage in giving it a showing during a theatre's down-time, was no doubt spurred by the *Doll*'s unexpected box-office success.[3] The prosperous middle-class home in which it was set must have been a further reassurance. In essence the play is a melodrama in which the background colour of turf lingo supplies the necessary working-class vitality. The three-act structure is text-book and somewhat creaky, as it drives the narrative forward by employing one device after another to assemble the characters fortuitously. But it has three good curtains; and there is no doubting the authenticity of the characters, whom Vernon was soon to carry into popular radio and television with series like *Bellbird* (which she originated) and *Certain Women*. The script published here is taken from the magazine *Theatregoer* and is clearly a working script. 'One of the clear merits', wrote Leslie Rees,

> was that the author caught the exact tone of talk and manners of this crudely ebullient Australian family—crude in the sense of having pitiably little inwardness or self-understanding or gift of the tactful touch, while living, at their best, according to a domestic code dictated by conscience rather than by reason, and supervised in her own vigorous, direct way by the sharp-witted Mum.[4]

Much the same could be said of most of the plays that survive from this period.

For me the most interesting aspect of *The Multi-Coloured Umbrella* is the sex, as personified by Katherine. This was a time before the pill, when girls from respectable families 'saved themselves for marriage'. Information about sexual conduct was hard to come by. Popular models were the 'it' girls

---

[3] The JCW Salary Book (4 October 1955–31 October 1970, held by the NIDA library in the Sydney G. Irving Papers in the SBW Foundation archives, Folio 54) shows that J.C. Williamson Theatres Ltd acquired the performing rights for two years for the payment of £100 advance to the author and 5% of the gross takings, less entertainment tax. And that the principal actors were paid £35 per week and the juvenile £25. Robert Earle, who played Kevin Donnelly, was given permission to return to Melbourne on Thursdays and Sundays during the Sydney run at the expensive of JCW, and they had the option to replace him after the first fortnight. Earle, one guesses, was cast in one of the popular radio serials of the time. Or possibly TV, which was centred in Melbourne and had begun broadcasting in 1956.

[4] Leslie Rees, *The Making of Australian Drama, A Historical and Critical Survey from the 1830s to the 1970s*. Sydney: Angus & Robertson, 1973, p.291.

PLAYS OF THE 50s VOLUME 2

of the movies but strict Hayes Office censorship confined relationships to the sentimental or threatening. Katherine is a flirt, deeply unsure of herself and fearful of her own body; but conscious that such power as she has lies in her femininity. The lines are drawn very strikingly: for the men, success in life is equated with wide sexual experience. For the women, sex leads either to social ostracism or to social position and domestic confinement.

For Ben, the elder and responsible son, promiscuity gives him the stamp of maturity. For Joe, the younger, in love with a wife from the educated classes, his sexual ignorance is directly the cause of his business failings. Katherine's models are her mother-in-law Gloria, resilient and generous in her willing servitude, and Katherine's own mother, a busy GP, who is punished for pursuing a career by losing her husband to a more 'feminine' woman. This has drastic impact on Katherine's teenage sister, equally fearful of adult emotions of which she has been kept in ignorance.

The play follows Katherine from her first appearance as a beautiful but coldly tiresome poseur to the beginnings of an understanding of herself and her hidden fears. It is refreshingly outspoken on these matters, which, according to Rees, led to a level of public protest when it was later broadcast on ABC TV. The scenes between Katherine and Ben are redolent of movie melodrama, with Ben alternately playing Clark Gable and Marlon Brando, and some of the dialogue is repetitious. But Vernon brings off the third act with splendid precision. While the younger characters' problems may lie in their 'little inwardness or self-understanding', they are hardly reticent in expressing their feelings.

Nor can the characters in *The Slaughter of St Teresa's Day* be accused of being inarticulate. 'This new play', wrote *Sydney Morning Herald* critic Lindsey Brown,

> brilliant in its wit and speed of hundreds of its lines, has the kind of power and colour and observation to give much incidental excitement immediately to an audience and to promise that Mr Kenna will go close to flooring even the coolest of his patrons when experience gives him the sensibility and the cunning to reject long-drawn irrelevancies and enlarge underbuilt matters of importance.[5]

Kenna applies to his characters all the wit, garrulousness and poetry with which his Irish-Australian upbringing had imbued him. *Slaughter*, in which the underworld figure Oola Maguire holds a party to celebrate her survival after a gunshot wound, is a recognisable domestic comedy-drama, but its roots lie more deeply in memories retained of his family and the movies, of which Kenna was a devotee. While Horrie Darcel, with his smooth talk and his flick-knife, may never before have ventured outside a Hollywood movie,

---

[5]   *SMH*, 12 March 1959.

the others in the play introduce us to a half-imagined, half-remembered world the author continued to explore for the rest of his life.

Unfortunately, it was the Darcel element that preoccupied the critics at its first performance. H.G. Kippax, writing in *Nation*, found parallels with *Summer of the Seventeenth Doll*, both plays having low-life characters, a resilient humour and a symbolic figure that is smashed, along with the household's tenuous life. But, like Hunt, he bemoans the lack of conflict, complaining that even the party is held offstage.[6] He might equally have noted that *The Multi-Coloured Umbrella*, too, has its smashes: first its peach tree, a childhood memento, and then the umbrella itself, which, according to Rees, is an object coloured with our emotions and desires, that shades us from the light of our real motives.[7] These symbolic objects were popular in drama of the period, encapsulated in titles like *Moon on a Rainbow Shawl*, *A Streetcar Named Desire* and *Come Back, Little Sheba*. But the post-war period also produced the poetic dramas of T.S. Eliot, Christopher Fry and Maxwell Anderson (and indeed *Waiting for Godot*). Such symbols may have derived from a need, in this transitional period out of realism, to elevate the ordinary, to pay attention, as Arthur Miller demands in *Death of a Salesman*. However, while the umbrella and the statue of St Teresa have an honourable collegiate, they amount to no more than a narrative device.

But such devices as the arbitrary gunfight and the unlikely death of Charlie are distracting. They break into the vivid inner-city demi-monde that Kenna has created. What we see in the play today, of course, is not Kenna's fictional world of prostitution and illegal starting-price bookmaking but the first fruits of a store of fluent and feckless Irish-Australians that culminated in his great portraits of Agnes Cassidy and the Cassidy brothers of *A Hard God*. Thelma's innocence and over-protection are hard to credit today but Oola Maguire and Essie Farrell are two of the lustiest characters in our dramatic literature and his achievement, in the love story of Wilma, Whitey and Paddy, of articulating the inarticulate is a rare one.

WILMA: I'm sorry, love.
WHITEY *doesn't respond, but begins to play 'I Love You Truly'.*
WHITEY: A man's a fool to take it from you.
WILMA: I'm a worrier, White. I worry all the time. But what would I do if I lost you again? I don't want to let you out of my sight for a single second. I'm scared when you're away. Humour me. Please.
WHITEY: A man's a fool. [p.81]

---

[6] H.G. Kippax, 'Assaying the New Lode: More Aussie Talk at the Elizabethan', in *Nation*, 28 March 1959. Reproduced in *A Leader of His Craft: Theatre Reviews by H.G. Kippax*. Sydney: Currency House, 2004, pp.43–47.
[7] See Rees, p.291.

Paddy Maguire's flowery account of the 'big blue in Warwick', on the other hand, (one of Kenna's 'arias' as he called them) was equally denounced as undramatic; but in subsequent productions has proved less arduous than the critics in 1959 made it out to be. There is evidence that the premiere production did not do justice to the play. In the professional theatre a raw new script was an alien thing. Such photographs as survive show an uncomfortable group of largely-radio actors, their body-language at odds with the milieu in which they found themselves.[8] Actors at this time were famous for their skills at reproducing any accent in the world—except their own.

The looseness of the play's narrative was also a sticking point for the critics. But it is possible today to see in the play the beginnings of experiment in form away from exposition, climax and resolution. As Kenna wrote thirty years later, in a note on the play, he was seeking to capture 'a moment of our history: a time when a particular type of person believed certain things were important and spoke about them in much the same way as they appear in the script'. The context of both *The Multi-Coloured Umbrella* and *The Slaughter of St Teresa's Day* is vividly old-style Catholic; but while the characters in the former belong intrinsically to the 1950s, the imaginative world of the latter has a wider resonance.

Eunice Hanger, in an excellent contemporary survey of the rising drama, defined Ray Mathew as a 'lonely playwright', one of those who did not 'join the school' of the *Doll*, and who, she wrote, received very limited opportunity in the way of production. These playwrights 'are not alike in many ways, except in being strongly individual: their unlikeness to each other is the great quality they have in common'.[9]

> The distance that separated the lonely playwrights from these is more than anything else a distinction in the use of speech. The realistic playwright establishes his characters, and from there on they behave consistently with themselves, speak as we expect they will, react to new incidents as we could more or less accurately predict. The lonely playwrights heighten or intensify as a poet does, but not by using verse, and not all in the same way; they resemble each other in that the speech protects the characters from becoming stock, predictable characters.

---

[8] Lindsey Brown opined that Neva Carr Glynn (as Oola) 'with voice rough and eyes gaping glassily and scrolled hair way up in a ginger edifice, went for the comedy of the central role with enormous vitality, but nowhere in the first act and not much in the last did she find a way of communicating the warm sentiment and wringing drama at work in this madam'. Patricia Conolly (Thelma) and Dinah Shearing (Wilma) 'gave the performance a few of the many moments of deep emotion that the play demands'.

[9] Eunice Hanger, 'Introduction' in *A Spring Song, a Comedy by Ray Mathew*. St Lucia: University of Queensland Press, 1961, p.10.

They all have techniques... which are the writer's method of putting into dramatic form the way people seem to him to betray themselves to the world. They may use patterns of repetition; catch-phrases said, as it were, in inverted commas; phrases that start as clichés and become something unexpected and more expressive at the end. They may use the trick of a character's answering the unspoken reality that lies behind another character's speech, instead of directly answering that speech. They may speak without answering at all, because they are carrying on, under the surface, a private conversation with themselves, running as counterpoint to the talk of the other characters. Such technique distinguishes the plays of at least three lonely playwrights as well as Mathew: Jack McKinney, Kevin McNamara and David Ireland.[10]

In the wake of the *Doll*'s winning formula, it was difficult for directors and critics to enlarge their appreciation of form, and for actors to conceive of a heightened style of acting; but what Hanger describes can be traced back to poet-dramatists like Louis Esson, Katharine Susannah Prichard and Douglas Stewart; and forward to Patrick White, Dorothy Hewett, Alex Buzo, Jack Hibberd, John Romeril, Stephen Sewell and Joanna Murray-Smith. These are not 'slice of life' writers; their characters are host to the words, as musical instruments are to their music; and their text is a score of subtle rhythms. *The Slaughter of St Teresa's Day* can been seen in this light as an apprentice piece through which, in the writing, Kenna discovered the poetic reality which became the canvas of his drama.

With David Ireland's *Image in the Clay* we enter another half-imagined, half-remembered world. Here we find again character and conflict but very little narrative and no resolution. Here we find, too, a smashed figure; but much more integral to the theme than the previous symbols. What is most radical about Ireland's approach is its writerly focus on capturing, as Kenna says, 'a moment in our history' and the almost clinical means he uses to do it. Ireland's moment is some time in the 1950s when he camped on a river bank and observed on the opposite bank an Aboriginal family. The play reflects that distance. He observes their daily habits, their quarrelling. He draws them as he sees them, without offering hope or pity or larger meaning: a day in their lives at the end of the road. 'They are people', writes Ireland. 'That is my interest.' Both their language and their actions are violent: violence is a kind of metaphor for survival—and understood as such by the family. There are contradictions: Gunner has adopted the deserted child Joy, who calls him father, but refutes that act of humanity by habitual rejections. The self is uppermost in each character and yet, when outsiders threaten they fall into polished

---

[10] Hanger, p.13. Jack McKinney's *The Well* is published in Katharine Brisbane (ed.), *Plays of the 60s Vol 1*. Sydney: Currency Press, 2000.

performance of mutual defence. The sons' homecoming is expected with anticipation; and yet the old patterns of rivalry and abuse are resumed. The play opens in the early morning and ends at midnight, by which time the family and their shabby home have been swept away. No resistance is raised, no attempt is made to change the course. The audience grasps this at the start. Gorooh, the elder, mourns the passing of his tribe but spends his days listening to the radio outside the pub; Billy, whom he sent on walkabout, has become a cadger and a drunk. Gunner, the former sniper who picked off Japanese in New Guinea, now chooses the 'freedom' of his fishing and ranting to a job at his white father's timber mill.

They break apart without a murmur, each acknowledging in turn that the white man's ways have won; each settling for least resistance as the bulldozers move in. Ireland sees it as a tragedy in the Oedipal sense that each finds in himself the seeds of his (or her) own destruction. Central to this is Joy and the clay figure she calls her Daddy. Child as she is, she has found in it an imaginary friend with whom to confide her condition. The figure is Gunner's, one of many he has made and buried, ashamed of the softness it reveals, perhaps a link with his own childhood. Today a gun is his secret totem; but perhaps it is this buried collection that keeps him at the river bank, hidden proof of his own secret self. Joy's 'Daddy' is crushed and with it her childhood. She moves without a murmur into the adult world of prostitution and drink.

Joy makes an interesting comparison with Kenna's wimpish Thelma. While Thelma has been protected from everything that could prepare her for real life, Joy's abusive existence has taught her little wiliness, only dependence. The implication from both authors is that these children are unformed human beings and that, deprived of adult protection, they will surrender to the worst the world offers.

Like the 'lonely playwrights' that followed, Ireland's form is dictated by his subjects and the rhythm of their lives. It is almost a contemplative approach, despite the outbursts of violence. But sadly, Australia had no theatre ready for such a play—neither the actors nor the audience. *Image in the Clay* was just one of the works that remained the possession of such forward-thinking theatres as the 66-seat Pocket Playhouse (1948–73). Up to that time there had been plays written about Aboriginal families, notably the work of George Landen Dann in Queensland. In 1960 Oriel Gray's play *Burst of Summer* won attention in Melbourne.[11] These two were probably the last plays that an all-white theatre group could in conscience perform before the civil rights movement of the 1960s awakened Anglo-Australians to the issue of appropriation. Like others before him, after this play Ireland turned to the novel to which he carried his exploration of form and rhythm further.

---

[11] See *Plays of the 60s Vol 1.*

The Life of the Party now makes the quantum leap out of the predictable world of realist drama. Ray Mathew's work is possibly the first to emerge from the provincial, predating even Patrick White (if one discounts the 1949 origin of *The Ham Funeral*). Eunice Hanger believed Mathew's reputation as a playwright would have been made before Lawler's had there earlier been a body to present his work professionally.[12] So it was no wonder that *The Life of the Party* saw its first stage in the United Kingdom. The play was a finalist in the London *Observer* contest in 1957, which gained Mathew a passage to London where *The Life of the Party* opened at the Lyric, Hammersmith, in 1960, followed in 1964 by *A Spring Song* (1958), firstly at the Edinburgh Festival and then at London's Mermaid Theatre. *The Life of the Party*'s cast was led by Alan Badel, had a distinguished director in Frith Banbury and design by Australia's legendary Loudon Sainthill. The critics, however, were not kind, most denouncing the work's verbosity. Bernard Levin in the *Daily Express* thought that,

> What with a lot of drink and a variety of suicides the whole thing puts me dangerously in mind of Robert Benchley's eager description of a 'great party, with fireworks and retchings'. But the quality is more serious and more difficult to define. It suggests, in its torrentially articulate incoherence, that this is what *Look Back in Anger* would have been like if Mr Osborne had been drunk when he wrote it.[13]

Penelope Gilliatt in the *Queen*, deduces that the play's wordiness is due to Mathew being a radio writer.

> The frenetic central character… is a radio dramatist who at moments of real self-loathing recites lines from his own scripts, appalled and pained by the awfulness of what he has written. Australia, one feels, is no place for this miserable farceur, for even King's Cross, the red-light district of Sydney where I assume the action to be going on, is palpably a far from over-sophisticated place. The implication is that the hero is a homosexual but the childishly aggressive promiscuity of his heterosexual friends leads him to have a series of affairs with girls who leave him feeling more foreign than ever. As played by Alan Badel, who sticks out like a healthy thumb in a company that is otherwise a pretty sore hand, he is a dynamic character to watch, subject to sudden attacks of *cafard* among the hypomanic capers; and he has some very funny lines.[14]

---

[12] Hanger, p.3.

[13] Bernard Levin, 'Down among these beatnicks Mr Badel really stirs', *Daily Express,* 23 November 1960.

[14] Penelope Gilliatt, 'Talking-Type Actors', *Queen,* 7 December 1960.

The veteran Harold Hobson in the *Sunday Times*, however, goes to the heart of the matter. He begins by quoting Pascal, 'the eternal silence of these infinite spaces frightens me…', and Robert Frost, 'They cannot scare me with their empty spaces…', and shows how Mathew's characters share their fears.

> For them these infinite spaces are no longer to be eternally silent: some say the Bomb will explode. Until it does they're lost people in a hopeless universe, in which God in the end kills Himself; they talk eagerly, wildly, madly to each other in order to fill the void they cannot bear to contemplate in sanity.[15]

Hobson admires the play and Badel's performance; but has a major reservation: 'Though he is a major character in the conversations, he is a minor one in the story, which disappointingly is concerned with one Jack, a bearish, boorish, bullish and boring fellow who wants to succeed in life, but never mentions what at'.

Forty years later the Cold War and the aftermath of World War Two transparently pervade the play. Alex and Jack are ex-servicemen who share a war experience of which they never speak; but which provides a bond. Having seen the worst that humanity can perpetrate they have returned to the only corner of their provincial home that is not absorbed in the getting and spending of post-war affluence. At the time the play was written Nikita Kruschev was Secretary General of the USSR. Stalin had died in 1953 and the process of de-Stalinisation had begun. In 1956 Maralinga was testing nuclear bombs. In 1957 Sputnik was in the sky. As Hobson says, space was no longer empty, the overwhelming threat of nuclear war had created a fever of uncertainty which ended with the Cuban missile crisis in 1963. The place of women was equally uncertain. Those who had kept family and industry alive during the war found their returning men estranged and their jobs confiscated.

Little of this appears overtly in the play: only a sense of frustration and of a world without a future. We know little of how they earn their living. Alex is a radio writer and actor, Marina a typist. The bohemian world described was not unfamiliar in the 1950s and reminds me of the stories of radio actors, who lived at a high pitch of histrionics around favourite Sydney pubs. The chief histrionics, of course, come from Alex, a homosexual with a sophistication that has gained him three women lovers. Alex is manic-depressive, death-possessed and in love with Jack, a pointlessly promiscuous young man and a gambler, married to Moira, who is desperately attempting to make order out of the chaos of their marriage. Through the frenetic dialogue run the themes of love, death, poetry and the bomb. Jack and Sylvie attempt a love affair while Alex compares them to Tristan and Isolde. Peg, an aged actress, fights

---

[15] Harold Hobson, 'A Week of Bewilderment', *Sunday Times*, 27 November 1960.

self-deception; the silent Tanya, one of Europe's displaced persons, commits suicide; one by one the characters awake—or are rudely shaken awake—from their dream and settle for the possible, as Marina does, by marrying an accountant; as Jack and Sylvie do, faced with a moment of near-death; as Moira does by bearing a child. In this respect the play makes an interesting comparison with *Coralie Lansdowne Says No* (1974), written at a time of similar trepidation[16] In a letter about the play Mathew wrote to me from New York:

> You feel/hear the Cold War! I would not have used that term, but I intended that un-suspenseful suspense, that dispiriting vision of unseemly alternatives, that pall to be the shadow in which they (we) lived. 'Let's pretend that we're spies. I don't know what for.' Does Alex have that in your script?
>
> It reads here and now silly, pretentious, politicians' portentousness, but in the poetry of the play it was the truth that went on creating itself. The party next door—the party next week, last week… For us they are all the same. We have no party. Whim, appetite, invention of need, a sense of unease, guilt, loss, embarrassment… That's us. And is there anyone other than one's self? Dare there be? Dare one admit there are? These are afterwards, afterwords, but that feeling really was there and somehow I hope it expressed itself. That feeling, those feelings— vague, half-felt, half-thought-on, were sharpened and saddened by what I saw of Frank Hardy, at some public do we sat together; I remember him as pale, and sounding pale, unable to comprehend (apprehend?) what the Law and the Press and the Party had done to him. He was party-less. He talked bravely enough; he was an Australian, and a Man, and a Good and Faithful Servant, but I thought he sounded lost, not sorry for himself, but sad—sad beyond self.[17]
>
> But all this is a babbling, blurting attempt to explain the obvious, which I have never done before. In my ignorance/arrogance I believed it was in the play, that it was the play, that it was what you took away from the play. I was wrong. The reviews—there were dozens— demolished me. It took me ten years sober and daily AA to admit that fact—and I still despise myself for being that vulnerable.[18]

Reid Douglas, in his entry on Mathew in *Contemporary Dramatists* 1973, calls him 'technically the most sophisticated playwright Australia has produced'.

---

[16] In *Plays of the 70s Vol 2*, (1999).

[17] Frank Hardy, novelist, journalist and prominent Communist, was author of the novel *Power Without Glory* (1950), which became the subject of a notorious libel suit. The trial lasted nine months before acquitting him.

[18] Letter from the author, 21 May 2001. In the possession of Currency Press.

He stresses how Mathew's work as poet materially influenced his drama:

> His dialogue is based on idiomatic syntax, built into rhythmic blocks and
> caesura and stresses placed as they are by the sub-group to which
> each character belongs. This leaves the impression of real speech but
> creates a denser texture and much broader emotional range.[19]

And Douglas grimly concludes:

> Ray Mathew's work was not maximised, either quantitatively or
> qualitatively, at its point of origin. His characteristic qualities need to be
> confirmed and consolidated by major Australian directors and actors.
> When staged in England, with that form of Cockney-cum-Loamshire
> which passes there for an Australian dialect, the plays—perhaps
> predictably—failed.

Douglas's put-down of the English production is probably as biased as any of
the commentators. The reader will draw his or her own conclusion about
whether what Ray Mathew avowedly intended is apparent in the text. *The
Life of the Party* was never (as far as we can discover) performed in Australia;
and Mathew never returned here. He continued to publish poetry, criticism
and journalism. In 1967 he published his only novel, *The Joys of Passion*,
which 'is partly autobiographical and draws on his talent as a social
comedian'.[20] He died in New York in 2003.

---

[19] Reid Douglas, 'Ray Mathew' in James Vinson (ed.), *Contemporary Dramatists*.
   London: St James Press; New York: St Martin's Press, 1961. White, Lawler and
   Seymour were the other Australians who made it into this first edition.

[20] William H. Wilde, Joy Hooton and Barry Andrews, *The Oxford Companion to
   Australian Literature*. Melbourne: Oxford University Press, 1985, p.471.

The Multi-Coloured Umbrella

Barbara Vernon

Barbara Vernon (1916–78) grew up in Inverell, northern NSW, and studied Arts at University of Queensland. She served in the Psychological Division of the RAAF in World War Two and later joined radio station 2NZ, Inverell, as an announcer. *The Multi-Coloured Umbrella* won second prize in the Sydney Journalists' Club competition in 1956 and premiered in 1957. In 1959 she moved to Sydney and in 1966 joined the ABC Drama Department as a script editor. She was a prolific writer for stage, radio and television. Her plays include *The Passionate Pianist* (1958) one of a trilogy of plays, *The Naked Possum*, and many one-acters and plays for children. *The Multi-Coloured Umbrella* was broadcast by ABC TV in January 1958. She originated the long-running TV serial, *Bellbird* (1967–76), wrote the acclaimed adaptation of *Seven Little Australians* (1973) and contributed to *Certain Women* (1973–6).

*Brenda De Lacy as Eileen and Marjorie Archibald as Gloria in the 1957 J.C.
Williamson production of THE MULTI-COLOURED UMBRELLA. (Courtesy of the
Performing Arts Museum, Victorian Arts Centre)*

FIRST PERFORMANCE

The Multi-Coloured Umbrella was first produced by the Melbourne Little Theatre and subsequently broadcast on ABC Television and national radio.

Produced by Sir Frank Tait for J.C. Williamson's, a season opened at the Theatre Royal, Sydney, on 9 November, 1957, with the following cast:

KEVIN DONNELLY	Robert Earle
GLORIA DONNELLY	Marjorie Archibald
JOE DONNELLY	Jeffrey Hodgson
KATHERINE DONNELLY	Pamela Greenall
BEN DONNELLY	Peter Aanenson
EILEEN HOWARD	Brenda de Lacy

Director, Peter Randall

CHARACTERS

KEVIN DONNELLY, Dadda
GLORIA DONNELLY, Mumma
JOE DONNELLY, 24
KATHERINE DONNELLY
BEN DONNELLY
EILEEN HOWARD

EDITOR'S NOTE

The Multi-Coloured Umbrella was first published in the magazine *Theatregoer*, February/April 1961, edited by the admirable Frank Harvey. The text reflects the careful explication usual among playwrights up to this time who wrote for a theatre that barely existed. I am grateful to John Senczuk who arranged a reading of the play in 2001 and made some small judicious cuts to some of the stage directions and the dialogue for the comfort of today's reader.

ACT ONE

It is a summer evening in Sydney.

The flat roof of the Donnelly house has been fitted as a sun deck. A flight of steps leads down to the small garden. Beyond the parapet we see a headland, closely built over, and below, the curve of the sand. A glass door, standing open with the breeze, leads from the sun deck into the upper storey of the house.

KEVIN DONNELLY *lies on a cane lounge, his shoes off. He is either asleep, or persuading himself that it is too early to move. He is partly shaded by a multi-coloured umbrella. There are other chairs and a table. A portable radio blares music and commercials. The furniture is of excellent quality and expensive, but it has been chosen directly from displays of such goods.* GLORIA DONNELLY—MUMMA—*calls from the living room beyond the glass doors.*

GLORIA: [*offstage*] Hey—Dadda!

> KEVIN *continues to slumber.*

Dadda—Dadda—you turn that wireless off! You're wearing out the batteries.

> *The radio continues to blare.*

I don't know why you can't jest open the windows, on account of we all know it almost blows you off the balcony now Ben got that hi-fi. But no, you gotter take the portable, and wear out the batteries.

> *She appears in the doorway.*

How you can sleep through it, I wouldn't have the slightest idea. You ain't even lying on your deaf side.

> *She turns off the wireless and slaps* KEVIN *companionably, but with resonance.*

Sit up, you lazy so-and-so bludger, and put on yer shoes. They'll be here in a minute.

KEVIN: If anyone had ever told me I'd marry a nagger, I'd 'ave said to get their 'eads read. [*He sits up, a good-looking, solidly-built man in his forties.*] What won the four-forty, Mumma? Honey Flow?

GLORIA: What do you care? You didn't have a bet on it?

KEVIN: No, but a coupla hundred suckers would. And Joe is jest the boy to 'ave laid 'em evens. [*He yawns.*] I sometimes wonder if it was only his looks that kid got from the iceman.

GLORIA: Well, a girl would've had to do something, married to a big lug like you.

> KEVIN *grins and fishes for his shoes.*

KEVIN: That's brazen me own wife is, she doesn't even deny it. [*Fishing*] Doesn't even deny it. How do you like that?

GLORIA: Don't you talk like that in front of Katey.

KEVIN: Aw—she wouldn't mind.

GLORIA: Maybe she wouldn't, but Joe would. You know he watches his language when she's around.

KEVIN: Never thought to see the day me own son would turn out to be a pansy.

> *He finds the second shoe on the last word and brings it out triumphantly.*

GLORIA: Thought you was jest blaming Joe on the iceman.

KEVIN: Iceman, milkman, postman, a man's got no security in a wicked world like this.

> *He begins to lace up his shoes.* GLORIA *begins to bring glasses, savouries and bottles from the room.*

GLORIA: Well, you heard me. Don't talk like that in front of Katey.

KEVIN: She's been living in this family for a year and she hasn't heard a word out of place yet, has she?

GLORIA: [*offstage*] Much!

KEVIN: Well, why should I watch me tongue for the benefit of a society duchess me younger son ups and marries? If she's so fussy, why did she marry Joe?

GLORIA: [*coming back in*] Joe's real nice-minded.

KEVIN: [*shocked*] Mumma!

GLORIA: I don't see what's wrong with it.

KEVIN: It makes him sound like a queer.

GLORIA: That's another word you can chop right out. Ben said it last night in front of Katey, and Joe went off properly.

KEVIN: Joe went for Ben when Kate was there?

GLORIA: After.

KEVIN: Doesn't she know what it means?

GLORIA: How would I know what she understands?

KEVIN: Then why are you so ruddy careful about her feelings?

GLORIA: Look, as far as I'm concerned I'd like to get up one day and say a few things that'd rot the little cotton socks right off her...

KEVIN: Why don't you, then? [*Twinkling*] You're the woman to do it, Mumma.

> GLORIA *stands beside him.*

GLORIA: [*seriously*] I don't on account of it'd hurt Joe.

KEVIN: Joe is twenty-four years old, Mumma.

GLORIA: Yes, I know. Married and everything. But you can't say things about a man's wife, Dadda. Especially when the man's Joe.

KEVIN: No. Give 's a drink, love, before they get 'ere. I got a mouth like the floor of a parrot cage.

GLORIA: Serves yer right. A man of your age out with the boys.

She pours him a drink.

KEVIN: Ah—ta!

He takes it gratefully.

GLORIA: Dadda—

KEVIN: Um?

GLORIA: Strike you as funny they don't have any kids?

KEVIN: No.

GLORIA: No?

KEVIN: No. Look at the hips on her. Too narrer. Not a bit like you, Mumma. You had two, and never give more than a coupla squawks.

GLORIA: How would you know, all that you did was booze until I was well enough to come home.

KEVIN: A man's got to wet the baby's head.

GLORIA: You might at least wait until he's here before you start. [*Pause.*] You think they've been trying… and can't?

KEVIN: I dunno. I sleep in me own room.

GLORIA: There you go again.

KEVIN: Look, the flamin' delicate petunia isn't here yet, is she?

GLORIA: You don't like her, either.

KEVIN: Like her? When Joe first bring her home I knew that me son was hooked. So I said to meself—Keep out of it, don't interfere. It's like on the racecourse, no interference. If you get in the way you're likely to get quite a bit of crowding, not to mention the nosiness of the stewards. [*He drinks.*] Them creeps! Look, Mumma, I wish you hadn't turned the wireless off. It might have made a hell of a lot of difference if Honey Flow won.

GLORIA: They'll be here in a minute and they'll tell you.

KEVIN: [*gloomily*] Tell me they done the whole bloody roll. Joe's too good-natured. I tell him to leave it to Ben, but will he?

GLORIA: Joe is too good-natured. That's what I'm complaining about. He never sees anything wrong with her.

KEVIN: Well, there isn't really—is there? Only that she isn't our sort.

GLORIA: It wouldn't matter so much about her family, if she was different herself. She isn't exactly a snob, that's what worries me.

KEVIN: You aren't suggesting she married Joe for his money, are you?

GLORIA: She could've, Dadda.

KEVIN: [*shaking his head*] No.

GLORIA: Why—no?

KEVIN: Because in that case she'd 've married Ben.

GLORIA: Perhaps Ben wouldn't be as easy as Joe.

KEVIN: No. But he'd be a hell of a lot more fun.

GLORIA: Joe's the one everyone likes, and you know it.

KEVIN: Since when has a girl wanted someone everyone likes? Ben's got plenty of what it takes.

GLORIA: Ben isn't…

KEVIN: Ben isn't what?

GLORIA: Ben isn't the marrying kind.

KEVIN: No, but he don't have no trouble finding women to go to bed with, not Ben.

GLORIA: You got the dirtiest mouth, Kevin Donnelly!

KEVIN: Look, I got to watch me tongue with my prissy daughter-in-law. All right, I'll watch it. But I won't watch it with me own wife. Especially when she can tell me a joke that still curls me 'air.

GLORIA: Who taught the dirty jokes to me?

KEVIN: The iceman.

GLORIA: I wish you'd lay off the iceman. We've 'ad a fridge for years.

KEVIN: We didn't 'ave one twenty-one years ago when Ben come along.

    Pause.

GLORIA: You don't think she's interested in Ben, do you?

KEVIN: I know damn well he isn't interested in her. He thinks she's a crab. Gimme another drink and forget it.

GLORIA: I—I can't forget it, Dadda.

KEVIN: Yes, you can. It's none of our business.

GLORIA: If she hurts Joe, Kev, so help me, I'll go after her with a razor.

KEVIN: Look, Mumma, it's none of your business. He's got to grow up sometime.

GLORIA: I'm not interfering. I'm not one of those women like your old woman.

KEVIN: [*piously*] Rest 'er soul.

GLORIA: There may be rest for 'er soul, but I bet no one else'll rest while she's got a tongue in 'er 'ead.

KEVIN: Wonderful old girl. Seventy-eight years of age and noticed everything that was going on 'round 'er.

GLORIA: I'll say she did.

KEVIN: And me dear, sainted mother is the reason that I keep outa this. [*With a decided twinkle*] Now if you could 'ave heard her when I said I was all set to marry Gloria Regan…

GLORIA: Old so-and-so. [*She rises and goes to the drinks table, then turns and speaks pleadingly.*] Kev, you don't think she could have had Ben, do you?

KEVIN: Not to marry.

GLORIA: You're sure, Kev?

KEVIN: You're worried that Ben's got a letch for her?

GLORIA: Well, if he has… you know what'll happen.

KEVIN: Joe'll paste 'im one, and serve him right.

GLORIA: Joe'll pretend not to notice, the same as he pretended about Hathaway.

KEVIN: [*warningly*] Mumma!

GLORIA: Well, there was more to that than handies-under-the-table, you know there was.

KEVIN: I hear no evil, see no evil and speak no evil. [*Pleadingly*] Love, give us a drink.

GLORIA: [*exasperated*] Sometimes I reckon all I married was a animated sponge!

She pours the drink.

KEVIN: You are a very fine figure of a woman, Mumma.

GLORIA: And you're a drunken sod. Why I put up with you…

KEVIN: [*cheerfully*] Me boyish charm.

GLORIA: [*submitting*] Oh, Kev, I do hope Ben isn't—

KEVIN: If he is, love, neither you nor me'll stop him. Nor Joe, if it comes to that.

A car horn is heard.

GLORIA: [*leaping up*] That's Joe.

She leans over the parapet and waves.

JOE: [*below*] How are you, Mum?

GLORIA: Fine, love.

KEVIN: How did you do, Joe?

GLORIA: For heaven's sake, Dadda, don't yell so loudly. [*She turns and speaks softly.*] Katey's with him.

KEVIN: [*grumbling*] Well, I wanta know if we done the whole roll on Honey Flow.

A car door slams. Voices are heard.

GLORIA: Kev, don't start asking Joe about what he lost the very minute he comes in the door. Give 'im a chance for once.

KEVIN: Look, is he making a book or isn't he?

GLORIA: He's not as good at it as Ben.

KEVIN: Look, Mum, is Joe making a book or isn't he?

GLORIA: Wait till Ben gets here—

KEVIN: That's all I want to know. And if he's making a book—

GLORIA: [*angrily*] You shut your trap! You hear me, Kevin Donnelly?

KEVIN: Look, is he making a book or—?

JOE: [*offstage*] Where is everybody?

JOE comes onto the roof, KATE is with him.

Mum—why didn't you come out? You could still have knocked spots off all the dames on the lawns, couldn't she, Katherine?

GLORIA: [*pleased*] Let me go, Joe, you great galoot. [*She pats her skirt down.*] How are you, Katey?

KATE: Very well, thank you.

JOE: [*exuberant*] Who do you think won a packet off the Tote? None other than little Katey! Wouldn't pass any business her old man's way. Not her. How are you, Dad? Getting a start on with the booze?

KEVIN: Did Honey Flow win?

JOE: Only turned to scratch itself a couple of times, and then ate a bit of grass, and still come in ahead of the field. That horse—that horse is another Phar Lap. I'm giving you the drum. It's another Phar Lap. [*To* KATE] What are you drinking, love?

KATE: Lemonade, thank you.

JOE: Oh, come off it, Katey. This is a celebration. It isn't every day my wife skins the blasted Tote, I can tell you. I'll give you a gin and ginger, eh?

KATE: I said lemonade, Joe.

JOE: But, love, you know you've got a headache, and a bit of gin and—

KATE: For heaven's sake, Joe!

JOE: All right, have it your own way. [*Pouring drinks*] What you drinking, Mum?

GLORIA: Gin and ginger.

JOE: Now there's a woman that knows what's good for her.

KEVIN: What did you give 'em on Honey Flow?

JOE: Evens.

KEVIN: Goddlemighty, yer wife 'ud need to win on the Tote.

GLORIA: [*warningly*] Kevin!

KEVIN: I didn't say anything, did I?

JOE: Now listen, Dad, you can't absolutely crab every chance the poor b's have got, can you? And I did get some information, confidential, at the last moment…

KEVIN: Where the 'ell was Ben?

JOE: He was laying some off.

KEVIN: How many times have I got to tell you—?

GLORIA: Kevin!

KEVIN: Oh, all right.

> *A slight pause.* JOE *glances at his father, shrugs, then swallows his liquor.*

GLORIA: Aren't you feeling well, Katey?

KATE: I had a sun headache, that's all. Joe always exaggerates everything.

GLORIA: I only thought—you drinking lemonade…

KATE: I often drink lemonade.

GLORIA: [*dashed*] Oh!

JOE: Now, Mum, don't you go dashing to conclusions. Told you you should have made it gin and ginger, love.

KATE: [*putting down her glass*] Would it make you feel better if I drank one?

JOE: You can drink whatever you like, when you like, because you like.

KATE: Thank you very much.

> *Pause.*

KEVIN: Where's Ben now?

JOE: Coming. He had to take Noreen home.

KEVIN: Why didn't he bring her here to have a drink? I like Noreen. She's a good sort.

JOE: I hope she and Ben make a go of it. Everyone should get married. Sign of me being a happy husband, isn't it, Katey?

KATE *rises.*

KATE: It's wonderful to get the breeze off the sea, Mrs Donnelly. It was so hot at the races.

GLORIA: It's always cool here.

KATE: Joe and I are going to try and get a house over the water. It's so hot where we are.

GLORIA: You want to get out of that flat. Not that it isn't convenient, but you want something a bit bigger.

JOE: Just to encourage us to see about a few grandchildren, eh Mum? [*With a laugh*] Read you like a book, don't I, old girl? How about it, Katey?

KATE: [*lightly*] Man proposes, God disposes.

JOE: You're right, though, Mum. Kate's too cooped up there. We want a decent big place. It isn't as if we can't afford it.

KEVIN: Is that that man that laid evens on Honey Flow talking?

JOE: Well, I tell you, I had good information.

KEVIN: I got a very good mind to wring Ben's neck.

JOE: It was my doing, Dad, and Ben went through me himself about it.

KEVIN: He wants to keep his mind on what he's doing.

JOE: Judging from what Noreen was saying he did that a bit too thoroughly.

GLORIA: What do you mean?

JOE: Well, you know Ben. He took Noreen and then left her to chase another skirt. Phew! Did the fur fly! That dame's worse than my little woman when she sees green.

GLORIA: But I thought Ben was keen on Noreen.

JOE: Oh, Ben's in no hurry, Mum. Why should he be? I'm the only faithful one in this family. I gotter be. If I wasn't, Katey here would scratch me eyes out, wouldn't you, love?

KATE: [*with her first smile of the afternoon*] Yes.

She puts her hand up and touches JOE's *cheek. His face transforms.*

JOE: Can I pick 'em, or can I pick 'em? Gee, Mum, did you ever see anything lovelier?

A phone is heard ringing inside.

Sit down, Mum—

He dashes inside. Pause. KEVIN *pours himself another drink.* KATE *sits on the parapet and* GLORIA *sits in one of the cane chairs.*

[*Offstage*] Hello—hello—hello— [*Pause.*] Your fourpence, chum...

GLORIA: Where was you getting this house, Katey? Around here?

JOE: [*offstage*] Fred? Fred Watson?... Well what's up with you, Fred...?

KATE: We thought further out. Where it's quieter.

JOE: [*offstage*] Look, Fred, I told you about it, didn't I? At the time I told you...

GLORIA: But, love, it isn't natural for young people to be in the backblocks...

JOE: [*offstage*] Well, Fred, I told you that a chap told me... I don't know his name... Charlie something...

KATE: We'd hardly be in the backblocks, would we? Just a bit further up the coast.

JOE: [*offstage*] Well, how am I supposed to know he was talking through his mullet head?

GLORIA: You know best, of course, but it's nicer to be near enough to do a bit of shopping.

JOE: [*offstage*] Well, tell Ben I'll explain it. For the love of— No one's blaming you, Fred... All right, Fred... Yes, all right. If you want to... Yes, Fred. G'bye, Fred.

> *The phone is hung up.* JOE *emerges, somewhat crestfallen.*

[*Somewhat unnecessarily*] That was Fred.

KEVIN: [*sarcastically*] We would never have guessed. What's up with him?

JOE: Bellyaching about the price we give on Honey Flow.

KEVIN: Well, you musta been outa your damn mind. Why the hell didn't you leave it to Ben? He's got a business head. Now Honey Flow...

GLORIA: [*passionately*] If anyone says Honey Flow to me again I'm going to throw up, right over this balcony. The firm won't go broke just because Joe made a little business mistake, will it?

KEVIN: Well, he'd better not do it too often.

> KEVIN *drinks morosely.*

GLORIA: [*working herself up*] You been nagging about that blasted horse all the afternoon. You been nagging about that blasted horse all week. Is it the first time a book's been skinned on one mount? You never ask how they did on the others. They could have won on every other blasted horse at the meeting, but you don't ask about that! You just got a fixation on Honey Flow!

KEVIN: If you're suggesting I'm nagging, what do you think you're doing this very minute?

GLORIA: Well, I told you not to talk bookmaking, bookmaking, bookmaking!

KEVIN: When I am dead and gorn, you'll be sorry!

> *He declaims this with some passion. Then he drinks; then he twinkles; then he pinches* GLORIA*'s bottom.*

GLORIA: Kevin Donnelly!

KEVIN: Sorry, love. Lost me 'ead.

GLORIA *laughs.* JOE *moves back to* KATE *who has been watching this scene without much expression.*

GLORIA: Ben is coming out, isn't he, Joe?

JOE: I think so.

KEVIN: What did Fred Watson want, anyhow?

JOE: Wanted the gen on a nod bet.

KEVIN: Whose?

JOE: [*somewhat unwillingly*] Fraser's.

KEVIN: Don Fraser's?

JOE: Yes.

KEVIN: Well, his name's as safe as a bank.

JOE: Well, I know it is. It was something about a cheque Ben paid him. Without the nod bet.

KEVIN: What did Ben pay him in such a hurry for?

JOE: Look, Dad, why don't you ask Ben? [*Pause. Somewhat angrily*] Look, I'm not going crook, but I'm getting a bit fed up with this. The way you're going on, it's as if you didn't trust me.

KEVIN: Don't talk such rot. Not trust me own son.

GLORIA: Told you so. Keep you mouth shut, you great boob.

KEVIN: What everyone needs is another little drink.

JOE: You've said it, Dad.

A car horn is heard. KATE *waves.*

GLORIA: That's Ben.

KEVIN: Has he got Noreen with him?

JOE *looks over the parapet.*

JOE: No. That argument musta got into serial form.

GLORIA: He ought to be ashamed, taking a girl to the races and leaving her on her own.

JOE: Oh, well, you know Ben. Not like me. I know how to pick 'em.

GLORIA: [*somewhat sharply*] There's not a girl I'd sooner have for a daughter-in-law than Noreen. [*Pause.*] Excepting you, Katey, that's to say.

JOE: Good old Mum!

A car door slams.

KEVIN: [*over the parapet*] You bring any extra beer with you, Ben?

BEN: [*below*] A dozen.

KEVIN: Cold?

BEN: [*below*] As an Eskimo's bottom.

KEVIN: Bring 'em up then. [*Turning back and speaking with satisfaction*] That's the boy for my money. Real grip on the essentials.

GLORIA: You didn't ought to shout at him like that over the parapet.

KEVIN: [*surprised*] Huh?

GLORIA: The neighbours are real nice.

KEVIN: Well, they're welcome to a glass, if they want it.

GLORIA: Have some more lemonade, Katey?

KATE: No, thank you. [*She takes a cigarette from a tiny gold case.*] Joe—

JOE: [*turning instantly*] What's up?

KATE: Will you light this for me?

> *He does so. A door slams in the living room.*

GLORIA: [*raising her voice*] All right, Ben, leave a bit of plaster on the walls.

BEN: [*emerging*] To match the plaster on me. Hello, you gorgeous creature, I'm pie-eyed.

> BEN *embraces* GLORIA.

GLORIA: I'll say you are.

> *She kisses him fondly. He is very well worth it—handsome, virile, with a long cheek scar. He speaks rather better than the rest of the family.*

BEN: Hello, Dad. [*He puts the beer down.*] Hello, you financial genius. [*He has very slight trouble with 'financial'.*] Hello, Katey, my orchid. How are you?

JOE: What did you call her?

BEN: An orchid. Doesn't she look like one? Very beautiful and expensive, but no smell. Not any smell at all. Only a very expensive perfume to take its place.

> *He has the same trouble with 'expensive'.*

JOE: [*sharply*] Here, lay off, Ben. You can't talk about Katey like that!

BEN: I was paying her a compliment. You gotter admit, Joe, that she looks more like an orchid than anything else. Noreen now, she looks like a rose, one of those big red ones. And her sister Nancy looks like a pansy, and Mum here, she looks like a wattle tree. Beautiful yellow wattle tree. Chock full of bees.

KEVIN: [*from experience*] You've got yourself a skinful, Ben.

BEN: Father, you are so right. And it was all to prove a point. Noreen, now, she said I was with another woman, but I should have thought I could have proved differently. I wasn't with a woman, I was with a beautiful bottle. In fact, quite a lot of bottles.

GLORIA: You should be ashamed. It's a wonder you weren't given a blue, driving in that condition.

BEN: The fuller I am, the better I drive, it's immoral but perfectly true. Besides, you have to get over the stage where things worry you. Then you can do anything. And I'm not drunk. Only I'm rather full... I'm rather full, all right?

KEVIN: You got my head, that's what it is. Very few people could carry what you carry and hardly show it.

GLORIA: It's nothing to boast about. You better go and have a shower.

BEN: And lose the head start I've got? No thank you, Mum. It took me all afternoon to get this— Waste not, want not.

GLORIA: [*resignedly*] Well, I'm going to get dinner.

GLORIA *rises.*

KATE: Can I help, Mrs Donnelly?

GLORIA: It's nothing much to do. I'll manage, Katey. [*She suddenly claps her hand to her head.*] Well, if I'm not the dumbest blonde that ever came out of— Dad, I never got the chow mein.

JOE: I'll drive you, Dad. It won't take more than five minutes. I never knew you yet, Mum, that you didn't forget the chow mein.

GLORIA: Look, it don't matter if it's right at the top of the list, I forget it…

They move inside. A door slams. Pause.

BEN: Well, Katey?

KATE: Well, Ben?

BEN: Satisfied with the experiment? You said I'd get drunk, and I've got drunk all right. [*Savagely*] But that's all I've got, Katey, in case you haven't noticed. I haven't come crawling after you, licking your feet, like Joe does.

KATE: I don't want you to kiss my feet, Ben.

BEN: Lick your feet, I said. Like a puppy dog that's too young for the bitch, and isn't sure if it'll bite him.

KATE: That is a disgusting way of putting it.

BEN: I wouldn't talk like that to a lady. I wouldn't even talk like that to most tarts I know. But it's the sort of language for you.

KATE: You are drunk.

BEN: I'm not nearly drunk enough. If I was I'd tell Joe that his beautiful young wife, the woman he'd die for, came to me with a suggestion. Me— his own brother.

KATE: Well, why don't you?

BEN: Because I wouldn't hurt him that way. Joe's something you just can't understand. He's decent. The only wrong thing he ever did was mixing up with you, and how was he to know what he was in for? Amateur. You don't take money, not your sort; only a man's guts and brains.

KATE: [*gently*] You don't mean any of this, Ben. It's because you're drunk.

BEN: And why do I get drunk? I just wanted to go to the races, I just wanted to have me a good time with Noreen, and my brother, and my pretty sister-in-law… You must have been crazy. Joe could have heard. Anyone could have.

KATE: Have you finished talking now?

BEN: For the moment, yes. There isn't anything more I can trust myself to say. [*He gets up.*] We Donnellys are pretty loud-mouthed, I suppose, compared with those fancy types you get around with, but we don't do each other dirt. Apparently that's something they never taught you at your fancy finishing school.

KATE: You aren't fair when you say that. If I did I wouldn't have married Joe.

BEN: For Joe's money, Kate, I think you would have married King Kong.

KATE: I had money of my own.

BEN: A hundred pounds a year. What you might spend on smokes. [*Quietly*] Keep out of my way, Kate. Right out of it.

KATE: All right, Ben, if that's what you want.

BEN: Because I'm not a gentleman like Hathaway. I won't just back out when the party's over.

>   KATE *does not answer him, but gives a long measuring glance.*

At least you aren't trying to tell me I misheard or anything.

KATE: You didn't mishear. But I do love Joe, Ben. I love him too much to let him be wasted.

BEN: Wasted?

KATE: Over protected. Made the boy of the family.

BEN: Joe?

KATE: Isn't he?

BEN: You know, Katey, you're good. You are damn good. You're so covered up with your own superiority that you really believe it.

KATE: Yes, I believe it.

BEN: Joe was all right until you came along. He was a bit too open-handed, a bit too ready to listen to a hard luck story, but he was all right. And you snapped away every bit of confidence he had with your—'I'm better than you'.

KATE: [*with sudden anger*] That isn't true!

BEN: My oath, it's true.

KATE: I didn't sap Joe's strength. I tried to help him. It's you. It's this family of his.

BEN: You hate the family.

KATE: No I don't. I think I— But I love Joe.

BEN: Ha, ha, ruddy ha.

KATE: [*regaining her calm*] I do love him, Ben. But I want him to be strong. I want him to be somebody.

BEN: He was somebody. He was the best bloke in the world. But you had to dirty it all up. How can a thing that looks like you—an orchid—be like you are inside? That's what you are. Growing in filth...

KATE: I don't think you'd better say any more, Ben.

BEN: ... shaded from the light.

KATE: [*superbly*] Am I afraid of light?

>   *The sun illumines her as she sits on the parapet.*

BEN: You got your own umbrella—a multi-coloured one. A big one, Katey. To keep you from seeing what you don't want to see.

KATE: If this moves you so little, Ben, why did you get drunk? It seems to me, for a man who is behaving so self-righteously you have a few things to explain.

>BEN *moves, angrily.*

Oh, not to me. To yourself. [*Pause. She looks at him.*] How's your own umbrella?

BEN: I don't need an umbrella. When I do something rotten I know it's that way. I don't lie to myself, Katey. It's only other people I tell lies to.

KATE: Then you are—

>*A telephone rings. Pause.*

Are you going to answer it?

>BEN *goes to the door, but* GLORIA *is heard approaching.*

GLORIA: [*well offstage*] It'll be for me. I bet you it's for me. [*Closer*] I always know who it's for. [*In the next room*] And I know who it is too.

>BEN *sits on the lounge.* GLORIA *picks up the phone.*

Hello, Mary… I beg your pardon…? Oh, Mr Fraser… Yes, he's here. Do you want to talk to him…? Okay, Mr Fraser. [*Calling*] It's for you, Ben!

BEN: [*rising*] Who is it?

GLORIA: Don Fraser.

BEN: Fraser? It's that nod bet. Joe can sort this one out.

>*He goes into the room and starts to talk on the phone. The two conversations continue more or less together.*

Hello… Yes, Mr Fraser… Yes, that's right… evens on Honey Flow… You didn't? I took it myself, Fraser… Oh— Oh, I see… Well, I'm very sorry but there's some sort of slip-up… It's very decent of you to draw our attention to— Yes, yes. That's quite true, Mr Fraser…

GLORIA: [*on the patio*] It was funny about that phone call, I coulda sworn it was Mary. I'm psychic, you know. Read the teacups and everything. I'll read yours for you sometime if you like.

KATE: Thank you.

GLORIA: Though last time I read them it said twins for Dadda, and he was annoyed. But it turned out to be a daily double, and then he got me to read them for weeks, with nothing more than a coupla drownings turning up. Laugh! That was one time I pulled it off.

BEN: [*inside*] Yes, thank you— Goodbye.

>BEN *hangs up the telephone and comes out. He is thoughtful.*

GLORIA: What's up, love? Trouble?

BEN: Bit of confusion about Fraser's bets today.

GLORIA: Not that Honey Flow again?

BEN: Yes.

GLORIA: If you could spare the time, Katey, I was wondering if you'd just make the salad pretty. You've a gift for it, and Joe's got so he doesn't appreciate plain stuff.

KATE: I'd be glad to, Mrs Donnelly.

They move towards the kitchen.

GLORIA: [*hastily*] Wait till I'm out of the way before you start arguing.

BEN: Yes. [*He frowns.*] Mum...

GLORIA: What?

She comes back. KATE *hesitates, looks at* BEN *and then exits.*

What's the matter? You aren't gonna be sick, are you?

BEN: No.

GLORIA: I thought you might like a bit of Worcestershire?

BEN: No thanks. Don't mention this to Joe, Mum.

GLORIA: Am I likely to?

BEN: Don't ask him about it or anything. Please.

GLORIA: All right. And we'll keep it from your dad. You'd never dream he had a couple of sons running the business for him.

BEN: No.

GLORIA: I won't split, love.

She pats his face, absently. The living room door opens and bangs shut.

Joe, will you stop giving that door such an almighty shove? You'll crack all that plaster.

JOE: [*emerging*] Tell you what, Mum, I'll put an anti-slam thing on it. They're the idea for a door like that.

GLORIA: Put an anti-slam thing on you 'ud be better. Get the chow mein?

JOE: Kate took it into the kitchen.

GLORIA: Where's your dad?

JOE: He went into the kitchen too.

GLORIA: He'll eat all the hors d'oeuvres.

She hurries out. The door slams.

JOE: There she goes. Crack the plaster herself most of the time, bless her heart. How you feeling now, Ben?

BEN: I have felt better.

JOE: Well, you know when you mix grogging with business, boy, you gotter expect to pay for it.

BEN: You have many drinks today, Joe?

JOE: Not when I've the little woman with me.

BEN: Then how do you account for the telephone conversation I just had?

JOE: Who with?

BEN: Don Fraser.

JOE: Fraser? What's he want?

BEN: He wants to know why he got a cheque for one hundred and fifty quid.

JOE: I never gave him the cheque. He's always paid or billed at the end of the month. What the hell would he be given a cheque for?

BEN: Because he was short. Because he asked me for the dough to carry on with.

JOE: Fraser was short?

BEN: Even men as well-heeled as he is—they can miscalculate.

JOE: [*angrily*] You didn't ought to have paid him. It's my job to do the paying. Now you've made the hell of a mistake. We only owed him fifty on this meeting.

BEN: One hundred and fifty according to the penciller. You took a nod bet on Honey Flow—for one hundred. According to the books.

JOE: Well—well, you know how it is. There's a ring around you. You can make a mistake. Can't you?

BEN: It's by way of being serious if you take a nod bet for a hundred pounds just on the shake of a man's head. Suppose Honey Flow had lost? Where would we have been then? Sure, we're big time, but we ain't so big we can just ignore a bet for a hundred.

JOE: 'Ell, I'm sorry. I can't say more than that, can I now?

BEN: No, but it occurs to me there was only about half a dozen nod bets there. You took 'em all. All big names that don't pay cash ever. All evens on Honey Flow. That's a bit funny, isn't it? You don't often make a mistake like that, Joe. [*Deliberately*] And I don't reckon you made one this time.

   Pause.

JOE: What are you getting at, Ben?

BEN: If you're a bit short, why the hell didn't you say so?

JOE: You suggesting I'm welshing?

BEN: On the firm's money? Yes.

JOE: [*resentfully*] You're stretching brotherhood a bit bloody far, Ben Donnelly.

BEN: I'm not the only one with elastic ideas. Look—why would you offer evens? You knew he was a certainty. He could have thrown a first-rate fit during the race and still won. And why did only half a dozen people—all good clients—all nod bets—get that good price?

JOE: They came at the right time.

BEN: They didn't bloody well come at all. You knew that Honey Flow was a certainty, and you gave yourself that price, and laid it on in their names.

JOE: Look, Ben… you're forgetting that I'm part of the firm. Some of that money's mine.

BEN: A third of it. Not the trading part. Joe—what did you want it for? You've got plenty of dough.

JOE: If you feel like this, I'll pay those bets, outa my own pocket.

BEN: Oh, come off it, Joe. I'm not drunk enough I tell you. I'm at the stage where everything sorta falls into place, like a plan drawn out on paper.

I'm drunk enough to talk and I'm drunk enough to keep on at you. Tell, me, or I'll bloody well keep on nagging. I won't want to, but I will. I'll nag in front of Dad and Mum. And I'll want to cut my throat then. So tell me quickly, and get it over with. You wanted the money and you worked out this damn awkward way of getting it. [*Pause.*] Look, Joe, either tell me or gimme that whisky bottle, because I'm beginning to sober, and I don't want to get too sober. If you don't tell me, I jest gotter get too drunk to say anything at all. [*Pause.*] You did try to work it, didn't you?

JOE: Yes.

BEN: And I thought you were just a sucker. [*Pause.*] How long?

JOE: About a month.

BEN: How the hell did you think you'd square the auditors?

JOE: I do the paying off. They'd be—paid off.

BEN: I oughter break your flaming neck.

JOE: You don't understand.

BEN: I understand you've been getting away with money that's partly Dad's, and that's crooked in any language. Who put you up to this? Katey?

JOE: Katey? [*Urgently*] You wouldn't let on to Katey? She'd never forgive me.

BEN: She'd never forgive you? Why don't you tell that dame where she gets off? She leads you by the nose.

JOE: Maybe she does, but she's like you called her—an orchid—and you mustn't touch it too hard or it'll bruise.

BEN: Did you want this money for her?

JOE: [*simply*] Yes.

BEN: But why?

JOE: I can't talk about it.

BEN: You've got to talk about it.

JOE: She—she doesn't always understand that I'm not a millionaire.

BEN: And rather than disappoint her, you'd—

JOE: [*simply*] I've got to.

BEN: But don't you see what she's doing to you? She's like, sort of—she's like she's between you and the light or something.

JOE: [*simply*] She is the light.

BEN: It's as if you're hypnotised. Didn't even Hathaway pull you out of it?

JOE: There was nothing between Kate and Hathaway.

BEN: Now look, Joe—

JOE: There was nothing between Kate and Hathaway. [*Dangerously*] Now, Ben, don't say any more. Granted you're my brother, granted you're so full you're splashing, granted you got a right to take a crack at me over the business, but you've no right to talk about my wife. So don't say any more.

BEN: [*miserably*] I wish to hell you'd listen.

JOE: I said—shut up! I'll never believe the filthy lies they spread. They aren't true.

Pause.

BEN: [*regarding* JOE *thoughtfully*] Suppose I won't shut up?

JOE: [*quietly*] Don't, Ben. Remember when we was kids, and that scooter?

BEN: I ought to. I got a mark to remember by.

    He touches the cheek scar.

JOE: Dad gave me the only belting I ever got for that. He said I went on like I could have murdered you. And I remember it, Ben. Not just the hiding. But the red mist—everything. It took a lot of strop to clear that mist. I was more frightened of the mist than of the strop! Then and now.

BEN: [*slowly*] A mist of any kind is dangerous. You gotter see things clearly. Without any umbrella between you and the light.

JOE: What?

    Pause.

BEN: Somehow I'm going to get you out from under that umbrella, Joe. I pulled you off that day with the scooter. Remember?

JOE: Yeah. I hated you like giddy hell for it, then, but boy, am I glad you did. I reckon I woulda done him in.

BEN: Yeah. Yeah, I think maybe you would have. But maybe I can pull you out again.

JOE: [*embarrassed*] God, I'm sorry about that, Ben.

BEN: The money…? Oh—yeah… the money.

JOE: Well, aren't we talking about the money?

BEN: I'm talking about a multi-coloured umbrella.

    JOE *shakes his head.*

JOE: [*affectionately*] You sure are full.

BEN: Not nearly full enough, Joe. Not nearly full enough.

    JOE *shakes his head again and grins.*

END OF ACT ONE

ACT TWO

It is about eight o'clock. Neons are everywhere on the skyline. Headlights run up and down the promontory like lizards on a wall. The patio is cooler than the rest of the house, but that does not say a great deal, as a storm is coming and the air is heavily charged with electricity. Lightning flickers out over the sea where dark clouds are massing. GLORIA, *who hates lightning, sits with her back to the coming storm, but* KATE, *who finds it exciting, sits facing it, her face lit now and then by the flashes.* BEN *is in a vicious mood,* JOE *is sullen and* KEVIN *nurses a suspicion which grows every minute. They are drinking coffee.*

GLORIA: Want another cup, Ben?

BEN: I think I'd better…

GLORIA: How's the head?

BEN: Better now.

KEVIN: Saw your old man yesterday, Katey.

KATE: Oh?

KEVIN: He was sitting in the car waiting for your mum. Classy car, that one your mum's got. You seen it, Joe?

JOE: No.

KEVIN: I said to your old man how long had she had it, but he said he couldn't remember exactly. Had other things on his mind.

KATE: [*lightly*] Daddy always had other things on his mind.

GLORIA: Your mother's a real marvel though, Kate. How she manages all those committees and meetings when all the time she's got her practice beats me. Dad was all for getting her in professionally last time I threw a seven. But he brought me round himself with the good old ammonia bottle. Didn't you, Dadda?

KEVIN: Wouldn't hear of havin' the quack. That's one thing you got up on us, Joe, havin' a doctor in the family. That'll be real handy for you later on. Won't cost you half as much when the little bits of nuisance start putting in an appearance.

KATE: Mother isn't an obstetrician.

KEVIN: Ah! [*He drinks coffee, then splutters.*] Mum, you never put one grain of sugar in this.

GLORIA: Sorry.

She passes the sugar. KEVIN *puts two brimming spoonfuls in his cup and stirs noisily.*

KEVIN: I can't stand coffee unless it's made to the old recipe. You ever hear it, Katey?

GLORIA: [*warningly*] Kevin!

KEVIN: The clean version I'm going to tell, love.

GLORIA: Oh!

KEVIN: Sweet as love, black as sin and hot as hell.

KATE: That's extremely accurate.

BEN: What's accurate about it? There are lots of things blacker than sin. Folly and selfishness and lack of insight.

> *He lights a cigarette.*

GLORIA: [*amused*] Here, I thought you was sobering up.

BEN: Mum—I was being clever.

JOE: [*sulkily*] Too damn clever, if you ask me.

BEN: But I didn't ask you.

JOE: Pull your head in, Ben.

BEN: Don't be unsociable.

JOE: Well, don't start getting clever.

BEN: Was I? How very flattering.

KEVIN: [*coldly*] You two, break that right up!

BEN: [*with exaggerated surprise*] Us?

KEVIN: You heard me. Break it right up. I never took any bickering from you two, and I'm not intending to start. Chop it right out.

BEN: Don't get quarrelsome, Dad.

KEVIN: And don't take that tone with me, me boy, or big as you are I'll land you a thick ear.

> KEVIN *leans back.*

BEN: I believe you would, too.

KEVIN: I'll say I would.

BEN: I'd drink to you, Dad, if my cup was full of anything stronger than coffee.

KEVIN: [*curiously*] What are you on this binge for?

BEN: You call this a binge? It's a family dinner, isn't it, Mum?

JOE: Ben always gets this way when he's got a couple in.

GLORIA: [*glancing at her sons*] Well, you aren't exactly making it pleasant for Katey and me, either of you. You're not the same as your Dadda. Drink never turned him sour. Made him cheerful. You shoulda had that Worcestershire I offered you.

BEN: [*with mock gravity*] I'm sorry, darling, I'm sorry, Dad, I'm sorry, Joe, I'm sorry, Kate. [*The last expressed is even more ironic than the others.*] I'm particularly sorry for Kate because she's not used to these lower-class scenes. It must be so trying for her. Drunkenness isn't the sort of vice you've seen, is it, Katey? And I must remember that Joe gets very worried when you see anything out of place, because it might put you off him—

JOE: [*angrily*] That's enough, Ben.

BEN: [*sickly*] Do you really think you are in a position to tell me what to do, dear brother?

JOE: I'm in a position to make you, Ben, and if you keep on nagging—

 KEVIN *leaps to his feet.*

KEVIN: [*loudly*] Goddammit, I said for the two of you to shut up this row, and I meant it. I'm master in me own house, and if you two boys want an argument, you can get up off your backsides and I'll damn will give it to yer!

GLORIA: Kevin—pipe down!

KEVIN: I will not pipe down! Here's Joe looking as if he'd been kicked in the face by a horse, and Kate as quiet as a canary, and Ben making every crack he can lay his tongue to. I tell you, I will not have it. I'll—

GLORIA: If you'll stop yelling, maybe they'll oblige you by saying what's wrong.

 KEVIN *subsides and she continues quietly.*

Anyway, I know what's wrong. Something happened at the meeting, that's all. Joe's upset about the business about Honey Flow and the way you went on at him about it. Ben's upset because he's had an argument with Noreen, and Kate never talks much, and she's got a headache anyway. And it's that oppressive it's no wonder everybody's got the wind up. There is going to be the mother and dad of a storm before the morning. You can feel it working up.

 There is a brief pause, then BEN *rises, crosses to his mother and kisses her lightly.*

BEN: Darling, you have poured oil on the troubled waters, and we all adore you. And if you'll get me another cup of coffee, I won't make another crack all evening.

GLORIA: [*embarrassed*] Don't be such a ruddy fool, Bernard Donnelly!

 She pours his coffee.

KEVIN: [*brooding*] You don't want to wash these things now, do you, Mumma?

GLORIA: I should. Why?

KEVIN: I forgot to tell you that Mrs Ransome down the street is going to hospital soon and she said you had a magazine or a book or something that you wanted to send up.

GLORIA: That's right. I did.

KEVIN: Why don't you take Kate and the book up to her? Joe'll drive you.

GLORIA: Kate and Joe and me?

KEVIN: Yes.

GLORIA: Subtle as a carthorse, you are, ducky. Come on, Katey. Dad wants to have a word with Ben.

KATE: Very well.

 She rises, stooping to pick up JOE's *cup as she passes.*

JOE: [*doubtfully*] Here, I dunno…

GLORIA: Come on, son. But, Dad, jest remember that Ben's a grown man, won't you? He happens to have outgrown the razor strop.

KEVIN: [*with great dignity*] I want to discuss business, Gloria!

GLORIA: Gloria! I'd better get moving. Whenever he stops calling me Mumma the fur flies! [*She goes to the door.*] Lemme give you one word of advice, Katey. Don't let Joe make a habit of calling you 'Mum'. After a bit you forget you were christened anything else.

> JOE *hesitates at the door.*

JOE: Sure you don't want me, Dad?

KEVIN: I want to talk to your brother.

JOE: Er… well… okay…

> JOE *follows his mother and wife into the living room. The inside door closes.*

KEVIN: [*quietly and grimly*] All right, let's 'ave it.

BEN: What's up, Dad?

KEVIN: That's what I wanta know. Just what's up? There's something funny about this whole meeting. You don't put as many years away in the game as I have without sensing when it's time to take a swab.

BEN: We went down on Honey Flow. We offered evens.

KEVIN: Ah—that isn't everything. Joe's often made little mistakes of judgment before. So 'ave you, Ben. You wouldn't be at him over a little thing like that. I told yer mum earlier in the day that I'm not one who believes in interferin', and so help me, I don't, but when you go on like you've been goin' on… And you're a cheerful drinker usually, as yer ma jest implied. There's something wrong and I wanta know what it is.

BEN: I think you'd better leave it to us, Dad. Thanks all the same. Mum's right. There was a row with Noreen, and perhaps the storm is getting on all our nerves. You know what it's like at a big meeting. Hot and dusty and your throat's as dry as the Sahara. I'm the one you oughter be cracking down on. Not poor old Joe!

KEVIN: You always protected Joe, didn't yer? Even when you was little nippers you was always the one that did everything—according to you. You was always the one that bust the vases and forgot to take out the garbage. You was always the one the cops chased—according to you. But I always belted both of you for all that. [*Pause.*] Look, Ben, it isn't a good idea to try and keep on protecting someone all the time. Some day they gotter stand up for themselves.

BEN: [*rising restlessly*] Well, I'm sorry, Dad, but it's no good coming to me. I can't tell you anything else.

KEVIN: Joe hasn't been up to anything with the books, has he?

BEN: Now what's got into you?

KEVIN: Less lip! Has he?

BEN: Damn it, Dad, he owns a third of the business.

KEVIN: He's been pouring out dough on that wife of his. That ring she was wearing wasn't paid for with peanuts, it damn well wasn't. [*Grimly*] Now look here, I'm not goin' to keep on naggin', but if there's anything funny goin' on, you stop it—quick! I'm givin' you the drum, you stop it, Ben. [*Pause.*] I'm not worrying about the money, if you get me. I reckon the Donnellys is in a position to buy their wives di'monds if they wanter, but there's something funny about this set-up. Joe didn't oughter behave as if she was china, and he didn't ought to have to bribe her.

BEN: 'Bribe' is a strong word, Dad.

KEVIN: It's an ugly one, I grant you. [*Pause.*] Well, if I'm wrong, I apologise. And if I'm right, you bloody well do something.

> *Pause.*

BEN: Why didn't you talk to Joe yourself?

> KEVIN *makes a protesting gesture.*

KEVIN: [*unhappily*] Joe ain't always easy to talk to, and you and him were always such mates. And I reckon that little prissy bit is well mixed up with this. And I might say something and then...

> *He trails off.*

BEN: And you aren't game to interfere, is that it?

KEVIN: I don't like damn nosiness.

BEN: But you're prepared to have me do it for you? Or to see him finish himself off for want of it? Look, Dad, when we were kids you were never frightened of giving us the strop when we needed it to straighten us out. You weren't frightened we'd think less of you then? Why the hell now?

KEVIN: I dunno. Be gettin' old and soft, I suppose. Joe's so... Joe's so damned easy to hurt. Damn it, you try to protect him, yourself. You've no grounds for slinging off at me.

BEN: [*sharply*] Maybe there's times when I get bloody well fed up with him being babied!

> KEVIN *shoots him a surprised glance.*

Maybe I'm bloody well fed of it! You say I always took the blame when we were kids, but you and Mum were always after me to look after the baby brother. Not that Joe wasn't the gamest little tyke in the district, but there was times I got fed up with—'Is Joe all right?'

KEVIN: You never talked like this before, Ben!

BEN: Maybe I got a bit fed up with Mum always kissing him first!

KEVIN: [*uncomfortably*] Gee! I'm sorry.

> BEN *shoots him a look, then grins, rather crookedly.*

BEN: Aw—it's the liquor still talking. Mum oughter make stronger coffee. [*He drinks, then shudders violently.*] That's as cold as a ma-in-law's kiss.

> KEVIN *still looks unhappy.*

Don't look like that, Dad. I'll straighten young Joey out if I gotter do it with brass knuckles. But just remember, you asked for it, and don't go blaming me afterwards.

KEVIN: I'm not likely to, am I?

BEN: Well, there might be one or two opinions on that... You see, I've a notion to get to the heart of the trouble.

KEVIN: [*cordially*] Good on you.

BEN: You think so, do you?

KEVIN: [*placating his conscience*] Not that I believe in interference, not with adults I don't.

BEN: Look, Dad, who are you kidding?

> KEVIN *makes a humorously threatening gesture.*

Little Mister Fix-it, that's you. And yours truly.

GLORIA: [*offstage*] Yoo-hoo.

BEN: Come on out, Mum.

GLORIA: [*emerging*] Was coming anyway, on account of I wanter wash up.

KEVIN: You take that magazine?

GLORIA: No. I didn't wanter see Monica with the kids along. Too cramping to the conversation. [*She looks back over her shoulder and grimaces.*] Did you ever see such a blight on a party? Don't that girl ever let her hair down? Going on as if she'd swallowed a poker.

BEN: You wouldn't be talking about little Katey?

GLORIA: I wouldn't be talking about Marilyn Monroe!

> BEN *throws the coffee dregs over the parapet.*

You stop pouring that on me peach tree. It's no wonder the poor thing never gets a real go on. When you was younger you was always climbing it, and now all you do is fertilise it with cigarettes, coffee and beer.

KEVIN: [*leaning over*] Does look a bit mangy. I saw the cat at it yesterday.

> GLORIA *pauses in gathering the dishes.*

GLORIA: Where is Kitty?

KEVIN: I wish you'd stop calling that cat 'Kitty'. It's been on the tiles for years.

GLORIA: It's never had no other name that I know of. Excepting the time Ben christened it with brandy on New Year's Eve. What did you call it then, love?

BEN: Too many girlfriends ago, Mum.

KEVIN: You called that cat after a girl? Didn't anyone ever explain the facts of life to you?

BEN: Not that I remember, Dad.

JOE: [*offstage, below*] Hey—Ben—

BEN: [*leaning over*] What's up?

JOE: [*offstage*] Dad finished belly-aching?

KEVIN: Less lip!

BEN: Yeah, he's finished.

JOE: [*offstage*] Is it safe for us to come up?

BEN: I reckon it is.

JOE: [*offstage*] Good.

GLORIA: Now I'm going to wash the dishes.

BEN: Avoiding the little woman, Mum?

JOE: [*offstage*] Wait on, love, I'll hold the door for you.

KATE: [*offstage*] Thank you, Joe.

GLORIA: I suppose I should be glad me son 'as nice manners. [*Somewhat wearily*] If I've said what I shouldn't, Ben, then forget it, will you? [*Looking out to sea*] I 'ate these blasted storms. They give me an 'eadache.

BEN: [*gently*] It'll break soon.

GLORIA: Well, I wish it would, and get it over with. When they're comin' everything gets so still you'd swear you could 'ear the storm breathin'.

BEN: [*gently*] Take an Aspro, Mum.

GLORIA: I've already taken two.

JOE: [*entering*] If you're really worried about that storm, Mum, you'd better bring that fancy umbrella in. [*He is uneasy. With him, it takes the form of riotous behaviour.*] It's going to come down by the bucketful before the night's over. Is it long enough after dinner for us all to have another drink? Let's 'ave the radiogram you're always boasting about, Ben.

BEN: All right.

> BEN *strolls inside.*

JOE: [*calling after* BEN] Something dreamy and romantic so's I can cuddle me girl.

> *He hugs* KATE, *who remains passive.*

Come and sit here, Katey... Move over, Mum.

> *He pulls* KATE *down on the lounge, sitting between her and* GLORIA. *He embraces both.*

Me two best girls! Prettiest girls in the whole of Sydney. What am I talking about? Sydney? Prettiest girls in the whole blasted world!

GLORIA: [*wearily*] Give over, Joe love. I've a splitting head!

JOE: [*with instant and genuine sympathy*] Sorry! Gee, Mum, why didn't you say? Can I get you anything for it? APC or anything?

GLORIA: It'll be better when the storm breaks.

JOE: You always did hate them. You know, Katey, when we was little nippers Mum always used to get under the eiderdown with us, all cuddled up like three kangaroos in a pouch. She always reckoned we was three little joeys...

KATE: I love storms. They excite me.

> *Music suddenly pours from the inner room: 'Jesu, Joy of Man's Desiring'.* GLORIA *leans back, closing her eyes.* BEN *emerges and leans in the doorway—smoking, looking at* JOE *and at* KATE *who leans forward.* KEVIN *leans back in his chair, sighing deeply.* BEN*'s musical leanings have always made* KEVIN *slumber. The music plays for about sixty seconds.*

JOE: Is that your idea of something cheerful, Ben? [*Loudly*] Haven't you any pop stuff? 'Moonlight Serenade' or something?

BEN: I'm playing this for Mum and me. Afterwards I'll play something for you… and Kate…

KATE: I love this, Ben.

BEN: Do you? And you're the one who likes storms. You are a continual surprise to me, Katey. Or perhaps you mean to be. Perhaps you consider that surprise attacks are always the best. They take the opponent off balance.

KATE: [*ignoring* BEN, *turning to* GLORIA] Do you really like this, Mrs Donnelly?

GLORIA: [*without opening her eyes*] Yes. When Ben first played it I didn't, but then after a while it was like winding a ball of wool, all coming out straight and smooth and lovely. [*Opening her eyes*] Only I can never get my tongue around what Ben called it. Latin or something.

BEN: Never you mind, Mum love. You don't listen to music with a Latin accent. [*Returning to the bantering tone*] But I'm surprised at you, Katey. I should have thought you would have preferred something with more kick in it. Like Joe does. After all, a husband and wife should appreciate the same things.

JOE: It'd be a pretty drack turn-out if Katey here had to accept my taste in music. All my taste is in my mouth.

> *The door bell rings—a two-toned gong type.*

GLORIA: [*sitting up*] Now who could that be?

JOE: [*getting up*] Stay still, love—

> JOE *goes out.* BEN *switches off the radiogram. The inner door slams.*

GLORIA: [*raising her voice*] Don't slam the door, Joe!

BEN: [*offstage*] You were a bit too late, Mum.

> BEN *comes back to the patio.*

KEVIN: I'm going to put an anti-slam on that door.

GLORIA: You boys've been going to put an anti-slam on it for years now.

KEVIN: Well—you should remind us when we're in town. We gotter buy it, haven't we? Anyone seen the evening paper?

GLORIA: In the dining room.

> KEVIN *rises.*

Wait a minute, Kev. This might be somebody for you.

KEVIN: Well, I don't want to see 'im, unless he happens to owe me a quid.

GLORIA: [*without conviction*] You know, I oughter do the washing up.

KATE: I'll help you, Mrs Donnelly.

There is a low growl of thunder from out at sea.

GLORIA: [*shuddering*] I do 'ate it.

BEN *sits beside her, taking her hand.*

BEN: It's all right, darling. The storm will break soon and then it'll be all right.

GLORIA: I hope it will, Ben.

JOE: [*offstage*] Come through this way, Eilie.

KATE: [*sitting up*] Eileen?

GLORIA: Your little sister, is it?

JOE: [*coming out*] Come on, Eilie, don't be shy. No one out here'll eat you. Here's a little lady with a great load of trouble, Katey…

JOE's *bluffness hides his sympathy for* EILEEN HOWARD *who is struggling with tears.*

EILEEN: [*sobbing*] Kathie—oh, Kathie…

KATE: Eileen—what's the matter? Why didn't you ring if you wanted me? What are you doing here?

EILEEN: It's really terrible, Kathie. I couldn't stay home… Mummy…

KATE: What's the matter? Stop crying at once and tell me.

EILEEN: I—I—

GLORIA *has risen. She embraces* EILEEN, *who is momentarily startled, but then abandons herself to the comfort.*

GLORIA: There, there, love, you'll make yourself real sick if you cry like that. But it'll do you good all the same. You have a good cry and tell us all what's the matter. Come on, love.

She pilots EILEEN *to the lounge and sits down, drawing the girl to her.*

[*To* KATE] Whatever can the matter be with the child to bring her up here, with the storm and all? There, there, love! Have you got a hanky? Then take mine.

KATE: [*sharply*] Stop it, Eileen—stop. Is Mother ill? Is that what you're trying to say?

EILEEN: No. Not ill.

She pulls away from GLORIA *a little, trying to control herself.*

It's Daddy. She says that Daddy—that he doesn't love her anymore. That he's going away from our house.

KATE *rises angrily.*

KATE: Really, Eileen. Can't you see you're embarrassing Mr and Mrs Donnelly? [*To* GLORIA] I'm really so sorry, Mrs Donnelly. It's disgraceful of Eileen to behave like this.

GLORIA: [*quietly*] You needn't be afraid that any of us will be embarrassed, Katey, or think any the less of her that she feels like this. We'll go in and you can talk to her here, and I'll get her a little bite to eat, because I'm sure you've had no dinner, have you, dear?

She kisses EILEEN.

And as soon as you've talked it all over with Katey, you come right down to the kitchen and have a little snack with Dadda and me. [*She rises commandingly.*] Dadda! Come and help me wash up!

KEVIN *rises.*

KEVIN: Okay, Mum. [*With a knowing look*] Joe, Ben. Beat it, can't yer?

The boys rise. BEN *gathers up the tray with the cups.*

GLORIA: [*to* KATE] If I may say so, it's more comfort she needs than scolding. Come on, boys.

She marshals her men before her.

BEN: [*offstage*] Careful the door doesn't come back, Joe. If it does these cups are goners.

JOE: [*offstage*] Righto.

The door slams.

EILEEN: [*nervously*] I'm sorry, Kathie. I suppose I shouldn't have blurted it all out like that.

KATE: I suppose Mother told you about the separation?

EILEEN: You know about it, then?

KATE: Of course. They've been talking about it for years, but I never thought Daddy would have the nerve.

EILEEN: But, Kathie—you—you can't take it so calmly. It's a sin.

KATE: You're quite old enough to understand that Mother and Father haven't really been in love for ages—not since you were born, I should think.

EILEEN: You mean it's my—it's my fault?

KATE: Of course not. But Daddy thought Mother ought to have stayed home and looked after us. And she wouldn't. And of course he had to give in to her. Why do women have to try to dominate their husbands...?

EILEEN: But, Kathie—

KATE: What?

EILEEN: Don't you?

KATE: Don't I what?

EILEEN: Try to—dominate— [*She stumbles a little on the word.*] Try to dominate Joe?

KATE: What?

EILEEN: Well, don't you?

KATE: Of course I don't. It's just that I don't want him to be weak like Daddy,
I couldn't bear that. Because— Look, we aren't talking about Joe and me.
We're talking about Mother and Daddy. What reason did Mother say he
was leaving for?

EILEEN: Another woman. Mother says she's—she's loud.

KATE: Well, perhaps he feels like something loud and exciting. Anyone would,
after Mother.

EILEEN: She isn't the one who's breaking up the marriage.

KATE: Well, as I see it, it is her fault.

EILEEN: Don't you—don't you care for her at all?

KATE: Much cause she's given me to love her—since I married Joe.

EILEEN: She didn't think that Joe was good enough for you, Kathie.

KATE: She's in a wonderful position to tell me who I should marry. At least
my husband hasn't grown tired of me. And he won't, if I can help it.

EILEEN: Oh, but Joe wouldn't. I think he's awfully nice. And then he's got the
family. [*Pause.*] I am rather hungry. Mother was too upset… and it seemed
sort of heartless, me eating. [*Pause. Shyly*] It's going to be awful at school,
Kathie. All the girls will know. They always find out things like this, and
Sister Ursula will look sorrowful.

KATE: It has nothing to do with Sister. She doesn't understand anything about
being married. How could she?

EILEEN: But—but it is sin, Kathie. He is with this other woman—as if she
was his wife.

KATE: Well, it's his sin. Not ours.

EILEEN: But we're his children. Besides I—I love Daddy.

KATE: Well, if you take my advice, you should get right away from Mother's
influence. You've got to grow up sometimes. Don't let her do to you what
she did to Daddy.

EILEEN: [*with a spark of spirit*] It's all very well for you. You're married to a
lovely man, and you've got Mr and Mrs Donnelly. I haven't got anyone.

KATE: I've got Mr and Mrs Donnelly all right.

EILEEN: Don't you like them?

KATE: Oh, for goodness sake, stop asking me questions. And if Sister Ursula
says anything, tell her to discuss it with Mother.

EILEEN: But I don't understand why Daddy would go. He always seemed
fond of us. It isn't as if he was angry—or anything. He was fond of us. He
gave us presents and everything.

KATE: Oh, Eileen! Look— Being married isn't being sentimental about
someone. It means—it means you're lifted up to a sort of ecstasy. And if
someone can't give you that, you've got to find some way to rouse them.
Because wanting it and not getting it… is hell.

EILEEN: [*shocked*] Katherine!

KATE: What?

EILEEN: That's the first time I've every heard you say anything like that!

KATE: It's a wonder I don't swear all the time, living with people like the Donnellys. [*Sharply*] You're not going to tell them anything about this, do you understand? Don't discuss our affairs. It's the Howards' business, not the Donnellys'.

EILEEN: They won't ask, will they?

KATE: I wouldn't put anything past that old gossip.

EILEEN: I'm sorry, Kathie.

KATE: Well, don't start worrying about it now. You've got to be firmer. You've got to understand that it's no good weeping and being sorry over families. They can look after themselves. You'll find that out when you get married.

EILEEN: I don't, ever. I hate men. I don't want to get married.

KATE: That's what you think now. Mother never satisfied Daddy. That was what was wrong.

EILEEN: Satisfied him? But—but why don't women satisfy men?

KATE: It isn't always the woman's fault. It happens when outside things— like families, or religion, or other people—get in the way.

> EILEEN *continues to gaze at her.*

Don't look at me like that, it's true. I'm explaining so you'll know when you get married. Take a man who can satisfy you. Or one that you can make strong.

EILEEN: I'm going to be a nun.

KATE: Every girl thinks she's going to be a nun when she's fifteen years old. I thought so myself. Everyone does.

EILEEN: I mean it. What you've been saying, it makes me feel sick!

KATE: Why? Why should it?

EILEEN: [*hesitating*] It's so—cold. Men and women making love in a little world to themselves. It's as if you've got to—to own someone.

KATE: It isn't owning someone. That isn't right. It's being owned by someone completely. Whether you want it or not.

EILEEN: If that's marriage, I don't want it. I thought it was—it was nice and friendly and having babies and—

KATE: Eileen, you sound exactly like my mother-in-law.

EILEEN: Well, it is like that to her. Not hungry—like you make it.

KATE: Perhaps I am hungry.

> EILEEN *rises quickly. She draws away from* KATE.

EILEEN: I'll go now. [*She pauses at the door.*] Which—which way is the kitchen?

KATE: Don't you speak to them about this!

EILEEN: I won't. I don't even want to think about it… [*She goes, then hesitates.*] I'm sorry, Kathie. I am sorry.

With a childish dignity, EILEEN *goes.* KATE *stares after her.*

KATE: I hope I never have any children.

> *She picks up her purse and takes out a powder compact. Having studied her face, she begins to powder if carefully.* JOE *enters.*

JOE: Darling, I'm so sorry. It must have been rotten for you.

KATE: She was in a very strange mood. She's very silly to come all this way with a storm blowing up.

JOE: [*kissing her*] Don't fret about it, love. Your old man isn't really the sort to walk out on your mother. It's just a passing row. Mum hit Dad with a standard lamp once. Laugh!

KATE: I very much doubt if the cases are parallel.

JOE: Well, I can't quite see my ma-in-law letting him have it, but he'll come back all right. He's just skating another skirt. Your mum must've been real pretty, Katey. Like her daughter.

KATE: [*stiffly*] Are you comparing me to Mother?

JOE: Well, of course, I don't know her too well, because she didn't exactly open her arms to yours truly, but you do look like her. Small and dainty, like a flower. Like an orchid, like Ben says.

> *He kisses her. She remains passive.*

And you got her brains. Everyone says she's the smartest doctor in this suburb. It's damn lucky for me your brains were asleep the day we met up, or I'd never have been able to persuade you. And there wasn't ever anyone else for me after I had seen you, Katey.

KATE: [*with a slight impatience*] I wish you wouldn't talk like that. You aren't ignorant. You've given out a lot more life and intelligence and money than my father ever had. And you were the man I wanted, the only man I ever wanted.

JOE: I'll look after you, love. Honest I will. [*Pause.*] This kid sister of yours... young Eilie... Mum was just saying that it won't be too nice for a kid in all this mix-up. What say we have her with us for a bit? Make her laugh, show her a good time? Until things settle down a bit with your dad and mum.

KATE: Mrs Donnelly suggested it?

JOE: Well, she said it wouldn't be too nice for the kid. She wasn't putting her oar in, Katey. You know Mum never does. She was only talking.

KATE: I wish you wouldn't discuss my affairs with your family, Joe.

JOE: Look, Katey, I never. But with the kid coming here and everything...

KATE: Because an hysterical child gets absurd notions you have to make it an excuse to drag the family into it. I want just us, Joe. Aren't I enough for you anymore?

JOE: Awmigosh, Katey, don't be Uncle Willie. [*Huskily*] Gee, Katey, you're so lovely I reckon a man could be happy with you on a desert island.

KATE: I wish we were on a desert island. I wish there was only you and me in the world. Then I'd have nothing to be afraid of.

JOE: Honey, what is there to be afraid of now?

The storm is coming closer. There is a roll of thunder.

Here, I thought you was the one who wasn't afraid of storms? Lovey, you're trembling!

KATE: It isn't the storm. It's other people, Joe.

JOE: Yeah, baby, but I don't know what I'm going to make a book on, on a desert island. Coconuts and monkeys? [*He chuckles.*] Monkeys! Look, honey, I reckon I oughter drive the kid home. She shouldn't go on her own.

KATE: I suppose you'll have to. Joe...

JOE: What?

KATE: You see why I don't want her with us, don't you? I don't want anyone but you. Not anyone.

JOE: Yeah, but we can't be on our Pat Malone forever. There'll be a time when you'll change your mind about kids. Then a babysitter like young Eilie'll come in real handy.

KATE: Oh, Joe, do stop it! [*Suspiciously*] Has your mother been talking to you again?

JOE: Well, you know Mum.

KATE: I wish you wouldn't discuss our affairs.

JOE: But, honey, Mum isn't like a stranger.

KATE *moves away from him.*

KATE: Are you going to drive Eileen home?

JOE: Yeah. [*Pause.*] What's up, Katey? Have I made you mad or something?

KATE: No. No. Of course not.

JOE: I want to be on my own with you as much as you want to be with me. You know that.

KATE: Then why can't we go away? Away from the family? To another city? Melbourne? Brisbane?

JOE: Here, love, we gotter eat. I happen to have an interest in the firm.

KATE: You could get another job.

JOE: F'r instance—what?

KATE: You're young and you're intelligent. You don't have to be a bookmaker. It isn't as if you'll ever get anywhere in the firm. Mr Donnelly still runs the firm, you know he does. And even when he does retire, Ben will still hold the reins.

JOE: Yeah, but I like working for Dad and Ben. And Ben's much better at it than I am. [*Quietly*] I been meaning to speak to you about this. We'll have to pull up a bit. We been going through a lot of dough lately.

KATE: [*instantly defensive*] Well, I haven't... You owe money? Who to?

JOE: Don't you worry about it. I'm kind of sorry I told you.

KATE's *face hardens.* JOE *throws away his cigarette and embraces her.*

Hell, if you knew what it does to me to say 'no' to you.

KATE: I'll help you save the money. Then we'll be free and we can go somewhere else.

JOE: Well, look, love, let's not discuss it now, eh? Pretty soon we'll have enough to have a holiday up the coast. Southport, eh? We'll have ourselves a real time.

KATE: [*obstinately*] I don't want a holiday. I want to get away.

JOE: Well, let's not get ourselves all het up, eh? We'll talk about it later. [*He kisses her.*] Anyone ever tell you you was a proper peach? [*Releasing her*] Well, I'll take the kid home. [*With a laugh*] You know, this business of not wanting anyone else in our flat—just as well I'm not the suspicious kind. Don't let it get yer down. And don't take no bad change till I get back.

> *He goes out, slamming the door.* KATE *looks after him, then there is a roll of thunder and a brilliant flash of lightning. She looks out to sea, her hair blowing back from her face. Then, feeling she is being watched, she looks at the door.* BEN *regards her cynically.*

BEN: I thought I'd mention, Katey, that if you still wanted me, I'm here.

KATE: Don't start anything now, Ben. You aren't sober yet—

BEN: Would you rather go out in the car? To the park? Or on the promenade? Would you like me to tumble you in the sand, or in your own flat? That'd be a nice, piquant little touch of sauce on your meat, wouldn't it? Having your brother-in-law in your own husband's bed?

KATE: [*looking at him steadily*] I'll forget this, Ben, because you're drunk. When you're sober you'll apologise.

BEN: I haven't had a drink since before dinner. I wanted to keep sober. Otherwise I might muck it up. You wouldn't appreciate a drunk.

KATE: How long is it going to take to penetrate through your conceit, your boorishness, that I don't want you? Just because every little floozy on the racetrack falls under the charm of the irresistible Ben Donnelly, that doesn't mean I've got to follow suit, does it?

BEN: Let me tell you that there's a mighty few little floosies who'd give me the come-on in the terms you did. I still don't know how you got away with it, without Joe hearing. The devil takes care of his own, is it? Or the angels protect the innocent. That's what I'd say if I was religious, like Mum.

KATE: Religious? Mrs Donnelly?

BEN: There's not a Sunday morning that Mum doesn't pray for the souls of Dad and Joe and me. And for you too, Katey, Heaven forgive you. But this is a time when more than prayers are needed. When Joe gets to the stage where he cheats and lies and steals for you, then it's time someone showed you up.

> KATE *laughs.*

Have I said something funny?

KATE: You are incredible. You're the one who's got the nerve to criticise my reasons and my emotions and my thoughts. And you're justifying your own actions by pretending that you're doing it for Joe. Joe would kill you if he heard what you were saying.

BEN: He'd probably try. But he wouldn't bring it off. And he'd see you then through something besides rose-coloured glasses, sweetie.

KATE: You aren't doing it for that. You're doing it because you can't bear to think one woman didn't want you. One woman stood up against your inflated ego, your vulgar womanising.

BEN: I'm not pretending I won't get a certain amount of fun out of it. It'll be wonderful seeing you off that pedestal.

He moves quickly. In sudden panic she dodges.

KATE: You can't behave like this here. Your mother—

BEN: Mum is trying to comfort your little sister. Poor little bitch—another one to be twisted and turned and frozen into shape like you. If I'm sorry for anything, I'm sorry for that kid.

KATE *pulls herself together. She walks to the glass doors.* BEN *remains between her and the inner door.*

KATE: Let me pass, Ben.

He does not move.

Let me pass!

BEN: [*jeering*] Trying to push me off now, Katey? Getting nervous about it? Why should you be? You were willing enough to let Hathaway make a play for you. What's up? Game getting a bit out of hand?

KATE: Please let me pass, Ben.

BEN: If you want to play A-Grade, baby, you'd better be prepared for the tackling.

KATE: [*desperately*] I didn't mean you to take me seriously. I only wanted to make Joe jealous.

BEN: You wanted to make him jealous? Look, Katey, you can't whistle me up like a puppy and then say, 'Get to heel, dog!' I'm not your puppy dog, doing what I'm told—

KATE: [*with rising hysteria*] If you come near me I'll scream...

BEN: Go on then, scream. Scream your silly lungs out.

He grabs her.

Scream now, Katey! Scream!

KATE: [*faintly*] Ben—Ben, you're hurting me!

BEN: And you're loving it, every minute. If Joe had got his belt off and beaten you buckle end, you would have loved it. You picked the wrong brother— you should have married me. I would have obliged.

KATE: Ben—Ben—don't! Please don't!

BEN: What's up with you? Pretty as a flower and yet you love this, you know you do. Were you beaten as a kid? Joe and I got leathered now and then, but it didn't send us queer. And yet when I'm with you, I want to hurt you... to strike you and kill you maybe...

> KATE *sees* JOE *first.*

KATE: Joe—Joe—help me! Please, Joe...

BEN: Joe!

> *There is a curious note of triumph in* BEN*'s voice. He swings* KATE *completely around, not releasing her, so that she is between him and his brother.*

JOE: Let her go, Ben. If you don't let her go, you'll regret it.

BEN: Come on, then.

> *He pushes* KATE *back and she falls against the parapet, crouching there.*

This is what you like, Kate. Men fighting over you.

JOE: I warned you, Ben.

> *He closes in. His first blow takes* BEN *over the eye, but he shakes his head and clinches.* JOE *breaks and they cannon into the lounge. The umbrella stick snaps and they become entangled. They break.*

BEN: [*with somewhat hysterical mirth*] We busted the damn umbrella, anyway.

> JOE *rushes him, but* BEN *sidesteps.* JOE *collects the drinks table in his rush. When he straightens, his hand is around the neck of a bottle.*

[*Warningly*] Joe—No!

> JOE *advances.*

Don't do it, Joe!

> *He dives desperately aside as the bottle comes down on the parapet. It comes up shattered, but* JOE *still grasps the neck end.*

KATE: [*screaming*] Joe!

> JOE *is not diverted.* KATE *rushes forward and grabs him, but he backhands her off.*

BEN: [*shouting*] Get out of this, Kate. This is a Donnelly brawl.

> JOE *comes at him.* BEN *backs rapidly and collides with the drinks table. As he is off balance* JOE *lunges. For a moment* BEN *flails on the parapet, then he goes over.* JOE *stands quite still, grasping his unused weapon.* KATE *rises slowly. There is a sickening cracking sound and a thud. The door of the living room bangs and* GLORIA *hurries on.*

GLORIA: Joe!

> *She races to the parapet and halts, seeing what is below.*

Ben! [*Pause.*] Ben—Ben—

She is still screaming his name as the curtain comes together.

END OF ACT TWO

ACT THREE

The same—some ten minutes later. Cars are still moving on the headland, but fewer of them, because the rush is over. JOE *sits, his head in his hands.* KEVIN *paces, glancing now and then at the place where* BEN *had fallen.* EILEEN, *awed and excited by the drama, sits and watches them both.*

KEVIN: [*muttering*] How lucky can you be... My Gawd, how lucky can you be... Why he didn't bloody well break his— I still don't know how he come to do it— You ruddy fool, Joe, I've always told you boys that you'd kill each other— No wonder your wife's screamin' the place down... How did he come to go over, anyway?

    JOE *does not answer.*

We shouldn't have moved him. I told your mother we shouldn't have moved him. But he's such a pig-headed fool. Walking in. Walking! We should have bloody well carried him in on a stretcher.

EILEEN: [*solemnly*] It is often the moving of the patient that does the damage, and not the accident itself.

KEVIN: What? [*He looks at her.*] What's that you say?

EILEEN: In the first-aid lectures they always say not to move the patient.

KEVIN: I told him. I said, you lay right there where you are, Bernard Donnelly, till we find out if your backside's in one piece or two. But he didn't listen. He never listens. Nobody in this house listens to me!

EILEEN: [*sadly*] No one listened to me either.

KEVIN: Not that anyone could 'ave 'eard with that ruddy fool Katey yelling her lungs out.

EILEEN: She can yell, too, can't she? When we were children she used to drum her heels as well.

KEVIN: Joe tried that once, and I fetched 'im a clip that straightened his blasted temperament. [*To* JOE] Listen, Joe, I tell you to paste her one in the way of kindness, and you wouldn't. It's the only thing to do with hysterics—you gotter let them have it. Now, when you was a little nipper—

    JOE *rises and moves away.*

JOE: Oh, for God's sake, stop going on about it.

KEVIN: And it looks as if I oughter clout you a ruddy sight more often!

    He leaves JOE *and comes down towards* EILEEN.

There's one thing. He ruddy well ruined Mum's flowering peach. That tree's 'aunted. Ten years it's been in, and something happens every year!

EILEEN: If it hadn't been for the peach tree, he would have still been lying there. You ought to be grateful to the peach tree, Mr Donnelly.

KEVIN: I am, I'm givin' you the drum, I am. And to think not an hour ago his mum was at him for pouring coffee on it. [*He shakes his head sadly.*] And him never thinking in so little time they'd both be goners. That is, nearly.

GLORIA *enters. She looks desperately tired.*

GLORIA: She's quieter now. Poor girl, it give her a dreadful shock.

She goes back and pats JOE's *arm.*

It'll be all right, son, jest keep a good grip on yourself.

KEVIN: Did the doc say anything?

GLORIA: Not a thing. [*She sinks in a chair.*] Kev—will you give me some of that brandy? Gracious Heaven—what's happened to the drinks table?

She looks at JOE *and her eyes widen.*

[*Innocently supplying the alibi*] Those ruddy boys horsing around. I tell you, Ben'll pay for that brandy. It was nearly full and it stood me back three blasted quid.

KEVIN: Never mind, Mum, I'll make us all a cuppa in a minute.

EILEEN: There'll be some coffee in the kitchen, Mrs Donnelly. Shall I get you a cup?

GLORIA: Oh, would you? Bless you, Eilie. It's a real pleasure to have you, love. Your mum's a very lucky woman.

EILEEN: [*without emotion*] Yes.

GLORIA: I always wanted a daughter meself. Pretty little daughter I could dress frilly.

EILEEN: I'll get the coffee.

On impulse she embraces GLORIA *as she passes.*

Don't you worry, Mum, I'll take care of you.

GLORIA: Bless you, Eilie, you're a good girl, you are.

EILEEN: [*kissing her and straightening*] Anyone else want a cup?

KEVIN: I want a good stiff drink, but I won't have one for a bit, and coffee'd be better than nothing. You want a cup, Joe?

No answer.

Joe!

JOE: What?

KEVIN: Do you want a cup of coffee?

JOE: I don't think— [*Somewhat surprised*] Yes. Yes, please.

KEVIN: Well, make up yer flamin' mind.

The loud wailing of a tom cat is heard.

GLORIA: That's Kitty.

KEVIN: Out on the tiles. [*He listens.*] Ben won't be out on the tiles for a day or two. How he didn't break 'is damned neck…

GLORIA: [*sighing*] I wouldn't mind so much if he'd been having fun when it happened, but he wasn't. Just drunk, and not even cheerful drunk at that. I've always been at him to watch out for some jealous husband—

She breaks off.

KEVIN: This was his mullet-headed brother. And his mullet-headed self.

GLORIA: Well, I wish he was out on the tiles this minute, I do.

The cat wails again.

KEVIN: The doctor didn't say anything?

GLORIA: No, and we can't go in. [*She looks around to see if* EILEEN *is out of earshot.*] That Doctor Howard! 'It is most desirable that the patient should be relaxed and quiet.'

She grimaces.

KEVIN: We oughter had one of the others. I never did trust that mealy-mouthed female.

GLORIA: She's Katey's mother. We can't very well change.

KEVIN: And that dear little kid's mother too, and a nice job she done of that, I don't think. I don't blame Ted Howard for walking out on her. She musta had him under chloroform when he proposed, I'm telling you. Don't you let her get near me, if anything happens to me, that's all.

GLORIA: Dad… you don't think—

She hesitates.

KEVIN: Don't think what?

GLORIA: You don't think he's broken anything, do you?

KEVIN: If he hasn't it's a miracle. He come down on his back.

GLORIA: That's what I mean. He come down on his back. He come down real hard. I was wondering… if Ben's hurt himself badly it'll go hard with him, Dad. I mean—Ben…

The tom cat howls despairingly.

KEVIN: I know what you mean… Look, if I had a gibber handy I'd get that damned cat fair in the slats. Where is he?

He peeps over the parapet.

GLORIA: [*leaning back and closing her eyes*] Next door. You know they got a blue Persian female.

The cat howls.

KEVIN: It's enough to drive a man crazy, that row. I tell you, Mum, we oughter've got him fixed.

GLORIA: [*hysterically*] Don't, Kev, don't! We don't want anybody—fixed!

JOE *and* KEVIN *turn hastily.* JOE *immediately relapses into brooding,* KEVIN *hastily hugs* GLORIA.

KEVIN: Look, love, you aren't going to be damned silly about this, are you? Granted, he took an awful cropper, but he never hit concrete. Just keep on remembering that he never hit concrete. And he's a big, strong feller, Ben is. He's got a lotter guts.

GLORIA: Yes, I suppose so. It's only—her not letting us in and all that.

KEVIN: And the whole blasted evening. [*He turns grimly.*] Now listen, Joe. There's one thing I want straightened out. Here and now. Are you listening to me?

JOE: Yes, yes, I'm listening.

KEVIN: Was you or weren't you cooking the betting books?

GLORIA: Kevin— What?

KEVIN: Jest a minute, Glory. Well, son?

JOE: Yes, I stole nearly eight hundred pounds.

GLORIA: Joe!

> *She crosses herself.*

KEVIN: [*setting his mouth grimly*] And was Ben having it out with you when he went over the balcony? Was he?

JOE: [*shaking his head*] No.

KEVIN: You're lying, Joe. You're lying like you've lied before to get you out of things.

GLORIA: Kevin!

KEVIN: He has, Mum. Like the time he and Ben pinched the car, and the time they bust the radiogram. A lousy, little sneak thief. That's what I've reared.

GLORIA: That's why Ben was so cranky drunk. I thought it was Katey...

KEVIN: Katey... Ben don't care anything for Katey—why the hell should he? Ben's always got any girl he ever wanted. He wouldn't go after his own brother's wife.

JOE: No. No, he wouldn't. I know he wouldn't.

GLORIA: Well, I tell you, one of them was making up—I tell you, if it wasn't Ben, it was her. She was 'round them like a Persian cat, and them like a couple of toms... I tell you, Joe would never go for Ben like that with a bottle over money— You can't tell me—

KEVIN: A bottle!

> GLORIA *stops in mid-breath. She gazes in terror at* KEVIN.

GLORIA: [*hysterically*] No, no, Kev! I didn't mean it! He never—he didn't... I never saw anything...

KEVIN: A broken bottle.

GLORIA: Oh no, Kevin, no...

KEVIN: He went for Ben with a broken bottle.

GLORIA: He's your own son…

KEVIN: You—

> *He flails a blow at* JOE *which, taking him by surprise, fells him.* KEVIN, *reverting to street fighting, kicks him heavily, then hauls him up and strikes him viciously, open-handed.* JOE *deliberately refrains from fighting—holding his hands back from his body, accepting what* KEVIN *deals out.*

You rotten, little mobster, fighting dirty—I'll teach you to fight dirty, I'll show you…

> GLORIA *seizes* KEVIN, *hauling him away.*

GLORIA: Kevin—you'll kill him—Kevin—

KEVIN: [*with utter distaste*] Get out of my house. Get out and take your wife with you.

GLORIA: Kevin—don't. He's your own son.

KEVIN: My son… a rat who'd use a bottle—

GLORIA: Get out—Joe—go away—

JOE: [*breathing hard but on his feet*] It's all right, Mum. It's all right, darling…

KEVIN: [*turning on* GLORIA] You—you was always at me not to be hard on the boys. Now look! No thanks to you, he isn't a murderer—

GLORIA: No thanks to me—and it's no thanks to you, you didn't kill him.

KEVIN: Ben dying and you worrying about this little—

GLORIA: Ben—Ben! Don't you think Joe is suffering, don't you—?

KEVIN: I only think about Ben—all you think about is Joe! Baby Joe! And all we done is damn well baby him along every inch of the way—baby him into murder—

GLORIA: We never! We never! We always treated them exactly alike—

KEVIN: You didn't… You always kissed Joe first—

GLORIA: [*bursting into tears*] Oh—I wish I'd never got married. I wish I'd gone into the convent, I do. I wish I was dead—

KEVIN: [*breaking into high-flown drama*] Better dead than the mother of a—

> BEN *enters, his hand to his head. He walks stiffly. He is evidently in a certain amount of pain, but is ignoring this.*

BEN: [*crossly*] Shut up, shut up… Isn't it enough me having a hell of a headache without you two making enough row to waken the dead?

> GLORIA *and* KEVIN *turn.*

GLORIA: [*horrified*] Bernard Loyola Donnelly, what are you doing outer bed? You get right back there this minute!

KEVIN: You didn't oughter move at all! [*To* GLORIA] See what your yelling's done? Now he's probably done himself in! [*To* BEN] Back to bed, you ruddy fool!

BEN: [*crossly*] You cheese it, Dad. I'm not going back to bed. That blasted bed is made of cast iron. [*He comes down gingerly.*] This is the worst backside I've had since you strapped me for pinching fruit.

KEVIN: It wasn't the pinching I minded, it was your habit of throwing the green bits back through the winders. Where's the doctor?

BEN: Sitting in the lounge, carefully keepin' the truth from me in case it upsets me. Someone oughter tell her something, and for a minute I thought I was elected. But I'm in— [*He groans.*] I'm in no fit state.

KEVIN: Sit down, sit down.

BEN: [*doubtfully*] You think so? Well, move the cushions.

> *They hasten to obey.*

Not under my head, under me. What do you think I fell on?

KEVIN: If you had fell on your head you wouldn't have hurt anything—

BEN: [*plaintively*] Mum—

GLORIA: I'll fix it, Ben. You—Kevin Donnelly—get your great carcase outter the way.

> *She arranges* BEN.

Son, did you take an aspirin or sleeping pill or anything?

BEN: [*moving his head sensuously*] Aspirin.

GLORIA: Lovey, you oughter be in bed.

BEN: Soon.

> BEN *closes his eyes, enjoying her tenderness.* EILEEN *comes out and nearly drops the tray of coffee.*

EILEEN: Oh, Ben! Honestly, Ben!

BEN: I felt so terrible in bed, Eilie. I felt all alone.

EILEEN: Oh!

> *She puts the tray down on the drinks table and runs to help* GLORIA *tend the wounded* BEN.

Oh, poor, poor Ben. Let me help you—let me get you some coffee. I'll hold the cup for you.

BEN: [*shamelessly*] Steady my hand.

EILEEN: Oh, you shouldn't have got out of bed.

BEN: The bed's too hard. It hurts. [*Confidentially*] When I have to go back I'm going to lie on me stomach and suck air through the piller.

> EILEEN *giggles, gazing at him entranced. In her eyes he is a wounded hero, impossibly romantic.* JOE *is looking at* BEN *too—a loving look.*

[*Glancing at* JOE, *whispering*] Eilie, please take a cup to Joe.

EILEEN: Joe— Oh, yes.

> *She rises and pours a cup, carrying it to* JOE. BEN *manages to support his own cup without undue effort.*

BEN: The doc wants to see you people. She has to make sure you don't kill
me off. Though if that tumble didn't do it, I don't know if a pickaxe would.

GLORIA: Oo—I'd forgotten her. [*Pleadingly to* KEVIN] Dad...

KEVIN: We'll both go, love.

He places an arm around her waist as they go out.

BEN: Eileen...

EILEEN: Yes, Ben?

BEN: Will you do me one more favour?

EILEEN: Yes, Ben?

BEN: Go and get Katey. Ask her to come here.

EILEEN: But she had hysterics.

BEN: That's why I want you to get her. Ask her to come out here. Say Joe wants
to talk to her. I want you to go because you're a born nurse. And if Mum
sees her it might upset the two of them again. You ask her to come here and
then go and help Mum. We all need you, Eilie.

EILEEN: [*shyly*] Do you—do you really think so, Ben?

BEN: We do need you. And, Eileen—tell Katey Joe wants to speak to her. Joe.
You understand?

He winks.

EILEEN: Oh... Yes, of course, Ben.

She hurries out.

JOE: What was the idea of that?

BEN: Get the kid out of the way, of course.

JOE: What?

BEN: Come down where I can see you without dislocating the back of me neck,
will you?

JOE *comes down and sits.*

Now look, Joe. It wasn't Katey's fault, entirely—that scene you busted in
on.

JOE: No, it wasn't entirely Katey's fault. It was mine.

BEN: I don't know how you work that one out. I made a pass at her. She socked
me. Quite rightly.

JOE: There's more to it than that, Ben. You aren't like that.

BEN: How do you know what I'm like? Maybe Katey was right when she said
I couldn't keep my hands off a woman. Any woman. Anyone's woman.

JOE: Go on.

BEN: Go on what?

JOE: You never touched a woman that didn't want it, Ben. Oh sure, you've
got the name for being a bit of a hot hands... but not with another man's
wife... not you, Ben...

BEN: Come off it. I can remember a barney with—

JOE: Yeah, but his wife was willing. And you despised him. [*Pause.*] So, I'm wondering if… well, if the same applies.

BEN: I don't despise you, Joe. You know damn well I don't.

JOE: Well, I despise myself. I'm really something all right. I let my wife behave like a street-walker, and then I try to kill my own brother for trying to open my eyes.

BEN: You… What do you mean, you let her? Get this straight, Joe. I made a pass at Katey. Damn it, you saw me, Joe. I made a pass at Kate.

JOE: Yes, I saw you. And I saw her at the races, too.

Pause.

BEN: Look, Joe—

JOE: Don't. Ben, please don't try and make me think I didn't see it. I've been lying to myself too long, too damn long. Katey and me, we've built a whole marriage on lies, and closed eyes, and make-believe. [*Pause.*] What is she, Ben? If she wasn't my wife, if she was someone we'd just met, what'd you reckon she was? What's she want? To make me into a gigolo—

BEN: She stopped me, Joe. I give you my word she stopped me. She didn't want me when I grabbed her. I'm not lying to you.

JOE: I wouldn't be surprised. She's done that to me more than once. The come-on and then go away. This has been quite a day, ain't it? The races, then the bets on Honey Flow, then the barney. [*Almost casually*] Dad knows about the bets on Honey Flow, Ben.

BEN: I might ha' known you'd split, you ruddy fool.

JOE: I didn't actually, he caught on. There's no flies on Dad.

BEN: What did he do?

JOE: [*ruefully*] What do you think he did? Nearly busted me in two.

BEN: Served you damn well right. [*Pause.*] If I'd done that it might have been better. Then you wouldn't have any ideas about Katey.

JOE: Well. I did get ideas about Katey. [*Quietly*] We're through, Ben.

BEN: You and… me?

JOE: Me and Katey.

BEN: Divorce? Well, that'd jest about break Mum's heart, that would.

JOE: We can separate. There's some things a man can't take.

BEN: For the second time I'm saying it. I tried for her. She's only guilty—of a little foolishness maybe. I misunderstood her.

JOE: Misunderstood her?

KATE *appears at the back.*

KATE: [*coldly*] Joe—

JOE *turns and looks at her.*

I think you might have come to me. But I suppose you were so worried about—about your brother…

There is a world of scorn in the words 'your brother'.

JOE: That's right, I was.

KATE: And what about me? I suppose you never thought of me?

JOE: Since you ask—no.

KATE: [*to* BEN] What have you been telling him?

BEN: Actually not a great deal, darling.

KATE: [*coldly*] Are you better?

BEN: Still in one piece.

KATE: I'm glad of that.

BEN: Well, thank you, darling…

KATE: Glad of it because Joe would have been blamed if you were hurt, and you deserved it. You deserved that, and more.

JOE: Come off it… no one deserves to fall over a balcony.

KATE: You defend him? After what he tried to do to our marriage? I said you lied to him, Ben. What have you said?

JOE: He said it wasn't your fault.

KATE: Oh.

>BEN *laughs.*

You think it's amusing, don't you? Amusing to break up a marriage. It's lucky you are hurt, because if you weren't Joe would hit you again—hit your lying mouth. He's man enough for that, even if he's not man enough for—

JOE: That is enough, Katey.

KATE: Don't you dare talk to me like that!

JOE: Shut up, then. Shut up and I won't. And don't start screaming again, do you hear me—or so help me—so help me, Katey…

KATE: Joe. [*Her lips tremble.*] Oh, God in Heaven! Joe—what's happened? Why are you behaving like this? Because you saw me in Ben's arms? I was fighting him off, in case you don't remember. I asked you to help me.

JOE: Yes, I remember that, all right. I remember most everything about it. That's what's so funny about a temper like mine. You know what you're doing but you can't stop. But I reckon this'll stop me, this'll stop me if anything will. I nearly killed my own brother. I nearly killed Ben.

KATE: But what about me? You struck me, too. My face is bruised. Joe—Joe, please don't be angry with me. It wasn't my fault.

JOE: It's never your fault, is it, Katey?

KATE: But it isn't, it isn't. What have I done?

JOE: You lied, that's what you've done. Lied and cheated, and held me off. You know, I reckon I could understand this if you was really warm… warm the way Ben is… if you wanted men the same way some women do. But you're a cold fish. You aren't even angry now. You're just whingeing.

KATE: Joe—Joe—

BEN: Joe.

> JOE *fails to turn.*

Joe, if I tell you again this was my doing, will you believe it? I did attack her. She did try to fight me off.

JOE: Yeah, yeah, I know she did. But what you're forgetting is she asked for it. Otherwise, why would you?

BEN: Because I'm no good, and because she's beautiful.

JOE: Come off it. She isn't as pretty as all that. Not pretty enough to tempt you.

KATE: Joe…

JOE: Well, you aren't. I think you are. Of course. Because I'm young and romantic, and I like—liked the idea of it. I was too damned uncertain myself to want to get too close. In case she saw me too clearly, I suppose. But not you, Ben. You're game to see things at close range. Close enough to get the scent of them. You said she had no perfume this afternoon. You said an orchid. But you're wrong, you know. Not an orchid—an artificial flower. More perfect than life.

BEN: I'll tell you what's wrong, Joe. You're wrong.

> *He reaches up and hauls* KATE *over so that her face is in the light, brilliantly illuminated.*

She's beautiful all right. Beautiful with a bruise on her cheek, and her tangled hair. And don't you know those tears are real? Artificial flowers don't get dew on them.

JOE: [*looking closely at her*] She is beautiful—now.

KATE: [*pulling away, furious*] How dare you—how dare you? You're despicable, humiliating me this way, Joe. Siding with Ben. Blaming me. That's just like you Donnellys. You all hate me. And now you've succeeded in turning Joe against me… because I'm educated and… and because I don't yell and call names and hit everybody…

BEN: [*pleased*] Now that's more like it!

KATE: You—you—

BEN: [*suggesting the words*] Drunken lecher?

KATE: Smug beast! You think you're too good for me. You think Mum's the only damned woman in the world. You'll never get married because you'll never find anyone who'll manage to put up with you. I wish I'd cut my tongue out before I asked you to…

JOE: To what?

> *Pause.*

BEN: Like me to answer? To let you prove yourself. That was it, wasn't it? Because in spite of your beauty, in spite of spending every penny on clothes, in spite of cutting Joe off from all his friends, from every distraction, Joe wasn't too good in bed, was he? He didn't satisfy you and you didn't satisfy him. You couldn't bring yourself to, could you? Because a man shouldn't want a woman only to go to bed with—he should admire her for her soul, eh?

KATE: Be quiet—don't talk like that—be quiet!

BEN: And so you froze Joe off, didn't you, and then something awful happened. Joe started getting uncertain—he started getting like your father, didn't he? But it still couldn't be your fault. Not if her name's Katherine Howard. So it was Joe's fault. It was Joe that was the matrimonial failure. And you could prove it, couldn't you? Because didn't other men want you...? Hathaway and—

KATE: [screaming] Be quiet!

BEN: But you couldn't quite bring yourself to let Hathaway, could you? And you still didn't know, until you thought about me... Ben Donnelly—the proved lady's man. Because if you failed this time it just might be you... [Pause.] You know, Katey, that's by way of being a bitter blow, that is... me... Ben Donnelly... a pacemaker.

    Comprehension comes over JOE's *face.*

JOE: Pacemaker! Of course! Pacemaker. That's it—of course. Of all the ruddy fools.

KATE: [desperately] It isn't true. I love you. I love you, Joe.

JOE: Well, Katey, I reckon that if I hadn't been in love with you I wouldn't be as churned up as I have been, either. Listen, love, you've been trying to prove you're all right. How's it for me? I went to a whore house a coupla weeks ago. To prove it wasn't me. How's that?

KATE: [horrified] Joe!

JOE: That's when I cooked the books to buy you that ring. I felt so ashamed afterwards—so ashamed to touch you. That's what you did to me, Katey, you made me feel ashamed.

KATE: But why? Why should I? I only wanted to be loved, not to lose you. I wanted to be proud of you—and the fact that you were mine. Mother and Father—

JOE: Oh, to hell with your mother and father. What have they got to do with this? Why were you so scared of having kids?

KATE: I'm not—I'm not—

JOE: You are!

    He seizes her.

Damn you, answer me.

KATE: I'm—I'm afraid of other people.

JOE: You are not. You're afraid of yourself and the fear of failing—failing to have a man you could be proud of—failing to hold the man you'd chosen... Couldn't you see that I love you—that I want you as you are—?

KATE: No. If you see me as I am I'll lose—

JOE: I'm seeing you as you are now. Young, and lovely and warm. Katey, I don't want to worship you like a saint in a church. I want you out in the sun and air with me.

KATE: But you—if you don't respect me—if I can't rouse you—

JOE: Respect you? Rouse me? I was so jealous you nearly killed me—and Ben. Come down on the beach with me.

KATE: It's going to rain—I'll look terrible if my hair—

JOE: Katey, your hair don't matter, and if you wear that goddam dress again I'll tear it off you. Right on the race track. And if you look at another man, ever, I'll belt the living daylights out of you. And we'll have kids, see, and a big house, and we'll fill it with friends, and we'll know and trust each other. Now, do you want that, or not?

KATE: I don't know if I can. I'm not like you... I can't let go all of a minute, I can't—

JOE: It's now or never.

He goes to the steps, waits a moment, then turns to go.

KATE: Joe—don't leave me—Joe—wait for me, Joe...

She runs after him, tripping on the steps falling into his arms. JOE *sweeps her up triumphantly and they go together into the darkness.*

GLORIA: [*entering*] Ben—Ben, you've gotter get to bed, you know.

BEN: Yeah. [*He lifts his head.*] Rain's coming. You can hear it on the roof.

GLORIA: The storm's broken. Where's Joe?

BEN: On the beach—with Katey.

　　　GLORIA is surprised.

Don't worry, Mum. Joe'll look after his wife.

He holds out his hand and she comes to him. He speaks childishly.

Love me, Mum?

GLORIA: I love all of you.

BEN: Love me better than Joe?

GLORIA: Joe needs me more than you do.

BEN: Not anymore. Joey's grown up, Mum. You've lost your baby boy. You know, Mum, you're the only decent woman I ever met.

GLORIA: Except Noreen—

BEN: [*tenderly*] Yeah. Except Noreen.

　　　Pause.

GLORIA: [*listening*] That's solid. Those kids'll get soaked. Did they take coats or umbrellas or anything?

BEN: No coats. No umbrellas. But don't worry—maybe that's what this marriage needed. A little bit of sun and rain on it.

KEVIN: [*offstage*] Glory.

BEN *rises stiffly as* KEVIN *appears in the door. The* DONNELLYS *stand together looking out at the storm. Then* BEN *shrugs and together they go into the house. The light picks up the tattered remnants of the umbrella.*

THE END

The Slaughter of St Teresa's Day

Peter Kenna

Peter Kenna (1930–87) was one of thirteen children brought up in an Irish-Catholic family in the working-class Sydney suburb of Balmain. A radio and stage actor, he first attracted national attention as a writer in 1959 when *The Slaughter of St Teresa's Day* won a General Motors-Holden National Playwriting Competition. He moved to London in 1959 where he wrote *Talk to the Moon* (1963) and *Muriel's Virtues* (1966). He returned to live in Sydney in 1971 debilitated by a chronic illness. Nevertheless the 70s proved to be his most fruitful decade: *Listen Closely* (1972), *Mates* (1975), *Trespassers Will Be Prosecuted* (1976) and *The Cassidy Album* trilogy—*A Hard God*, *Furtive Love* and *An Eager Hope* (1973–82).

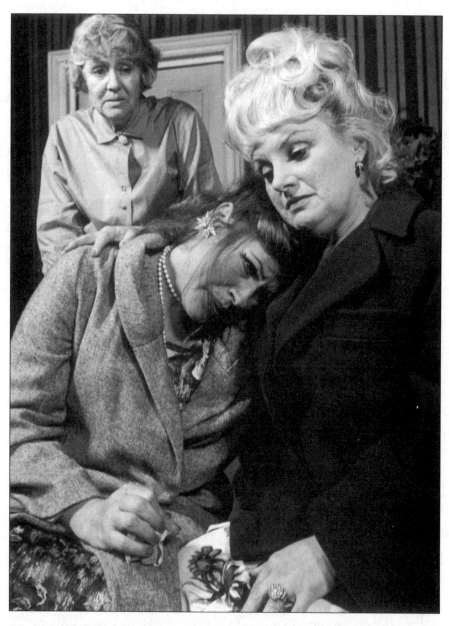

Marion Johns as Essie, Carole Skinner as Wilma and Gloria Dawn as Oola in the 1972 Community Theatre production of THE SLAUGHTER OF ST TERESA'S DAY. *(Photo: Leon Gregory).*

FIRST PERFORMANCE

The Slaughter of St Teresa's Day was first presented at the Elizabethan Theatre, Sydney, on 11 March 1959, with the following cast:

OOLA MAGUIRE	Neva Carr Glynn
ESSIE FARRELL	Dorothy Whiteley
CHARLIE GIBSON	Des Rolfe
HORRIE DARCEL	Grant Taylor
SISTER MARY LUKE	Philippa Baker
SISTER MARY MARK	Mary Mackay
THELMA MAGUIRE	Pat Conolly
WHITEY MAGUIRE	Rodney Milgate
WILMA CARTWRIGHT	Dinah Shearing
PADDY MAGUIRE	Frank Waters

Setting designed by Phillip Hickey
Directed by Robin Lovejoy

AUTHOR'S NOTE

One afternoon in the mid-1950s I was thumbing through the illustrated magazine *Pix* and came upon a photograph of Tilly Devine, the notorious Queen of Sydney's underworld, presenting Kate Leigh, her equally notorious peeress, with a statue of St Teresa of Lisieux. The ladies had had a falling out and the statue was Tilly's peace offering to Kate. The incident took hold of my imagination and out of it I began to fashion *The Slaughter of St Teresa's Day*. But, of course, I knew nothing about Sydney's underworld except what I had read in the papers. The substance of the play is drawn from what I did know; the Irish-Australian working-class milieu I had been brought up in and still belong to.

The nice part of Oola was personified by a deeply religious mother-of-four who seemed always to be throwing grog-free parties at which simply everybody was called upon to entertain. At home I frequently heard my Uncle Raphael perform Paddy's Story, parts of it word-for-word as it is now written down. At a party somewhere else I saw a Wilma dance the Hula.

It is nearly thirty years since I wrote the piece and, after so long, I believe I am able to look at it objectively. Its virtues and failings aside, I think I did manage to capture a moment of our history: a time when a particular type of person believed certain things were important and spoke about them in much the same way as they appear in the script. One thing is certain. I've become a more serious person than I was at 28. I'd give a lot to recapture the spirit of fun I then possessed.

Peter Kenna
March 1986

To Ray Cook

CHARACTERS

OOLA MAGUIRE
ESSIE FARRELL, her aunt
CHARLIE GIBSON, Oola's lover
HORRIE DARCEL, a visitor
SISTER MARY LUKE, nun of a Roman Catholic teaching order
SISTER MARY MARK, nun of a Roman Catholic teaching order
THELMA MAGUIRE, Oola's daughter
WHITEY MAGUIRE, Oola's cousin
WILMA CARTWRIGHT, Whitey's girlfriend
PADDY MAGUIRE, Oola's uncle

SETTING

The action of the play passes in Oola Maguire's sitting room at her home in the Sydney suburb of Paddington.

The time covers the third of October and the following morning of the year 1958.

The architecture of Oola Maguire's house is Victorian. The particular room we view is not the largest or the most formal in the building. But it is here that Oola conducts a thriving SP bookie business and entertains her friends. A doorway on the right of the stage leads out to a kitchen. When the double doors at the back are opened, a hall and the beginnings of a staircase leading up to a second storey are visible.

The decoration of the room sets Oola's character immediately. She has chosen the fittings she lives among at the dictates of a heart wallowing dangerously in irrepressible nostalgia. Here is the memory of this event, the memento of that: the raffle prize, the wedding present, the curio she was clever enough to find. Colours and styles clash alarmingly but one gets the immediate impression of both comfort and cleanliness. The room is decorated with vases of poinsettia.

Out of all the confusion three details must emerge, for they are referred to in the plot. The first is a gold-framed photograph of Oola's late husband Boxer, who was a prize fighter. This greatly-enlarged press print depicts him in ring attire sparring up to the camera. It is set above a sideboard on the back wall. The second detail is a plaster statue of St Teresa of Lisieux placed among flowers on the mantelpiece, a small votive lamp burning before it. The third detail is a spent bullet framed in black on a large white mount and set on the wall on the right side of the stage as close to the front of stage as possible. Apart from these decorations the other necessary properties are four telephones set out on a desk, a piano and stool against the wall on the left side of the stage, and a mirror.

ACT ONE

Afternoon. The curtain rises to discover OOLA *seated on the centre cushion of a sofa. She is most carefully dressed and groomed, so still she appears to have been set there as one places a doll. Her dyed blonde hair is too carefully waved, her pale face so heavily made up she appears to be wearing a mask. Her bare arms, in contrast, are mottled and brown, giving the expensive jewellery that clings to them a tawdry look. Her fingernails and even what we see of her toenails through high-heeled sandals are too vividly lacquered. Her slovenly figure is held in place by a strong corset, the construction of which is almost fully visible through the light, floral, jersey dress she wears. She is trying desperately to assume a graceful pose.*

She turns her head stiffly and observes a box of chocolates on an occasional table. She endeavours to ignore them, glancing around the room for distraction. But her eyes return to the chocolates.

She stretches her arm out to reach one, but cannot do so from her present rigid position. She struggles to rise but cannot manage that either. She falls back onto the sofa exhausted by her effort. Her pose crumbles.

A new set of features peeping through the veil of cosmetics like a photographic double exposure reveals a disenchanted woman of fifty-four. Excessive calculation, a lifetime of summing-up, has narrowed her eyes to slits. If the decoration about her reveals 'Oola Triumphant' then the downward droop of her mouth and the wobbly chins reveal 'Oola Outsmarted'.

She twists the rings on the fingers angrily; she takes a tiny hankie from her bosom and mops her forehead.

One of the telephones begins ringing. She waits for someone to come and answer it. No one arrives. She turns towards the kitchen and calls.

OOLA: Aunt Ess. Essie!

> *No reply. She boils to sudden anger and calls again, savagely.*

Essie!

> ESSIE FARRELL *appears. She is a small, gaunt woman in her seventies, reminding one of a tiny rat whose whole existence has been a quick, frantic scramble for crumbs. She is wiping her hands on her apron and is angry too.*

ESSIE: All right, all right, I heard you the first time.

OOLA: I'm yelling my lungs out for you!

ESSIE: I was turning out a sponge. Did you expect me to drop it in the middle of the kitchen floor and flash in here?

OOLA: Well, how was I to know?

ESSIE: Screaming like that, anybody'd swear you'd had your throat cut.

OOLA: Look, answer the phone. I didn't call you in here for a recitation.

ESSIE: Was that all you wanted?

OOLA: Oh, and you can pass me them chocolates.

ESSIE: Okay, okay. Now make up your mind. I'm not a bloody octopus.

OOLA: Pass me the chocolates and *then* answer the phone. Ain't that clear enough, you silly old bugger?

ESSIE: [*thrusting the chocolates at* OOLA] Great lump of a thing!

OOLA: Who? Who are you calling a great lump of a thing?

ESSIE: [*trying to decide which phone is ringing*] You! Great lump of a thing, Oola Maguire!

OOLA: How would you like a great kick in the—?

> ESSIE *lifts the phone, silencing* OOLA. *She speaks to the caller employing what she considers a refined phone voice.*

ESSIE: Hello. Oola Maguire's residence. [*Then, in her normal voice*] What do you mean: what am I bunging on side for...? Look, who is this...? Oh. I might have known... Cheeky lump!

OOLA: [*softly*] Who is it?

ESSIE: [*into the phone*] Wait a minute, I'll see if she's around.

> *She lowers the phone and extends it to* OOLA. OOLA *shakes her head indicating that she couldn't possibly get up to answer it.* ESSIE *returns to the caller.*

No, she's not here. She must have slipped up the street. Anyway, where've you been for the past fortnight? We been ringing and ringing that place... Oh, that's nice. When did they let him out...? Umm, fancy... Well, look, it's Oola's St Teresa's Day party tonight, can you come...? Oh... Hold on a minute. I'd better ask her... What...? Oh, well, she's just this instant come back.

OOLA: Gawd, I'd hate to have to depend on you for an alibi, Ess.

ESSIE: It's not the johns I'm talking to, it's Wilma Cartwright.

OOLA: Can she come?

ESSIE: Yes, but they let Whitey out of the clink a couple of weeks ago and she wants to know can she bring him too?

OOLA: Oh, I don't know, his father's coming. I don't want no blues. Tell Wilma Uncle Paddy's coming.

ESSIE: [*into the phone*] Hello, Wilma, Oola says to tell you Uncle Paddy's coming and she don't want blues... Yeah... Well, are you sure? [*To* OOLA] Wilma says Whitey won't start no blues.

OOLA: It isn't him I'm worried about. I suppose it'll be okay. You never know, get them here together they might make it up.

ESSIE: Pigs might fly.

OOLA: We can give it a go, can't we? Just remind her about the rules.

ESSIE: [*into the phone*] Hello, Wilma, Oola says that'll be okay but to remind you about the rules: no grog and any ironmongery to be parked in the hall. Okay...? About eight... Yeah. Ta ta.

> *She hangs up the phone and crosses Wilma's name off a notebook on the table.*

Wilma says lots of love.

OOLA: Where's she been?

ESSIE: Jervis Bay. She took Whitey down there to get a bit of outside air into his lungs.

OOLA: Oh. She was the last we had to hear from, wasn't she?

ESSIE: That's right. Now we know they're all coming.

OOLA: Good. [*Extending her hands*] Now, here, you can help me upstairs. I'm going to strip this corset off.

ESSIE: Oh, Oola, that's giving up.

OOLA: Well, one of us has to sooner or later and I know when I'm beat. I'm in agony. I bet I cracked a rib getting into these things.

ESSIE: Don't be silly. These are what they put you into in hospital when you do break something. And anyway, you haven't got time. Thelma'll be here any minute. You want to look stylish for her, don't you?

OOLA: I don't think she'll expect me to kill myself doing it.

ESSIE: You've probably only got a bit of skin caught between the bones. Wait till I jostle you about a bit.

> ESSIE *moves behind* OOLA *and shakes her about.* OOLA *cries out in pain.*

OOLA: Oh, stop it. Don't, Ess.

ESSIE: Is that better?

OOLA: Oh, fine. Now I feel like my bloody back's broke. Oh, God, I'm starting to sweat and I can feel my tinea coming on.

ESSIE: I'll dab a bit of calamine lotion between your toes.

OOLA: Not on your life. I bought these sandals special. I'm not going to be walking 'round in them with calamine lotion up to my ankles. People'll think I'm falling to bits.

ESSIE: Well, I'm warning you, you take those stays off and you will be.

OOLA: Don't you try bouncing me. I'm telling you, I'm taking them off and that's that.

ESSIE: [*moving towards the kitchen*] Okay. Go 'round looking like a bag of spuds. See if I care.

OOLA: And don't start any of your cracks.

ESSIE: Well, it's about time you started to think of your appearance. It's a wonder to me how you hold onto Charlie, getting about the way you do.

OOLA: You flaming old cow, I'm still a very attractive woman; that's how I hold onto Charlie. He tells me all the time, I'm still a very attractive woman.

ESSIE: [*continuing towards the kitchen*] Oh, yes, you're gorgeous.

OOLA: You can come back here and help me upstairs.

ESSIE: No.

OOLA: One of these days, Ess, maybe right this day, you're going to end up on that footpath outside with your bags beside you. Just as sure as God's there, you will.

ESSIE: And do you think I'd care? It's no picnic for me, slaving around here. You can't even open your mouth. Don't think it wouldn't be a pleasure to get out.

OOLA: Well, go on, go to your room now and pack. Anybody'd swear I had you on a chain.

ESSIE: I'm staying right here until it suits me to go, but when that day arrives I'll sweep out of here on a cloud of dust so big you'll think a bullock dray's passed through the place.

OOLA: Yeah, I can see you getting out without me pushing you. Catch you walking out on free board and tucker and all the rest of it. Christmas presents and birthday presents—

ESSIE: That's right, throw up all the things you've given me. I think you only give me things so as you can sling them up at me afterwards.

OOLA: I'm only saying—

ESSIE: It's not them things that matter. It's how you treat a person every day that counts.

OOLA: That's what I'm saying: you and your cracks, you're biting the hand that's feeding you, that's what you're doing.

ESSIE: Anybody'd swear I didn't earn what you give me. I cook for you, run your messages, clean the place up so as you can loll around with that Charlie dirtying it up.

OOLA: What do you mean: dirtying it up?

ESSIE: I meant making a mess of it. If you thought I meant anything else—

OOLA: You'd better not.

ESSIE: Don't pick on me when your conscience is playing up.

OOLA: Can't you say one thing that isn't mean and nasty!

ESSIE: I never mince words.

OOLA: And neither do I. You've hurt me, Auntie Ess. I took you in and I thought I'd been good to you.

ESSIE: That's just your side of the story. You've never given me one little bit of respect, Oola Maguire, and that's a fact too. Bobbie Farrell might have been a bit rough with me—

OOLA: A bit rough! When you came to me you was just stuck together with bits of chewing gum.

ESSIE: Nevertheless, he wouldn't allow no one else to lay a finger on me, or talk to me the way you do.

OOLA: Aw, come off it!

ESSIE: [*beginning to sniff*] You'll see, one of these days I will get out. I'll go off on my own to a cosy little place, where I'll only have myself to look after, and I'll never be anybody's slushie again.

OOLA: [*relenting*] Oh, shut up, you silly old cow. Don't start bawling. [*Sniffing herself*] You only do it because you know it breaks me up too.

ESSIE: All I was thinking of was making you look pretty. I put a lot of trouble into it and you want to undo it all. It's like decorating a cake and having no one around to eat it.

OOLA: Well, that's a bit better than the bag of spuds crack. Now, blow your nose. You're dripping like an old tap.

> ESSIE *sits beside* OOLA. *She blows her nose loudly.*

And on top of everything else I'm worried like hell.

ESSIE: Why?

OOLA: I don't know whether I've done the right thing in asking those nuns to bring Thelma down for the party.

ESSIE: Oh, rot! She's got to get to know her own mother sometime. Stuck up there in that boarding school year after year.

OOLA: She's got everything she wants, hasn't she? And how can I have her home here? There's the SP and Charlie. I go up and see her six or seven times a year. I take her to Woy Woy every holidays.

ESSIE: All that might have been okay when she was a kid, but she's nearly sixteen now. She needs a mother to talk things over with. The nuns can only help her so far. For instance, have you any idea of what she wants to do when she finishes school?

OOLA: No, but—

ESSIE: Well, there you are!

OOLA: Well, I'll ask her when she gets here.

ESSIE: It's about time.

OOLA: Put those phones away, will you? I don't want her to see those. They'd be a dead giveaway.

> ESSIE *unhooks and packs three of the phones into the sideboard.*

I've got a premonition, Ess.

ESSIE: You and your premonitions!

OOLA: No, they ain't never wrong. I got one the night her father was killed and I was right about that, wasn't I?

ESSIE: You'd better call the party off then, hadn't you?

OOLA: It's no use. You can't run away from what's meant to be.

ESSIE: Then what's the use of griping about it? Everything'll be all right. You've been holding these St Teresa's Day parties for eight years and every year they've been getting quieter. They're a bit too quiet now, if you ask me.

OOLA: They're not meant to be rowdy. That's why I won't have no grog.

ESSIE: It's going too far not letting me put any wine in the trifle.

OOLA: A rule's a rule. But I didn't think when I asked Thelma down that, apart from Wilma and you and me, there was only going to be men here.

ESSIE: Just tell her all the girls you know work nights. You wouldn't be telling a lie at that.

They both laugh.

OOLA: Oh, don't make me laugh, Ess, it's agony.

ESSIE: Just think of the look on Charlie's face when he sees you all strung together in one piece.

OOLA: Now don't start that again.

ESSIE: You just don't know how nice you look, Oola. Real stylish. Honest.

OOLA: Am I? Well, I suppose I can try for a bit longer.

ESSIE: That's the girl. It's sure to get better before it gets worse.

OOLA: But I'm going to have to slip my shoes off for a while. I've got to get relief somehow.

She kicks off her shoes. The front door is heard slamming. CHARLIE GIBSON *calls from offstage.*

CHARLIE: [*offstage*] Ool! Oola! Where are you, love?

OOLA: In here, Charlie.

CHARLIE opens the double doors and leans in. He is a happy, weak-willed man of forty-five.

CHARLIE: Hey, Ool, I brought a bloke back with me wants to meet you. Can I bring him in?

OOLA: Who? Oh, Charl, I've got my shoes off.

CHARLIE: You can put them on, can't you?

OOLA: Well, give me a minute.

CHARLIE: Sure.

He disappears, shutting the door.

OOLA: Put my shoes on for me, would you, Ess?

ESSIE: It doesn't matter about your shoes. It can't be anyone important.

OOLA: No, I suppose not. Is my hair all right?

ESSIE: It's all right.

OOLA: [*calling*] Okay. You can come in now.

CHARLIE returns with HORRIE DARCEL. HORRIE is a good-looking, suave man of thirty-eight. OOLA is immediately sorry she hasn't put her shoes on. She attempts to hide her bare feet under the sofa. CHARLIE kisses her.

CHARLIE: How are you, love?

OOLA: You've been to the pub.

CHARLIE: Just a beer.

OOLA: It's St Teresa's Day.

CHARLIE: And the longest thirst of the year. Hey, I'd like you to meet Horrie Darcel.

> HORRIE *moves forward and extends his hand.* OOLA *takes it and they shake hands.*

OOLA: I'm pleased to meet you.

CHARLIE: And this is Oola's Auntie Ess.

ESSIE: [*to* HORRIE, *curtly*] Hello. [*To* CHARLIE, *sharply*] I thought you said you was coming home to lunch?

CHARLIE: I had a pie in the pub.

ESSIE: Gawd, you're on a good thing here. The day might come you'll be glad of that chop I just chucked out.

CHARLIE: I'll come 'round and ask for it then.

ESSIE: Ask away, I won't be here to give it to you. I'll be lazing in the sun somewhere and the likes of you will be cooking chops for me.

> ESSIE *exits into the kitchen.*

CHARLIE: Gawd, to hear her complain you'd think she bought the chop.

OOLA: Well, she had to cook it and she's got her work cut out with the party tonight and all.

CHARLIE: She'd try running us all if we let her.

OOLA: Well, don't worry about that. Sit down, Horrie. You'll have to excuse my bare feet but you took us by surprise, like.

HORRIE: I told Charlie I'd be butting in.

OOLA: Oh no, it's not that.

CHARLIE: People are always dropping in.

OOLA: If you don't mind them bare I don't.

HORRIE: I think they're very pretty feet.

OOLA: Oh, Gawd! Where'd you pick this one up, Charlie? The charm school?

CHARLIE: Yeah, talk about a talker. To listen to Horrie you'd think the whole world was his oyster.

OOLA: Why not? I got a lot of time for a man who's go ahead—providing he don't try to go ahead of me.

CHARLIE: [*throwing his arms around* OOLA] Didn't I tell you, Horrie?! Quick as a flash! Didn't I say that?

> *He kisses her sloppily on the cheek.*

OOLA: Charlie! Stop it!

CHARLIE: And the quickest head for business in the country.

> *He kisses her again. She pushes him away.*

OOLA: Charlie! Don't be such a bloody fool. Stop it.

CHARLIE: What's the matter?

OOLA: Well, look at me. I'm all done up. I don't want you slobbering over me. [*Coyly*] Besides, Horrie's here.

CHARLIE: Aww, I been telling him all about you. Couldn't wait to meet you, he said. Made me bring him straight home.

OOLA: I'll bet you had more than one beer. And I'll give it to you, talking about me in pubs.

HORRIE: I wouldn't mind, Oola. He was boasting.

OOLA: [*primly*] Well, I do not like it, Horrie. I will not have it.

CHARLIE: [*placing his arms about her waist*] Oh, come off it, Oola.

> *He becomes aware of her corset.*

Hey, what's this? I thought you felt a bit different.

OOLA: Now, shut up.

CHARLIE: Roped yourself in for the hurdling tonight, did you? Good old Ool!

> *He runs his hands over her corset as though playing a harp.*

Woo! Wooooo!

OOLA: [*exploding*] Now stop it! Stop it or I'll drop you.

> *She pushes him away. He continues to snigger.*

CHARLIE: Good old Ool. Good old Ool.

OOLA: I'm ashamed of you, I am. Go upstairs and have a shower. You smell like a stable. [*To* HORRIE, *sweetly*] Pardon me for mentioning perspiration.

CHARLIE: I smell all right.

OOLA: You don't. I told you what you smell like. I'm not having you coming to the party tonight reeking of beer. Now, go and have a shower. I want you out of the way when those nuns get here with Thelma.

CHARLIE: I know, you told me. Oh, can Horrie stay for the party?

OOLA: We'll be glad to have you, Horrie.

HORRIE: Thanks!

CHARLIE: You'll look after him, will you? He might like a cup of tea.

OOLA: He'll be all right. Now, go on.

CHARLIE: Tell her about some of your ideas, Horrie. He's got a million of them. Take the floor.

> CHARLIE *exits.*

OOLA: He always gets a bit silly when he has a few in.

HORRIE: It'll wash out of him under the shower.

OOLA: What were these ideas he was talking about?

HORRIE: Oh, just a few things we were discussing over the beer. Charlie was saying as how he'd like to be doing something.

OOLA: Why? Is he bored?

HORRIE: I don't know. He just said he'd like to be doing something. And I've got a few plans.

OOLA: In what line?

HORRIE: I'm good with a safe.

OOLA: Specialised business. Where you been operating?

HORRIE: I'll give it to you straight, Oola. I been in the jug for ten years. Just got out.

OOLA: That don't sound too promising.

HORRIE: Well, it wasn't my fault.

> OOLA *laughs.*

No, honest. The cockatoo let me down and I ran into some trouble with the night watchman. The safe went like [*snapping his fingers*] that.

OOLA: I see. I guess you've heard of me, have you, Horrie?

HORRIE: Who hasn't? You're famous, Oola.

OOLA: I got some influence. And, believe me, you can't have that unless you're determined.

HORRIE: I agree.

OOLA: Well, I got nothing much to be determined about these days. I kissed most of the rackets goodbye years ago. Run a bit of an SP just to keep my hand in. I'm comfortable, you understand? Settled down. So the only thing I got to be determined about is holding onto that comfort. And Charlie's part of it. He don't have to work. He don't have to do anything to get him tangled up with the johns. The day I have to worry about whether the bloke I'm living with is coming home in one piece is the day that bloke gets his walking papers. I just don't want to be bothered with any of that. So suppose you forget about asking Charlie in on any plans you might make, eh?

HORRIE: Just as you like.

OOLA: Good. I'm glad we understand each other.

HORRIE: I meant, if that's how you feel there'd be no point in asking Charlie. A bloke'd have to be crackers to throw you over for a job.

OOLA: Thanks.

> *A pause.* HORRIE *stares at* OOLA. *She becomes disconcerted.*

Look, we haven't met before, have we?

HORRIE: No. I'm sure we haven't. Why?

OOLA: You're looking so hard. Like you were trying to place me from somewhere else.

HORRIE: Was I? I'm awfully sorry, Oola. It's just that ten years in gaol, I'm still a bit starved for the sight of a real woman.

OOLA: Don't try to kid me I'm the sort you've been dreaming about.

HORRIE: Everyone to his own tastes. I've always been very selective.

OOLA: I can believe it. A set-up like yours, you could take your pick.

HORRIE: That's true. And it took me just a couple of years to get sick of the type of girl you think I've been dreaming about. Nowadays—

OOLA: Well, I'm not very interested in what you find attractive, Horrie. Where are you living?

HORRIE: I got a room just around the corner.

OOLA: Comfortable?

HORRIE: It'll do till something better turns up.

OOLA: I guess it will, if you're as handy as you say you are. Maybe I'll be able to fix you up with a few contacts.

HORRIE: If that's possible I would be grateful.

OOLA: We'll see.

HORRIE: Why do they call you Oola? It can't be what you was christened. It sounds like some sort of nickname. Like it comes from the fun of a little kid.

OOLA: Yeah. Imagine you guessing that. It's really Ursula, you see, but when I was little I couldn't get my tongue around it. Oola was what came out and it kind of stuck.

HORRIE: My name's the same. My people were French and I was called Henry. Only they don't say it that way. They said 'On-ray'. Well, nobody out here could get their tongue around that either. So I got Horrie.

OOLA: That was a bit of a comedown after a flash name like—what did you say it was?

HORRIE: On-ray.

OOLA: On-ray to Horrie.

They both begin to laugh.

I had a share in a horse once was called Horrie. We had to admit he was an outsider when he kept jumping the rails and finishing the race on the wrong side of the track. Gawd, what a mad horse. Horrie. Horrie the horse.

HORRIE *whinnies. He blows his jaws out and buries his head in* OOLA'S *neck.*

Oh don't, Horrie, don't. You're tickling.

She pushes him away.

Oh, you are a cheeky thing. Now that's quite enough of that sort of hanky-panky.

HORRIE: [*taking her hand tenderly*] Ten years in gaol is a long time, Oola.

OOLA: [*with a metallic smile*] Yeah, and I been in this business for thirty. I know a con man when I meet one. Let's hear what you really want, Horrie. I might give it to you anyway.

He moves away from her angrily.

HORRIE: Nothing. Nothing. I don't want nothing. I should have known better, I should have kept my mouth shut.

OOLA: [*nicely*] Now don't get sulky with me.

HORRIE: I'm not. It's just that I'm sorry if that's what you think. And I'm embarrassed. Maybe I'd better go.

OOLA: Oh, no you don't. Charlie'll be back in a minute.

HORRIE: That's what I mean. This is his house and if you think I—

OOLA: It's not Charlie's house, it's mine. Now sit down again and behave yourself. Or better still, can you see my shoes?

HORRIE: Here they are.

OOLA: My Gawd, I can't quite reach down that far myself. Would you mind slipping them back onto my feet?

HORRIE: Sure.

> *He squats at her feet and takes her foot in his hand.*

You got a tiny, graceful foot, Oola. Look, it just about fits into my hand.

OOLA: [*in danger of giving in to him*] Just put my shoes on, will you, Horrie?

HORRIE: Hey, did you ever play this game when you was a kid?

> *He pinches each of her toes.*

You know. This little piggy went to market—

OOLA: [*laughing*] Horrie! Horrie! Stop it!

HORRIE: And this little piggy stayed home. This little piggy had roast beef, and this little piggy had none. And this little piggy went...

> *He walks his fingers up her leg.*

... whee, whee, all the way—

> *She slaps his hand away.*

OOLA: Stop it. I never saw such cheek.

> *He walks his fingers up her leg again.*

HORRIE: Whee, whee, whee, whee—

> *The front doorbell is heard ringing.*

OOLA: Oh, Gawd, that'll be the nuns bringing my daughter home. Sit up here. Sit up.

> HORRIE *jams her feet into the shoes and sits beside her.* ESSIE *enters from the kitchen and crosses to the hall.*

ESSIE: That was the doorbell.

OOLA: I heard it.

ESSIE: Pity they had to break the party up.

> OOLA *turns sharply and opens her mouth to answer back.*

Ah! Ah! Remember there are women of God at the door.

> *She exits.*

OOLA: [*nudging* HORRIE] What you need's a good clip under the ear. Cheeky lump!

> HORRIE *nudges her back.*

Now stop it. Give us a hitch up.

HORRIE *assists* OOLA *to her feet. The front door opens to sounds of greeting.*

ESSIE: [*offstage*] Oh, there youse are. We been waiting and waiting.

THELMA: [*offstage*] Hello, Auntie Ess.

ESSIE: [*offstage*] Oh, hello. Give us a kiss. Hello, Sister. Come right in. Just put your bags down there. Your mother is in her study. Did you have a nice trip?

THELMA: [*offstage*] Not very. The train was awfully crowded.

SISTER LUKE: [*offstage*] And so hot.

ESSIE: [*offstage*] Oh, really? [*Calling*] Oola! Oola! They're here, love.

THELMA *enters the room followed by* SISTER MARY LUKE, SISTER MARY MARK *and* ESSIE. THELMA *is nearly sixteen, a pretty child glowing with youth.* SISTER MARY LUKE *is fifty and further along the road to spiritual perfection than* SISTER MARY MARK *who is still inclined to gush a bit over things.* MARK *carries a huge bunch of red poinsettia and can't help noticing that the room is already full of them.* HORRIE *moves away discreetly until the hellos are over.*

OOLA: [*opening her arms to* THELMA] Is this my baby? Is this my little girl?

THELMA: [*throwing herself into* OOLA's *arms*] Mum!

OOLA: Oh, but it's good to see you. Hello, Sister.

LUKE: Hello, Mrs Maguire.

THELMA: It's great to be home, Mum.

OOLA: It's great to have you, lovey.

LUKE: I don't think you've met Sister Mary Mark yet, have you, Mrs Maguire?

OOLA: No, I don't believe I've had that pleasure.

MARK *comes forward and they shake hands.*

OOLA & MARK: [*together*] How do you do?

There is a pause. Then ESSIE *steps in front of* MARK *and extends her hand.*

ESSIE: I'm Thel's great auntie.

MARK: How do you do?

OOLA: I'm sorry, Ess. I thought you two must have met at the door. Yes, this is our Auntie Ess. Oh, and this gentleman here is Mr Horrie Darcel. He's a friend of Charlie's—and Charlie's—a friend of mine.

HORRIE: How do you do?

OOLA: Sister Mary Luke and Sister Mary Mark. And this is my little girl Thelma.

THELMA: I've grown an inch and a half since the last time you saw me, Mum.

OOLA: Have you? Oh, that makes it sound like years since I been up. Can we put those flowers somewhere for you, Sister?

MARK: Oh, yes. They're for you, Mrs Maguire.

OOLA *and* ESSIE *gasp in surprise.*

OOLA: [*taking the flowers*] Oh, thank you, Sister. Thank you. I never seen nothing like them. They're beautiful, aren't they, Ess?

She dumps the flowers into ESSIE's *arms.*

ESSIE: Lovely. [*Gazing around the room, wondering where she can put them*] I've always had a special place for poinsettias. They'll be just right for the party tonight.

MARK: Thelma told us about the party, Mrs Maguire, and I think it's wonderful. A party for St Teresa!

OOLA: Well, it's sort of the least you can do.

ESSIE: I'll just put these into some water. And I've got a nice strong cup of tea made for you out there.

LUKE: Oh no, thank you, Mrs Farrell. It's a bit late for tea. The sisters are expecting us to supper at the local convent. We just dropped Thelma in, really.

ESSIE: Oh, what a pity.

OOLA: I'll tell you what, Ess, you can wrap up one of those cakes for the sisters. They can take it with them.

LUKE: Oh, Mrs Maguire!

OOLA: Now, it's nothing. A nice cream sponge, it'll do youse good.

LUKE: Oh, well, thank you.

ESSIE: I'll go and put it into a bag now. [*At* HORRIE] Would anyone else like a cup of tea seeing as how I've got one made anyhow?

A pause. HORRIE *is admiring* THELMA.

OOLA: Horrie?

HORRIE: Oh, sure. Sure. I'll have one. Thanks. [*He bows to the nuns.*] Well, it's been nice meeting you ladies.

LUKE: And you, Mr Darcel.

HORRIE: I may bump into you again sometime.

LUKE: Perhaps.

ESSIE: [*tugging at* HORRIE] Come on.

ESSIE *and* HORRIE *exit into the kitchen.*

THELMA: Mum, do you think I might go upstairs and change now? It's dreadfully hot in this tunic.

OOLA: Of course, love. And I've got a bit of a surprise for you laid out on your bed. It's something a bit special for the party tonight. Put it on and see if it fits you.

THELMA: Oh, Mum, thanks. [*To* LUKE] I'll say goodbye now, Sister.

LUKE: All right, dear. You're coming to the convent to see us tomorrow, aren't you?

THELMA: Oh, yes, I'll look forward to it. Goodbye, Sister Mark.

MARK: Goodbye, Thelma.

THELMA: [*to* OOLA] I'll be down again in a minute.

OOLA: All right, love.

> THELMA *exits.*

Well, Sisters, she's a credit to you.

LUKE: We've got no complaints at all, Mrs Maguire.

OOLA: She's so tall now. And look at this, Sister. I want you to have a look at this. There's her father. That's Boxer Maguire, that is. And she's the dead spitting image of him.

LUKE: Yes, there's a great resemblance.

OOLA: I might just as well've had nothing to do with it. That's Boxer Maguire, that is. Died with his gloves on at the age of thirty-two.

MARK: What a beautiful belt he's wearing.

OOLA: That's his champeen belt that is. I made it myself. He would have won a real one if he'd lived, but I couldn't wait for that. I wanted a good photo of him then. I must have known I wouldn't have him for much longer.

MARK: Oh, look at this, Sister. [*To* OOLA] Is it a bullet?

OOLA: It is. And there's another story attached to that. That bullet is the sole reason why I hold these St Teresa's Day parties every year. I copped it in the back eight years ago. Nearly finished me, it did. You should see the scar they made getting it out. You'd swear they used a pick and shovel for the job.

MARK: You were… shot?

OOLA: My word I was.

LUKE: What a terrible accident.

OOLA: No, it wasn't no accident. This fella I knew called Frankie Leonard, he did it on purpose.

MARK: But… you could have died.

OOLA: That was the idea he had. Got me one bleak and windy day coming down Hazel Street. Shot me into the gutter and left me for dead.

MARK: And, did they…? Is he…?

OOLA: Funny about that. Here's a sort of coincidence. He got it himself two days later, a couple of hundred yards from where he dropped me. Somebody that was a better shot than he was too. I've heard it said he was dead by the time he hit the asphalt. Of course, I didn't know anything about it at the time, I was in a coma for five days after I got mine. Just laying there in hospital having crisis after crisis till this particular time I can still vividly remember. I was having a dream. A nightmare. I was in a coffin and they was nailing the top on me. And I was alive, you see, but helpless. I couldn't do a thing but just watch them putting the planks over me. Well, the box got darker and darker and I was just about to close my eyes and give up the ghost when I caught the smell of roses somewhere. Something told me there was a beautiful wreath outside the box if only I could see it and I wanted to so much I fought to keep my eyes open. And then with all my strength I lifted myself up and squeezed through where they were putting the last plank on. And I saw them, the roses. And they got nearer and nearer as I looked at them. Then I realised I was sitting up in bed looking at a bunch of flowers the sisters had placed before a statue of St Teresa. And I prayed. I said, 'Oh, St Teresa, help me to live and I'll honour you all my life'. And she heard me. I sunk back and for another two days I slept peaceful. When I woke up the doctors said it was a miracle I was alive. And I said I knew it was. My oath it was.

THELMA *opens the double doors and re-enters. She is now dressed in a simple, white silk dress.*

THELMA: Oh, Sisters, I'm so glad you haven't gone. I wanted to show you this.

OOLA: Oh, you look lovely, Thel.

MARK: [*speaking together*] Isn't it lovely?

LUKE: [*speaking together*] Charming.

THELMA: [*hugging* OOLA] Oh thanks, Mum. It's beautiful.

OOLA: You deserve it for being such a good girl. I must say it fits you something lovely. [*Calling*] Ess! Ess! Come and have a look at Thel in her new dress.

ESSIE: [*offstage*] Oh, coming.

THELMA: [*spinning about*] The skirt is so beautifully flared.

ESSIE *enters with a wrapped cake.*

ESSIE: Oh, look at her. So grown up.

OOLA: Isn't she? I almost want her back in her tunic again.

ESSIE: All the wanting in the world don't stop them from growing up, Oola.

OOLA: I know, more's the pity.

ESSIE: [*giving the cake to* LUKE] Here's the cake, Sister.

LUKE: Thank you, Mrs Farrell. And now we really must be going.

OOLA: It's been lovely having you. Thank you for the beautiful flowers and for bringing Thel down.

LUKE: It was no trouble.

MARK: Goodbye, Mrs Maguire.

ESSIE: I'll show you to the door.

OOLA & THELMA: [*together*] Goodbye.

LUKE & MARK: [*together*] Goodbye.

ESSIE *exits with the nuns. In a moment the front door closes.*

OOLA: [*to* THELMA] Oh, aren't they nice things? Just like little saints themselves. Now come over here and sit beside me so I can have a good look at you.

THELMA *sits beside* OOLA. OOLA *takes her face in her hands.*

Well, well! Boxer Maguire's Thelma.

ESSIE *re-enters.*

ESSIE: They've gone.

OOLA: Oh. What kind of a cake did you give them, Ess?

ESSIE: A passion fruit and cream one. Why?

OOLA: I just wanted to know.

ESSIE: Did you think I'd slip them a rock cake or something?

OOLA: I was only asking. What's Horrie doing?

ESSIE: Talking with his mouth full. I bet he hasn't had a decent feed in months.

> ESSIE *exits into the kitchen.*

OOLA: [*calling after her*] Send him in here when he's finished. I want everybody to see how nice Thel looks. [*To* THELMA] Auntie Ess is a bit off today. She's been baking for the party. Now get up and twist around again like you did before. You did it so graceful.

THELMA: All right.

> THELMA *dances about the room humming a waltz.*

OOLA: Beautiful. Beautiful. Do they teach you dancing at school?

THELMA: Oh, yes. But just with the other girls, you know.

OOLA: Never mind, I don't suppose it'll be long before the young men are lining up. You're going to have a lovely figure, Thel. You're busting out all over like a young tree.

THELMA: [*lowering her head*] Oh, Mum.

OOLA: What's the matter? You'd like to have a pretty figure, wouldn't you? Every girl does.

THELMA: I don't... I don't care about those things.

OOLA: Oh, nonsense. You'll feel different a bit later on. And you come by your good looks honestly enough. Your father was built like a statue, and you mightn't think so to look at me now but when I was your age you could see the fellas' heads spinning like tops as I turned into Taylor Square.

THELMA: I don't care about those things.

OOLA: No? Well, what do you care about, lovey?

THELMA: I was going to have a talk with you sometime over the weekend. Ask you if you'd let me enter.

OOLA: Enter in what?

THELMA: The convent. Study to be a nun.

OOLA: A nun! Is that what you want?

THELMA: Yes, I'm sure I do. How would you feel about that?

OOLA: I don't know. You sprung it on me too sudden. I think I'd be glad. But are you sure? Are you sure it's not just because you've lived in the convent most of your life and now you've got to leave you're maybe a bit scared to face anything else?

THELMA: No. Most of the girls I know can't wait to leave school, but I don't feel that way, I just want to stay on there forever.

OOLA: Have you spoken to anybody else about this?

THELMA: Sister Luke.

OOLA: And what does she say?

THELMA: She said I had to have a talk with you first, and even if you said 'yes', I was to come out into the world and just see what it had to offer. She said that later on, if I still wanted to come back, maybe they would take me.

OOLA: That sounds like real good sense. Though I don't think there's much outside here to make you change your mind. It's a hard world, Thel. Maybe you would be better off safe inside a convent.

THELMA: I thought... you might mind a bit.

OOLA: No. Anything you want, that's what I want too. We'll talk about it again later on.

HORRIE *enters.*

HORRIE: Can I come in?

OOLA: Oh yes, Horrie. This is what I wanted you to see. Stand up, Thel.

THELMA *rises.*

HORRIE: Well, isn't that pretty! Nice enough to eat.

OOLA: Isn't she?

ESSIE *enters with a bowl of poinsettia.*

ESSIE: Now where am I going to put these? The front room is already chock-a-block with them.

OOLA: We'll be holding the party in there. Are you sure you can't fit them in somewhere?

ESSIE: No. You'll be having the place looking like a cemetery.

OOLA: Then put them on the sideboard under Boxer's picture.

ESSIE: I'll try.

OOLA: And then we're going upstairs so that you can get me out of these bloody stays. [*To* THELMA] Oh, you mustn't mind Mum swearing, love. It was the way she was brought up.

ESSIE: Quitter.

OOLA: None of your cheek. [*To* THELMA] You talk to Horrie, love. And I'll bring Charlie down to meet you. Charlie... he sort of boards here. A very sad story. It's the only home he's got. All right, Ess, upstairs and shell me.

OOLA *and* ESSIE *exit into the hall.*

HORRIE: Well, Thelma, I just wouldn't know you was the same person.

THELMA: Well, I am. I'm still the same person.

HORRIE: Maybe you are and then again maybe you're not. New clothes do alter people, you know. How long is it since you looked in the mirror?

THELMA: I don't know. I wanted to get down here as quickly as I could so as I could show the sisters how I looked.

HORRIE: [*leading her to the mirror*] Then you just come over here. Come on. I'm not going to hurt you. Stand there. Now.

He stands behind her and places his hands over her eyes.

THELMA: Oh!

HORRIE: It's all right. This is like a trick I learned when I was by myself for a long while. You see, if you want to be a new person inside as well as outside you've got to put a bit of work into it, think away all those stale old thoughts and make some new ones.

THELMA: Oh, that's silly.

HORRIE: It's not. You just do like I tell you. First of all, make your mind a blank.

THELMA: You can't. You can't just think of nothing.

HORRIE: Try.

THELMA: [*after a moment*] Well, that's about as blank as I can get it.

HORRIE: Good. Now think of the prettiest thing you've ever seen. You got that?

THELMA: Yes, I think so.

HORRIE: Then, tell me about it.

THELMA: Well, last Christmas we were allowed to stay up for midnight Mass. Our school is in the mountains and on the way to the church it was dark. But when we passed through the pine break it suddenly got light. Then you could see the church all lit up, glowing like it had the moon inside it. The clouds were low and they looked like veils. Inside there were hundreds of candles and the incense smelled real sweet. The big bell was ringing and you could hear the echo of it as it came back through the pass. The little altar bells sounded like a song you couldn't quite catch the melody of. That's how it was. And the nuns looked as crisp as tissue paper; and the priests looked like their vestments were standing up without them. They were embroidered in red and silver and gold. That's how it was. I'll never forget it.

HORRIE: Right. Now hold onto that like it was all still there before your eyes. When I take my hand away look through it into the mirror. Now.

> HORRIE *moves away.* THELMA *gazes into the mirror.*

THELMA: Oh, it's just the same.

HORRIE: It's not. You know it isn't.

THELMA: All right, it does feel different. Am I really changed?

HORRIE: I promise you, you are.

THELMA: Gosh, I'm going to remember how to do that every time I'm sad or lonely. I'm going to do it often. I'm glad I met you, Horrie.

HORRIE: I got a dozen or so tricks like that. I can show you a few others you might be anxious to see.

THELMA: Gosh, thanks.

HORRIE: How much longer you got to go at school?

THELMA: I'm not certain. At least another six months.

HORRIE: And what are you going to do when you get out? No, don't tell me. I'll bet you're planning to be an actress or a singer.

THELMA: No. I've got a voice like a foghorn.

HORRIE: But you must have done some acting at school.

THELMA: Oh, yes. Last year we played some scenes from *A Midsummer Night's Dream* by William Shakespeare. It wasn't a very elaborate production but I had the leading role.

HORRIE: What part was that?

THELMA: Titania. She's the queen of the fairies.

HORRIE: Yes, I can imagine that. Why don't you say a bit of it for me? I'm a pretty good judge of acting. I'll tell you whether you're any good or not.

THELMA: Would you?

HORRIE: You bet.

THELMA: Well, there was this part I always loved. It was where she woke up and saw Bottom changed into an ass.

HORRIE: [*laughing*] Bottom?

THELMA: Yes. He's the clown. And he's singing to her, you see. And she opens her eyes and says:

> What angel wakes me from my flowery bed?
> I pray thee, gentle mortal, sing again:
> Mine ear is much enamour'd of thy note;
> So is mine eye enthralled to thy shape;
> And thy fair virtue's force, perforce, doth move me,
> On the first view, to say, to swear, I love thee.

HORRIE *affects great feeling at her recitation and kisses the top of her head.*

HORRIE: That was beautiful, Thelma. Beautiful.

THELMA: Honest? I'm glad you liked it.

HORRIE: It was beautiful.

He kisses her on the forehead. She draws away.

THELMA: Well, I'd better go and change now. I don't want to crush this dress before the party. I'll see you later, Horrie.

HORRIE: I'll see you later.

THELMA *exits.* HORRIE *smiles after her. Then he sits and takes a stiletto from a band around the top of one sock. He begins cleaning his nails with it.*

END OF ACT ONE

ACT TWO

The evening of the same day. When the curtain rises Oola's room is in darkness except for the votive lamp before St Teresa. But there is a lot of noise coming from the main sitting room just along the hall. OOLA *is entertaining her guests in there. In a moment the double doors open and* OOLA *turns the light on. A few guests are revealed sitting on the staircase or leaning over the railing drinking coffee.*

OOLA: [*to the men*] Now, no one's to come in here. Charlie, you divide them into pairs. Horrie, you'd better come in. And Wilma and Thel too. You can help me write the things out. Come on.

> HORRIE, THELMA *and* WILMA CARTWRIGHT *enter the room.*

[*Shutting the door*] Now, see and behave yourselves. We won't be long.

> WILMA CARTWRIGHT *is a thin, nervous woman of forty. Her figure is good but her face too sharp to be pretty.*

I don't know, Horrie. Sounds like a sort of kids' game to me.

HORRIE: No, it's great fun. Treasure hunt. We used to play it all the time. The first thing we need is some slips of paper to write things down on.

OOLA: I think you'll find some paper in that drawer over there, Wil.

WILMA: [*going to the drawer and searching for paper*] Okay.

OOLA: What sort of things?

HORRIE: The craziest objects you can think of. A welcome mat or a pair of combinations. You have a wow of a time picking them up.

OOLA: You mean snitching them?

HORRIE: Now, who's going to worry about an old pair of combinations?

OOLA: It sounds a bit wild to me.

HORRIE: Give it a go. We've got to do something. It's slowing down something dreadful out there.

OOLA: Well...

THELMA: It sounds like terrific fun, Mum.

OOLA: Well, don't get any ideas into your head about you going out, Thel.

THELMA: Oh, Mum.

OOLA: No, love, it's too dangerous for young girls walking around the streets at night. Besides, I want you to stay and play the piano for us.

THELMA: But I'm only up to my chromatic scales.

OOLA: Sounds lovely.

WILMA: There's no paper here, Ool. There's some bits of pencils but no paper.

THELMA: I've got a writing pad upstairs.

OOLA: Oh, would you get that for us, love? I'll buy you a new one.

THELMA: Okay. But I would like to join in, Mum.

OOLA: No, love, no. I won't hear of it.

HORRIE: I'd take care of her, Oola. She could come out with me.

OOLA: No. Just go and get your pad, there's a good girl.

> THELMA *exits.*

WILMA: If there's going to be any trouble, Whitey's not going either.

> WILMA *exits.*

OOLA: Treasure hunt. Gawd. You've got a lot of funny ideas.

HORRIE: [*resting his hands on* OOLA*'s hips*] Yeah, all sorts of funny ideas.

OOLA: Hands off.

HORRIE: I see you managed to get yourself out of those corsets.

OOLA: You shouldn't have noticed I had any on.

HORRIE: It was either that or you had a broomstick laced up your back.

OOLA: If you aren't just the cheekiest thing.

HORRIE: I like a woman to be generously built.

OOLA: You let Charlie hear you say that.

HORRIE: You don't appear to be objecting.

OOLA: Show me a woman who will turn her back on a compliment. But that don't mean she'll be in anything that's going, either. You might lead her up to the water but just watch out she don't turn 'round and push you into it.

HORRIE: I'll take that risk.

OOLA: You're certainly sure of yourself, aren't you? You conceited bugger, you know you're good-looking. You know most women are only human.

> *They are about to kiss when* THELMA *returns with her writing pad. They move apart.*

THELMA: I've got my pad.

OOLA: Oh, good. Now I suppose we'd better tear it up into sheets.

HORRIE: That's right. Tear them big enough so as you can fold them over. They're not supposed to know what they've got to find until they get outside.

> *They tear the paper.*

OOLA: Where's Wil gone? She ought to be good at thinking up things.

THELMA: She's talking to Whitey.

OOLA: Oh. Okay. Here are the pencils. We'd better start writing.

> OOLA, HORRIE *and* THELMA *retire to different parts of the room and begin writing the slips.* WHITEY *enters with* WILMA *following. They are arguing.*

WILMA: Well, I'm telling you, you go out and I go home.

OOLA: Hey, Whitey can't come in. He's in it.

WILMA: No he's not. He's not going.

WHITEY MAGUIRE *is a surly, good-looking man of twenty-nine.*

WHITEY: I'll go where I bloody well like. You mind your own business.

WILMA: It is my business if you get into trouble and land yourself back in the jug.

WHITEY: You think I'm going to have a woman hanging around my neck telling me what I can do and what I can't do?

WILMA: All I'm saying is—

WHITEY: You better not say any more or I'll backhand you across your ears. You'd better just keep your mouth shut.

WILMA: All right then, go! Go! Land yourself back in the jug.

OOLA: Look, maybe you'd better stay, White. Your father will be here in a minute and then you can play the piano for us all. It's a long time since he's heard you play.

WHITEY: I don't want to play the piano.

WILMA: Gawd, you're sociable.

WHITEY: [*raising his hand at* WILMA] Didn't I warn you—

OOLA: [*moving between them*] Oh, White, White; do me a big favour, will you? Be nice to Paddy when he gets here. Give him a go.

WHITEY: Me give him a go! In all the time I been going 'round with Wilma he's never opened his mouth to say 'hello' to her. Not even once.

WILMA: Look, I don't care about—

WHITEY: It's got nothing to do with you. Him not talking to you, that's an insult to me. Let him talk to Wilma and then I'll talk to him.

OOLA: Well, just give him a go. Don't meet him in a temper. You might be surprised how he feels after two years.

WHITEY: Two years in the jug and neither of them came out to see me.

OOLA: You know how disappointed he was. You know how he loves to be respectable.

WHITEY: Well, I'll give him back just as good as he gives me.

OOLA: All right, that's only fair. But you will stay and play the piano for us, won't you? I'll give you a big kiss if you do.

WHITEY: Okay. [*To* WILMA] But I'm not giving in. I'd go if I wanted to.

WILMA: Sure, White. Yeah, I know.

> *She attempts to put her arms about him, but he moves away from her to the piano. He begins to play a sentimental song softly.*

HORRIE: Come on, Oola, they'll be starting to stamp their feet out there in a minute.

THELMA: Look at all I've got written.

OOLA: Oh, yes. Aren't you a good girl. It looks like that'll be enough. Come on, Wil, you write a couple out for us just for good measure.

WILMA: I haven't got an idea in my head, Ool.

OOLA: Gawd, what use are you! I'll have to do it myself, I suppose.

OOLA *sits and thinks.* WILMA *moves to the piano and places her arms about* WHITEY.

WILMA: I'm sorry, love.

WHITEY *doesn't respond, but begins to play 'I Love You Truly'.*

WHITEY: A man's a fool to take it from you.

WILMA: I'm a worrier, White. I worry all the time. But what would I do if I lost you again? I don't want to let you out of my sight for a single second. I'm scared when you're away. Humour me. Please.

WHITEY: A man's a fool.

She lays her head on his shoulder. They take up what is left of the song and sing it to the end, harmonising.

OOLA: That's lovely, Wil. [*Rising*] Okay. I got my two down.

PADDY MAGUIRE *opens the door and pokes his head in. He is a gay, seventy-year-old Irishman.*

PADDY: Is this where they're making the bombs?

OOLA *drags him into the room and embraces him.*

OOLA: Uncle Paddy!

PADDY: Hello, Oola. And, my God, that can't be little baby Thelma.

THELMA: [*kissing him*] Hello, Uncle Paddy.

PADDY: She's a woman.

OOLA: I know. You turn your back for a minute and they've grown a foot.

PADDY: They do. But where's the party? What are all those fellas doing standing 'round in pairs in the hall?

OOLA: Oh, it's just a game we're playing. You don't have to be in it. Just wait here till we pass these slips out and then we'll be back. Come on, everybody. Wil, come on.

PADDY *turns his eyes to the piano and sees* WHITEY. *Everybody exits but these two.*

[*As she goes*] We won't be a minute.

WHITEY *begins playing the piano again.* PADDY *sits on the sofa for a moment and endeavours to ignore his son's presence.*

PADDY: Well, when did they let you out?

WHITEY: [*still playing*] A couple of weeks ago.

PADDY: I thought you had longer to do.

WHITEY: [*bitterly*] Good conduct.

PADDY: Well, that's to your credit.

WHITEY *snorts in contempt.*

You might have called 'round to see your mother.

WHITEY: She didn't come out to see me.

PADDY: You think I'd allow her to visit you in a place like that? It was no fault of hers you was there. But she wanted to go.

WHITEY: [*ceasing to play*] And you bloody well stopped her.

> *Pause.*

PADDY: You was playing well. You haven't lost your touch.

WHITEY: They let me practise at the Bay.

PADDY: And don't say it like I sent you there either.

> WHITEY *begins to thump out 'Rule Britannia'.* PADDY *moves to the piano and slams his hands down on the keys.* WHITEY *stops playing.*

It's a pity they didn't let you practise your manners while you was out there.

WHITEY: My manners are good enough for the company I keep.

PADDY: That's always been my objection.

WHITEY: That's always been none of your business.

> *Pause.* PADDY *returns to his seat.*

PADDY: I see she's stuck to you.

WHITEY: What was it last time? Women don't change?

PADDY: They don't grow any younger, either. How many years is she up on you? Seven? Ten?

WHITEY: Fifteen! Twenty! It doesn't matter.

PADDY: No, it never did. You always liked the older women. And the cheaper the better.

WHITEY: [*threateningly*] Don't push your luck too hard, Pop. Don't push it too hard.

PADDY: Look at me, I'm quivering with fright. [*Angrily*] Don't you try to stand over me, boy.

WHITEY: For Christ's sake, what is the way to talk to you?

PADDY: Like you owed me some respect.

WHITEY: Then do something to make me respect you. Show a bit of bloody pity and... forgetfulness.

PADDY: What? Pat her on the head or something?

WHITEY: Yes. Just that. Aw, let's drop it.

> *He begins to play a sentimental tune on the piano again.*

PADDY: That's a pretty thing.

WHITEY: [*after a moment*] How is Mum?

PADDY: She misses you. She's not Irish, you know. She hasn't got a temper like me... or you. You could go and talk to her. She wouldn't let fly at you.

WHITEY: I'll take Wilma over to meet her, yes.

PADDY: Do you think I'll ever agree to her meeting that... that prostitute?

WHITEY: She's not.

PADDY: Well, she was.

WHITEY: She waited for me.

PADDY: You've only got her word for that.

WHITEY: [*moving away from the piano*] Oh, what's the use? You'll never be convinced.

PADDY: [*after a moment, grudgingly*] Well, if she did wait for you—

WHITEY: [*angrily*] I'm telling you she did.

PADDY: Don't yell at me. I'm trying, boy. But how can I change the way I feel?

WHITEY: You expect it of me. I can't change how I feel either. And it's Wilma and me, Pop. Right down the line.

PADDY: It's not a home without you, Whitey. Your mother and I just sit there. We don't talk much.

WHITEY: I wanted to come but I stopped myself. Not until I can take Wilma too.

PADDY: My God, you're as stubborn as—

WHITEY: You.

PADDY: Yes, but you're younger. I can't stay the distance anymore. I'll tell you what: I'll have another look at her.

WHITEY: She's a good girl, Pop. Just give her a go.

PADDY: I'll have another look at her.

> OOLA *returns, followed by* WILMA *and* THELMA.

OOLA: Well, they're off at last. I've got my fingers crossed.

> ESSIE *enters from the kitchen.*

ESSIE: Why, hello, Paddy.

PADDY: Hello, Mrs Farrell. My God, I don't know who's the prettier, you or little Thelma here.

ESSIE: Don't you blarney me, you old top hat.

OOLA: The trouble with Ess is she doesn't know how to take a compliment. [*Sitting*] Oh, it's good to get the weight off your feet.

ESSIE: Well, don't get too comfortable. We'll have to have supper ready by the time they get back.

OOLA: Gawd, you been out there all night. What else is there to do?

ESSIE: Put pickled onions on the savouries. And I hate making sandwiches before the time they're to be served.

OOLA: All right, well just forget all that for a minute. We'll give you a hand when the time comes. Come over here and give us another kiss, Paddy.

PADDY: Never have to be asked twice.

> As he moves to OOLA he passes WILMA.

And how have you been?

WILMA: [*stunned*] Who? Me? Oh, I'm fine. Fine thank you, Mr Maguire.

PADDY: Well... health's a wonderful thing. Look after yourself.

> He continues to OOLA and kisses her on the cheek.

OOLA: Thanks, Uncle Paddy. I love you. Come on now, Thel. Now we're all settled I want to hear you play. [*To* PADDY] Thel's been learning classical music at the convent.

THELMA: Mum, I told you; I only know my chromatic scales.

OOLA: That doesn't matter, love. Maybe some of us haven't heard it.

THELMA: Well, all right.

> She moves to the piano and plays a couple of chromatic scales. She pauses.

OOLA: What's the matter, love? Have you forgotten it?

THELMA: That's all there is. I told you—

OOLA: Well, that's the shortest piece of classical music I've ever heard. Gawd, the things they get away with!

WHITEY: It's just like a practice piece, Oola. To make you play better.

OOLA: People have still got to listen to it, haven't they? Couldn't they write them with tunes to them?

THELMA: No, Mum, you see—

OOLA: Oh, it doesn't matter, love. Mum's just probably dumb or something. You played it beautiful... what there was of it. Wilma will do us her hula now.

WILMA: Oh no, I couldn't, Ool.

OOLA: Don't be silly. You've got to be in it.

WHITEY: Onto your feet.

OOLA: Oh, Ess, get me a couple of spoons. I'll play them while Wil dances.

THELMA: [moving to the kitchen] I'll get them, Auntie Ess.

ESSIE: Thanks, love.

PADDY: [to WILMA] What kind of dance is this you're going to do?

WILMA: It's just a hula. You know.

OOLA: She does it so graceful. You wait till you see her, Uncle Paddy.

PADDY: Well, we'll have a look at it.

> In tribute to his father, WHITEY begins to thump out 'Ireland a Nation'. PADDY rushes to the piano and both men sing:

PADDY & WHITEY: [together]
> Ireland a nation!
> Ireland a nation!
> Ireland a nation!
> Sinn Fein!
> Sinn Fein!

OOLA: Oh, my God, they could run youse in for singing it like that.

> THELMA returns with two dessert spoons and gives them to OOLA.

THELMA: Here are the spoons, Mum.

OOLA: Thanks, love. Now, come on, Wil.

WILMA: [taking up a hula position] Well, I hope I remember it all.

> She looks around to WHITEY who is gazing at her tenderly.

Right?

WHITEY: Oh, yeah, yeah. Go for your life, love.

> WHITEY *plays 'Lovely Hula Hands',* WILMA *dances a very free version of the hula accompanied by* OOLA *on the spoons. When she gets into her stride* OOLA *begins running the spoons over her thighs and down her legs.*

PADDY: Woo! Look at her go.

THELMA: Isn't she good, Mum?

OOLA: Don't talk to me, love, I got to keep the rhythm.

ESSIE: It's a wonder to me she don't turn herself inside out.

PADDY: That's a wonderful dance. It is indeed.

WILMA: I could teach it to you if you like, Mr Maguire.

PADDY: [*leaping up and attempting to follow* WILMA] Right. How does it go?

WHITEY: That's the shot, Pop. Fall in and follow the leader.

ESSIE: You've got to be in everything, Paddy Maguire. A real lair.

WHITEY: Hey, Oola, watch it. You're losing the beat.

OOLA: [*putting down the spoons*] It's no use. I can't laugh and play too. I keep missing myself.

> *The song and dance ends. Everybody applauds.*

Well, I've got to admit you was marvellous at it, Paddy.

PADDY: There's never been nothing I've never been able to learn. The little lady was the best at it, though.

ESSIE: Big of you to admit it.

OOLA: Now don't get down again, Uncle Paddy. While you're up on your feet tell us about the big blue in Warwick.

PADDY: Surely you've heard it all two or three times?

OOLA: Wilma hasn't and neither has Thel.

ESSIE: Do you think she ought to?

OOLA: Maybe you're right. It's about time you was in bed anyway, love.

THELMA: Oh, it's not late, Mum.

PADDY: Will you have the child thinking I'm going to repeat something obscene? Why, it's a plain and simple story of heroism and bravery.

OOLA: That all depends on the language you intend using. Now, be a good girl, love. You'd be in bed earlier than this if you was at school.

THELMA: Okay. [*Kissing* OOLA] Goodnight, Mum. Thanks for having me down.

OOLA: Aw, goodnight.

THELMA: [*kissing* PADDY] Goodnight, Uncle Paddy. I hope I see you again soon.

PADDY: You will, my darling.

ALL: Goodnight, Thel.

THELMA: Goodnight.

> *She exits into the hall.*

PADDY: Now, you can run me out of the house if I so much as use a single curse.

ESSIE: Go on then and tell it.

PADDY: Okay. This is the way it happened. In nineteen hundred and nine or thereabouts. The time my sisters lived at Warwick looking after my old Dad, God rest his soul. Martin and I, he was my brother, Boxer's father, God rest his soul too; Martin and I was fencing and road-building and generally working at whatever came along to earn a crust. Sometimes we'd be together, but like as not we'd be apart. And this time I'm going to tell you about there was over a hundred miles between us. He was working on a road and I was out further engaged in more complicated employment, I being the stronger of the two.

ESSIE: Ha! To hear Martin tell it, it was always him who was the stronger of the two.

PADDY: God rest his soul, Marty had the best of intentions but no eye for details. He'd get carried away by a story and never know where to draw the line. This'll be the true version you're hearing now.

OOLA: Okay. We'll take your word for it. Tell us how alike you was.

PADDY: [to WILMA] As alike as two Chinamen in the dark. When we walked into some of those country dances the locals used to get up guessing competitions to decide who was who. Now, talking of country dances, brings me to the scene of the event. It happened at a ball that Mrs Munroe was holding to open her new hotel, the Warwick Royal. It seemed that everybody was going to it. I'd arranged to ride in from the scrub and join Marty and the girls there. God, I wish I had a drink, Oola. It's difficult to get into it without a drink.

OOLA: You know the rules. Get onto Hinchey.

ESSIE: Aw, I love hearing about that bruiser. It makes my flesh creep.

WILMA: Who was Hinchey?

PADDY: Hinchey! A great big black-hearted, carrot-topped, hairy, foul-mouthed bastard.

OOLA: Oh, there you go.

PADDY: That's who Hinchey was. He came from the North.

WILMA: North where?

PADDY: Ireland, of course. Where else is there a North? Martin was working with him on the road and they was bitter enemies, though none of it was Marty's fault. He was a peaceable lad. Always said his prayers at night and went to Mass on Sunday. And this was the beginning of the row with Hinchey. Every Sunday morning when he came back from Mass, all decked out in his suit with his missal under his arm, Hinchey would be lying in wait for him like a big goanna astraddle a log sunning himself. He'd get a crowd of other Orangemen around him, layabouts as rotten as himself, and they'd snigger and giggle and nudge each other as Martin passed.

Hinchey'd shout out, 'How's the Pope this morning?' And all the rest of the bludgers'd laugh and roll about on the grass thinking it was a great joke. Well, most of the time Marty used to ignore him. He'd just move on quietly. Oh, he had a beautiful dignity about him. But one morning his Irish got the better of him, and when Hinchey shouts out, 'How's the Pope this morning?' Marty replies, 'Fine, and praying for all the poor damned Protestants'. Oh, that Hinchey let out a yell. You'd have sworn he'd been hit. He could give it, you see, but he couldn't take it.

WILMA: What happened? Did they work him over?

PADDY: No, they was mean rats and too scared to start a real brawl. They wasn't so sure the rest of the camp'd be on their side. You see, Hinchey was the type that brooded and bided his time plotting and planning. And he saw his opportunity to get even with Marty on the night of Mrs Munroe's ball. He knew that Marty was considered to be the most honest man in Warwick and so he'd been asked to take the tickets at the door. Hinchey'd stated his intention of going to the ball without a ticket: 'And just let that Marty Maguire ask me for one'.

WILMA: Oh, wasn't he mean?

OOLA: Mind you, Wil, Uncle Paddy wasn't actually there for any of this.

PADDY: Marty told me all about it afterwards. Very vivid with his descriptions he was.

OOLA: That's a gift you both had... always. You could always tell a lovely story.

PADDY: You're right. It is a gift. Well anyway, on the night of the ball the whole town spruces itself up. They polish their top hats and they lace themselves into their bustles and button themselves into their shoes. Marty took his place at the door early and Bridgie, Boxer's mother, was in a cane chair beside him, feasting her eyes on the rich ones who were turning up in diamonds and emeralds and honest-to-God fur capes, though in fact the night was hot and they were only wearing them to show they had them. Well, while all this activity is going on I'm riding in from the scrub, lathering my horse into a foam so as to get there on time. But what with one thing and another, a fallen tree I had to get off and move, a river to ford with a stronger current than I'd expected, I get to the house late and was told they'd left without me. Determined to lose no further time, I begin to spruce myself up so as I can join them. Meanwhile, back at the ball, Hinchey has arrived with his mob and when they see there's no one about outside they stalk up those ten beautiful front steps of the establishment and try to get past Marty into the foyer. 'Hey there, Hinchey, where's your ticket?' shouts Marty. 'Friends of the management', snarls back Hinchey. 'You've never been the friends of anybody', quips back Marty. Well, that was as good an excuse as Hinchey needed to go for him. He rushes at Marty like a bull and Bridgie jumps out of her chair in panic and Hinchey collides with it and over they both go again and again until they come to those twelve beautiful front steps again and Hinchey is on his way down. And by the bottom of them he's out like a light. The outcry brought Mrs Munroe to the balcony and does she put a flea in those mugs' ears! She orders them off the premises and warns them not to come back. And she can see Bridgie's upset by the incident and she tells Marty to take her home and she'll get someone else to see to the door. So they all go off. Bridgie and Marty back to our place and Hinchey's bludgers carry him around to the coach yard and begin passing a bottle until he comes to. Now, as coincidence would have it, I pass the coach yard at this time and I see this fella prostrate on a seat and these bludgers all around him, so I pause for a minute to observe what's going on and one of the fellas shouts at me, 'You'd better be on your way before Hinchey comes 'round, mug'. I think, 'What the hell? Who's this Hinchey? And who's that calling me a mug?' So I move a bit closer.

OOLA: They took him for Marty, see. They was so alike.

WILMA: Oh.

PADDY: Now you wouldn't credit it, but the moment I was level with Hinchey, he opens his eyes. 'Mug', he snarls and the whole seven and a half feet of him gets off the seat and towers over me.

ESSIE: Oh, I always get scared at this bit.

PADDY: 'What was that you called me?' I says. 'Further around the back', he says and he pushes me toward a patch of ground out of the general view. 'Right', says I. I was a cocky lad, you see, ready for anything. 'I don't know who you are', I says, 'And by the time I'm finished with you neither will your mother'. The others make a kind of circle around us and I'm just halfway through taking off my coat when Hinchey makes the first swing, low down, dirty. I leaps away from him, comes up under his armpit and into his bread basket with a right. Then it was a left and a right and another left again. I got his style after the first swing and then it was just a matter of finishing him off. It was simple, like working a punching bag. He was swinging wild, of course, and the air around him was black with his cursing. Left, right! Ooff! Ooff! One to the head. He was staggering.

ESSIE: Don't forget he'd fallen down a flight of stone steps before this.

PADDY: Considering his size we was fairly matched like David and Goliath. He was seven and a half foot long and four foot wide. Ooff! Ooff! I was closing in for the kill when one of his mates, just to save him, I suppose, pretends the cops are coming. 'It's every man for himself', he yells and they all scatter like falling chaff. I give Hinchey one more punch and he goes down for the count. Then I scatter too.

WILMA: It's a pity you couldn't have stopped to count him right out.

PADDY: It was, but I thought the police was coming too and I didn't want to spend the weekend in the calaboose. I beats it up the back steps of the pub and into the ballroom, and you'd hardly credit it, Hinchey after me.

ESSIE: I thought you said he was taking the count?

PADDY: I never seen a man recover so quick. The skull of an ox.

OOLA: Don't keep asking questions.

ESSIE: Well, you're chipping in too.

OOLA: Shh!

PADDY: Well, there I was in the ballroom and everybody's waltzing around me like there was nothing going on in the world but dancing. I see a little room at the side and decide to duck in there until things cool down a bit. Hinchey arrives just in time to see me go in and close the door and he follows. I could hear the women screaming as he lumbered across the floor. He was a terrible sight. Bright red with rage and blood, from forehead to toetip. Now the room I'm in is where Mrs Munroe had stored all the bits and pieces of furniture and mirrors and things that she hasn't put into the rooms yet. I ducks behind a lowboy and waits, as still as a mouse. Then Hinchey enters and I can hear him breathing heavy as he drags the furniture aside to seek me out. But I was moving from one place to another, light on my feet as a bower bird. I hadn't bargained for those mirrors though. I come to one part of the room and it's like moving through a maze. I haven't any idea of what was reflection and what was real. I turn a corner and oh! There's Hinchey!

> WILMA screams.

'You Pope-worshipping ponce', he screams, and with all the strength left in him he swings at me. Well, of course, I wasn't there by that time and he goes straight into an eight-foot mirror. Holy Ghost! You should have seen that room shatter. He was swinging even wilder and there was bedsteads going and candlesticks and drawers all crashing about with the noise of a war in Hell.

WILMA: And was you hurt at all?

PADDY: No. By then I was outside sitting in a chair waiting for the police to come and collect him. And when they did come they carted him straight off to the hospital. In the end he had to pay for every scrap of damage he'd caused and you've never seen a sorrier man in the state of Queensland. That's the story.

WILMA: Oh, isn't it a pity none of youse got to dance at the ball, though?

PADDY: What do you mean?

OOLA: [laughing] Now, Uncle Paddy, leave off. Don't go too far. This bit's a real lie and you know it.

PADDY: It's the truth of the Lord. I have witnesses. I walked out of that chaos up to the first pretty girl I saw and asked her to dance with me. She agreed and within two ticks she was two-stepping across the floor with me. Inside a year she was Whitey here's mother.

> WHITEY plays a final dramatic chord on the piano and everybody applauds.

OOLA: Now that's what I call a story.

WILMA: What a time youse must have had.

PADDY: Oh, that was just the beginning of it all.

ESSIE: [*rising*] Well, before you begin again let's see how clever you are at making sandwiches.

OOLA: Oh, Ess, we don't have to all go out, do we?

PADDY: She doesn't want to miss anything, do you, Mrs Farrell? Well, I'll come and lend you a hand and we'll sing the time away.

OOLA: I suppose it'll be done all the quicker if we all pitch in.

ESSIE: Onto your feet then.

OOLA: [*to* PADDY, *as she rises*] I'll give you three guesses who runs this place.

> OOLA, PADDY *and* ESSIE *exit into the kitchen.* WILMA *and* WHITEY *linger in the doorway.*

WILMA: Hey, White, your father talked to me.

WHITEY: What's so funny about that?

WILMA: Aaw, White! Look, I'm so happy.

WHITEY: I knew he'd come around. He just had to get to know you.

WILMA: Look, I'm that happy, White.

WHITEY: Come on, I suppose you'd better find out what a kitchen looks like sometime.

> They exit into the kitchen.
>
> The lights die and then rise again to denote the passing of time.
>
> No changes are made to the set. Laughter and singing can be heard from the kitchen. In a moment the double doors open and CHARLIE looks into the room furtively. He enters the room, quietly followed by HORRIE.

CHARLIE: They're out in the kitchen. We must be the first back.

HORRIE: I told you we would be. We could have had another beer.

CHARLIE: No, you've had enough.

> He takes up a bowl of peppermints and pops one into his mouth. He offers the tray to HORRIE.

Here, have one of these peppermints. If Oola smells booze on our breaths she'll kill us.

HORRIE: [*pushing the tray aside*] Aaw, come off it.

CHARLIE: No, chew one. You don't understand how she feels about this party. She said no grog and she meant it.

HORRIE: We weren't drinking here. Stand up to her. Tell her that you came 'round to my place for a quick one and that's that.

CHARLIE: You don't understand. Hey, what about what we had to find on the treasure hunt?

HORRIE: Grab anything. Swipe a broom and tell her you had that written down.

CHARLIE: How can I get a broom? They're all out in the kitchen.

HORRIE: Say you had to pick up one of these.

> *He takes up the statue of St Teresa and tosses it to* CHARLIE, *who just manages to catch it. He replaces it on the mantelpiece.*

CHARLIE: Are you crazy? What's up with you?

HORRIE: I thought this was going to be a real lively party.

CHARLIE: I warned you it'd be different.

HORRIE: Well, I'm not the type to stand still. No grog, no women. I might as well still be inside. [*He takes a flask of alcohol from his back pocket.*] I don't know about you, but I'm going to have another one.

CHARLIE: What did you have to bring that back for? God! Put it away.

HORRIE: [*drinking*] Go to hell.

CHARLIE: Put it away.

HORRIE: [*shoving* CHARLIE] Shove off.

CHARLIE: I think you'd better get out, Horrie. I'm warning you, don't try to cross Oola or you'll come off second best. You'll get more than you bargained for.

HORRIE: [*smiling*] Is that right?

CHARLIE: You're on your own, then. But don't forget I warned you. I think I saw a broom up there in the spare room. [*He moves to the door, then pauses.*] Oh, God, just my luck, Thelma's up there.

HORRIE: I'll get it for you.

CHARLIE: You stay where you bloody well are.

HORRIE: What are you scared of? Think I'm getting in too good with Oola?

> THELMA *opens the door and peeps in.*

THELMA: Oh, I'm sorry. I didn't know anybody was back.

CHARLIE: It's all right, Thel, come in. What did you want?

THELMA: My writing pad. I loaned it to Mum to write the things down for the treasure hunt.

CHARLIE: Oh, it'll be somewhere around here then.

THELMA: There it is.

> *She moves to the pad.* CHARLIE *signals to* HORRIE *to keep her there for a moment while he goes upstairs. He exits.*

HORRIE: It's time you were asleep, isn't it?

THELMA: I'm so excited it's just impossible, so I thought I'd write a letter to my girlfriend Gloria back at school. Of course I'll get there before the letter does but it's all been so marvellous I want to set it down while it's still fresh in my mind. Excuse me.

HORRIE: [*blocking her path*] I suppose you'll tell her all about the new people you've met. Do you like them?

THELMA: Yes. Most of them.

HORRIE: Do you like me?

THELMA: Oh, yes. What you showed me this afternoon about looking in the mirror, I thought that was terrific.

HORRIE: And what about that other thing we were talking about, about you maybe becoming an actress? How did that strike you?

THELMA: Oh, well, do you honestly think I could?

HORRIE: I'm sure you could.

THELMA: Gosh!

HORRIE: In fact, I'd like to have a long talk with you about it sometime.

THELMA: When?

HORRIE: Any time you like.

THELMA: I'm going back to school tomorrow night. Could you write me a letter?

HORRIE: It's not the same as talking it over.

THELMA: Well, you see, I'm going to see the sisters at the convent in the afternoon.

HORRIE: What about the morning?

THELMA: I go to Mass, of course.

HORRIE: Well, couldn't you call and see me on your way home from there? I'm just around the corner.

THELMA: Well, I don't think Mum'd like that.

HORRIE: Does she have to know?

THELMA: I couldn't lie to her.

HORRIE: You don't have to say anything at all. That's not lying.

THELMA: No, I don't think so, Horrie.

HORRIE: [*stroking her hair*] Why not?

THELMA: I just couldn't.

HORRIE: Not even if I said your whole life may depend on it? What do you intend doing when you leave school?

THELMA: Oh, I had some plans.

HORRIE: They can't have been as important as the ones I have for you.

THELMA: Oh, Horrie, so much has happened today, I'm all mixed up. This morning I knew exactly what I wanted to do. I knew who I was, but now… I'm not so sure.

HORRIE: That's how things are when you're young. You change your mind all the time and it's always for the better.

THELMA: Is it?

HORRIE: I'm telling you.

> *He places his arm about her. She is reluctant to move away but tries.*

THELMA: I'd better get back to my room now, Horrie.

HORRIE: [*holding her tighter*] All right.

THELMA: I can't go if you're holding me.

HORRIE: Thelma?

THELMA: Yes?

HORRIE: Look at me.

THELMA: I can't.

HORRIE: Yes. Look at me.

> THELMA *lifts her face to him. He kisses her forehead and is about to kiss her lips when* OOLA *enters from the kitchen with a tray of savouries. She drops the tray and stands for a moment dumbfounded.* HORRIE *releases* THELMA *and she moves to the door. As she is about to exit* OOLA *finds her voice.*

OOLA: Thelma!

HORRIE: [*with a laugh*] She's an affectionate kid, isn't she, Oola?

> OOLA *smacks* HORRIE*'s face.*

OOLA: Get out of here, you filthy bastard.

HORRIE: Hey, what's up with you? Oh, Ool, you're surely not jealous?

THELMA: [*beginning to weep*] Mum...

OOLA: You! You think this is the right way to start being a nun?

THELMA: I only—

OOLA: What do you mean by coming down here in your nightdress?

THELMA: I wanted my writing pad.

OOLA: Get back to your room this instant. [*To* HORRIE] Didn't I tell you to get out of here? My God, I'll settle your hash.

HORRIE: Now hold on a minute.

> CHARLIE *enters holding a mop.*

CHARLIE: Hello, Ool. I'm back.

OOLA: Have you both been drinking? I can smell you from here.

CHARLIE: No.

OOLA: Well, you can get out too. Pack your things and get out.

CHARLIE: What's going on?

HORRIE: I'll tell you what's going on. Mother's had to face the fact that her sweet little daughter's as much a trollop as she is.

OOLA: [*to* CHARLIE] Get him out of here.

CHARLIE: All right, boy, you've been asking for this.

> *He swings the mop at* HORRIE. HORRIE *avoids it and reveals his knife.*

OOLA: Look out, Charlie, he's got a knife.

> CHARLIE *makes another swing at* HORRIE *with the mop. Again* HORRIE *avoids it and this time lunges back at* CHARLIE *stabbing the knife into his stomach.* OOLA *and* THELMA *scream.*

Charlie! Oh, God, no!

> ESSIE, PADDY, WILMA *and* WHITEY *come piling into the room from the kitchen.* HORRIE *opens the double doors and exits into the hall. We see him remove a gun from the drawer of a dresser against the stairway and run up the stairs.*

CHARLIE: You bastard. He's stabbed me, the bastard.

> *On* HORRIE's *exit, knocking begins at the front door. Shouts of 'We're back, Ool', 'Let us in' and 'Get that prize money ready' are heard from the guests outside.* WHITEY *rushes to the door.* WILMA *attempts to detain him.*

WILMA: No, White, not you too.

WHITEY: I've got to let the others in. Somebody has to.

> WHITEY *runs out into the hall.* OOLA *grabs* THELMA *who begins to scream hysterically and push her mother away.* PADDY *and* ESSIE *have taken* CHARLIE *to the sofa. He is writhing in pain.* HORRIE *shoots down the stairs at* WHITEY, *but* WHITEY *manages to get the door open and the guests rush into the hall. They take their guns from the dresser drawer and exchange shots with* HORRIE.

WILMA: Whitey, Whitey, come in here.

> WHITEY *runs back into the room.* WILMA *slams the door shut.*

Are you all right?

WHITEY: Of course I am.

OOLA: [*to* WHITEY] Play something loud on the piano. We don't want the johns in on this. Sing! Sing! Make as much noise as you can!

> WHITEY *runs to the piano and begins to thump out 'Come Back to Erin'. Everybody except* THELMA *and* CHARLIE *sing.*

That's it. Louder. Louder.

> *More shots from the hall. The people around the piano sing louder.*

END OF ACT TWO

ACT THREE

Early the following morning. When the curtain rises the room is deserted. All traces of the party have been removed. The poinsettia are wilting.

The front door slams. OOLA *and* WILMA *enter, both wearing topper coats* over their Second Act dresses.* WILMA*'s has clearly been borrowed from* OOLA. *They move into the room with the motion of people following a funeral.* WILMA *sits on the sofa.* OOLA *moves to Boxer's picture. It looks a little crooked to her. She straightens it.* WILMA *begins to cry softly.* OOLA *moves to her and gives in to tears herself. They fold their arms about each other and simply wail.*

ESSIE *appears from the kitchen. She has changed her dress and wears a clean apron.*

ESSIE: I thought I heard the door go.

> OOLA *and* WILMA *make no response. They go right on wailing.* ESSIE *turns to go.*

I'll put youse on a cup of tea. [*Pausing*] Oh, did poor old Charlie die?

> OOLA *nods her head: yes.*

Yes, I thought he would. Who else?

OOLA: Gary Cambridge, Freddie Dwyer and… him.

ESSIE: Horrie?

> OOLA *nods her head again: yes.*

It's a wonder to me only four of them copped it. The bullets was flying around like confetti at the last.

OOLA: Don't be disrespectful.

ESSIE: What's up with Wilma?

WILMA: They're holding Whitey. He didn't do nothing. He never stopped playing the piano.

OOLA: They'll find that out once they check everyone's story and then they'll let him go.

WILMA: But you never know what the others is going to say. Oh, and did you hear him giving them cheek? They'll hold onto him for as long as they can if he keeps going on like that. Why did he keep going on like that?

ESSIE: Nobody's got no reason to frame him, have they?

WILMA: Oh, I don't know. I'm nearly mad with worry.

ESSIE: They must be holding Paddy too, are they?

---

* Flared thigh-length coats fashionable in the 1950s.

OOLA: Oh, Gawd, yes. You can hear him all over the station. To hear him talk he's going to have everybody's badge.

ESSIE: Well, they won't hold them any longer than they have to if he's in with the mob. [*Brightly*] And I suppose things could be worse. It could be one of us stretched out in the morgue.

OOLA: Where's Thelma?

ESSIE: I put her to bed after the cops arrived. She's still asleep, I think.

OOLA: Did she calm down?

ESSIE: After a while. Poor little bugger, she was frightened out of her wits. I wouldn't be surprised if she never gets over it.

OOLA: Neither will I… what I saw.

ESSIE: Maybe you was just jumping to conclusions.

OOLA: I know what I saw.

ESSIE: Well, what if he was going to kiss her! You're a grown woman and you'd have gone off with him in a flash. How should a child of fifteen be able to resist him?

OOLA: It's the deception I can't bear. This butter-wouldn't-melt-in-her-mouth act she was throwing around.

ESSIE: Anyway, it was foolish of you to have her home among all those people, in the first place.

OOLA: What do you mean? It was you that was all for it yesterday.

ESSIE: Well, I've changed me mind about it today.

OOLA: Today's a bit too late.

ESSIE: Maybe, but we happen to be stuck with it. We've just got to pick up what we can and go on from here.

OOLA: [*weeping*] I can't. I don't even think I want to. I haven't got the strength. I just want to crawl into a hole somewhere and die.

ESSIE: Now, I'm not going to sympathise with you, Oola. It'll only make you worse. You pull yourself together. There's going to be a lot to be seen to today.

OOLA: I don't want any sympathy. I just want to die.

ESSIE: You'll change your mind about that after you've got some scrambled eggs and steak inside you. I'll get you some tea to start off with.

    ESSIE *moves into the kitchen.*

OOLA: She's a hard woman, that Essie Farrell.

WILMA: Oh, Ool, what am I going to do if they take Whitey away again? Two years he's been gone and I only just got him back. I can't lose him again.

OOLA: He'll be okay. He'll be back.

WILMA: Two years and I never looked at another man. That was tough considering what I'd been until I met Whitey. I'd sit in my room fighting down the need to be near someone, like any old boozer you'd see shivering in the gutter waiting for the pubs to open.

OOLA: Wilma, how can I help you? I got nothing to give, I'm a wreck myself.

WILMA: If he ever went away again I'd kill myself. I know I would. I'd kill myself.

OOLA: Stop it. That's wicked, that talk.

WILMA: [*hysterically*] I want Whitey.

OOLA: [*shaking her*] Do you want me to smack your face?

> WILMA *puts her arms around* OOLA *and rests her head on her breast.* OOLA *rocks her back and forth to comfort her.*

There, there.

WILMA: [*after a moment*] Ool, Whitey and me was married a couple of weeks ago.

OOLA: Was youse? Whereabouts?

WILMA: Jervis Bay. We had a sort of honeymoon there too. I wasn't saying anything. I thought youse'd all laugh at me.

OOLA: Just let me hear anybody laughing. Oh, Wil, I'm so glad for you.

> ESSIE *enters from the kitchen.*

Ess, guess what? Wilma and Whitey was married down at Jervis Bay.

ESSIE: Oh, isn't that marvellous! Give us a kiss, love. Congratulations.

WILMA: Thanks, Ess. And we was married in a real church too.

ESSIE: Was you a bride?

WILMA: Oh, no, that would have been too much fuss. I was just wearing ordinary clothes.

OOLA: Something special though, surely?

WILMA: Oh, yes. Coffee silk with a pink hat and beige accessories. Whitey bought me an orchid.

OOLA: Oh, why didn't you let us know? We'd have all gone up with you.

WILMA: Well, Whitey said he didn't think his mother and father would come and if they wouldn't we didn't see the point of inviting anybody else.

OOLA: Do you know if Whitey's said anything to Paddy yet?

WILMA: Not to my knowledge. But he mightn't mind as much as I thought. I was real pleased when he spoke to me last night and treated me so nice.

OOLA: He'll come 'round, won't he, Ess?

ESSIE: Of course. Now you're as honest as he is.

WILMA: That's how I've always wanted it to be. I want the best for Whitey. Everything out in the open.

OOLA: I know.

ESSIE: Tell us more about the wedding. Where did you stay?

WILMA: In one of those classy beach hotels. Oh, I can't tell you what it was like when I saw Whitey writing Mr and Mrs W. Maguire in the register. Of course, he'd done it lots of times before, but to know that this time it was fair dinkum... it was such a thrill.

OOLA: Wilma Maguire!

WILMA: I been saying it over to myself all week.

OOLA: Say it some more. That ought to cheer you up a bit.

WILMA: I do feel a bit better now that I've talked it all over with someone. And I'm sure you're right. They can't hold Whitey for something he didn't do. There's all of us to swear he was in here playing the piano. And if they don't believe us they'd have to believe a nice little kid like Thelma.

OOLA: [*sadly*] Oh, yes.

WILMA: What's up?

OOLA: I hadn't thought of her having to go through that. She'll find out everything, won't she? About Charlie and I and the rest of it. Oh, well, if it's got to be! Poor old Charlie, I liked him a lot. He went like a gent, Ess. Father Simpson was there to give him the last rites, a real send-off with all the trimmings. And when he'd finished Charlie shook hands with me and tried to smile a bit. Then he just closed his eyes, gave a couple of little shudders and he was gone. People surprise you. He went like a gent.

ESSIE: He was probably so drugged up he didn't know what was happening.

OOLA: [*angrily*] He knew all right and he went like a gent. You dare say anything else, you sarcastic old cow…

She sees that ESSIE *herself is weeping.*

Oh, Ess, I'm sorry.

ESSIE: I got me feelings. I don't go 'round whingeing and wailing about them. If you'd asked me I could have told you he'd go like a gent. Poor old Charlie.

The kettle whistles from the kitchen. ESSIE *moves from the room.*

There's the kettle.

OOLA: Wil, do you know what one of those coppers down at the station had the hide to say to me?

WILMA: What, Ool?

OOLA: He said I was the kiss of death.

WILMA: Aaw, coppers!

OOLA: Well, in a way it's true when you count up all the blokes who've known me that are dead. Boxer and Charlie and…

WILMA: Now don't get morbid. None of that was your fault.

OOLA: I was involved with them. I guess I been bad luck to everybody that knew me.

WILMA: You're getting morose.

OOLA: I'm not. But I've always had this feeling about myself, like no matter what I've done to other people it's really myself I've been hurting. I got the feeling that I was never really meant to be like this. Like, underneath it all, I was someone special. Like I was born with that and it couldn't be taken away from me. Like you're born with a certain colouring or born to be a queen. Something like that.

WILMA: I don't know what you're talking about, Ool.

OOLA: It doesn't matter. It's just this feeling. This feeling I get.

> ESSIE *enters with a tray of tea.*

ESSIE: This'll put some life into us all. [*To* OOLA] Move that great rump of yours over and let me sit down. Do you take milk, Wil?

WILMA: Nothing. Black, no sugar.

ESSIE: You're easy. Want a biscuit?

WILMA: No.

OOLA: I don't think either of us cares much about eating.

ESSIE: Remember what your mother used to say: 'Feed a crisis'. Now let's get organised. First off, is there anything we've got to get together on? Anything special we've got to tell the johns?

OOLA: Just tell them the truth. Oh, we don't have to say how the fight started. All we know is that it happened between him and Charlie and we were there.

ESSIE: Is that what you're going to tell the papers?

OOLA: Don't tell them anything.

ESSIE: If you don't they'll make it up.

OOLA: Let them.

ESSIE: Well, just make sure your hair's done in case they surprise you and take a photograph. Just look at it. You'd never know I set it yesterday.

OOLA: I got more to worry about than my hair.

ESSIE: It's the first thing that'd occur to you if you opened a paper and saw a picture of yourself looking like an old mop.

OOLA: It's Thelma I'm worried about. What am I going to tell her?

ESSIE: The truth too, I guess. A bit at a time, though. She's sure to find out for herself what you don't tell her.

OOLA: She's going back to school this afternoon. I could ask the sisters not to let her see the papers.

WILMA: There's the other girls, Ool.

ESSIE: You know you can't keep a thing like this quiet.

OOLA: Well, how am I going to put it? What will I say?

ESSIE: Just open your mouth and let it roll out.

> *The front door bell rings.*

It's started. I'll bet that's a reporter.

OOLA: Maybe you'd better not answer it.

ESSIE: Then again it could be the johns. You can't shut them out.

OOLA: Well, don't say anything if you can help it.

ESSIE: Just leave it to me.

> *She moves into the hall.*

OOLA: Leave the door open so we can hear.

ESSIE: [*offstage, opening the door*] Oh, it's youse. Come in.

PADDY: [*offstage*] Thank God, we're here.

WILMA: [*leaping up*] Whitey? Is Whitey there?

> *She runs to the door into* WHITEY'*s arms.* ESSIE *and* PADDY *move into the room.* WILMA *weeps.*

Oh, White! White!

OOLA: Are youse in the clear?

PADDY: Clean as whistles. I told them.

WILMA: [*angrily, to* WHITEY] Well, it's only luck, that's all. It's a wonder they didn't charge you the way you was talking to them. You want a hit across the head for going on like that.

WHITEY: We're out of it, aren't we?

WILMA: You make me bloody sick.

OOLA: Now, cut it out. Hasn't there been enough fighting already?

WHITEY: Did you think I was going to stand around with my mouth closed while they lumbered me for nothing?

WILMA: They was only making an investigation.

WHITEY: Aw, go to hell. You don't know when you're well off.

> *They separate and sit in different parts of the room.*

ESSIE: [*to* PADDY] Tell us what else is going on down there at the station.

PADDY: Holy hell, there's unlawful possession of firearms charges and attempted murder charges and God knows what else being read out.

ESSIE: It must be like Christmas for them. I'll get you a cup of tea.

PADDY: No, Ess, I'd better get straight home. I rang the old woman from the station last night and told her I'd sleep here. But I'd better get home now before the papers are delivered. I just called in to see if youse was all right here.

ESSIE: Everything's under control.

PADDY: Whitey?

WHITEY: Yeah?

PADDY: Will you be along a bit later?

WHITEY: Maybe.

PADDY: I'll tell your mother to expect you.

WHITEY: Look...

PADDY: [*to* WILMA] I've asked Whitey to bring you home to meet his mother this morning.

WILMA: Oh.

PADDY: He's told me about the coast.

OOLA: It's all right. She told Ess and me about it a minute ago.

WILMA: I'll make him a good wife, Mr Maguire.

WHITEY: There's no need to crawl, Wilma.

WILMA: [*angrily*] I was talking to—

PADDY: You'd better start by giving me a kiss, I think.

> WILMA *kisses him on the cheek. He turns to* WHITEY.

And don't come home quarrelling. That's a fine way to start a marriage. Goodbye, Oola. It was a lovely party till it fell to pieces. You see. It'll go with a swing next year.

OOLA: Oh no, I've finished with parties. I'm never going to throw another.

PADDY: Of course you will. But take my advice, put a bit of wine in the trifle next time. Stops the boys from getting restless.

ESSIE: I'll let you out.

PADDY: No, I can find my own way. Good day, Ess.

ESSIE: Good day.

> PADDY *exits into the hall.*

Come on now, Ool, I'm going to put you to bed. You look dead on your feet.

OOLA: I couldn't sleep.

ESSIE: Try laying your head down, you'll drop off. I'll wake you if anything happens.

WILMA: You ought to try, Ool. You do look exhausted.

OOLA: Well, I might try.

ESSIE: Good girl. Put your arms about me.

OOLA: I can walk myself.

ESSIE: All right, be independent.

OOLA: [*to* WILMA] When will I see youse again?

WILMA: We'll give you a ring and tell you how everything goes today.

OOLA: Yeah, do that.

ESSIE: I'll be back in a moment.

WILMA: Thanks for everything, Ess.

ESSIE: What did I do?

WILMA: Well, the cup of tea and all. You've been run off your feet.

ESSIE: I'm run off my feet every day. You kids today don't know what keeping a house is.

WILMA: I'll have to ask you around to give me some lessons.

ESSIE: It wouldn't be any use. They just don't make them like me anymore. I'll be back in a minute.

> OOLA *and* ESSIE *leave the room and move slowly up the stairs.*

WILMA: Well, come on. I suppose we'd better be on our way.

WHITEY: Sit down there. You'll sit down there until I'm good and ready to go.

> WILMA *sits for a moment.*

WILMA: Well, how long are you going to be? Your mother'll be expecting us. I want to change my clothes and freshen up.

WHITEY: They can take us as we are.

WILMA: You'll spruce yourself up too. They'll think I been letting you go to the pack.

WHITEY: It doesn't matter what they think.

WILMA: My God, there's no doubt about it, you're just a big kid.

WHITEY: No woman's ever bounced me.

WILMA: That's the trouble with you. You need a woman to keep you toeing the line.

WHITEY: I suppose you think that you're up to the job?

WILMA: Who knows? Anyway, you're stuck with me.

WHITEY: Yeah, I'm stuck with you.

WILMA: Don't say it like you regret it, White. Don't say it like that. [*After a moment*] Do you regret it?

WHITEY: [*after a moment*] No.

WILMA: Well, say it like you mean it.

WHITEY: You know I got no time for soft talk.

WILMA: Then tell it to me rough. Just remember to say it sometimes. That's all I need.

WHITEY: What you need's a good clip under the ear. Come on.

> WILMA *moves to him. He kisses her.*

That's what you need.

WILMA: Oh, White.

> THELMA *enters from the hall. She is still in her nightclothes.*

THELMA: Oh.

WILMA: Hello, Thel. You just got up?

THELMA: Yes. Where is everybody?

WILMA: Auntie Ess is putting your mother to bed. We've just got home from the… hospital.

THELMA: Was anybody badly hurt?

WILMA: Your mother will tell you all about things later. You don't have to worry about anything.

THELMA: Horrie's dead, isn't he?

WILMA: Don't you worry your head now.

THELMA: I saw them carrying him out. I'd never seen a dead person before, but I was sure he was dead. He looked so empty.

WILMA: Why don't you go back to bed for a little while?

THELMA: No. I've got to change.

WILMA: What for?

THELMA: I'm going up to the convent to stay with the nuns. I can't stay here. Auntie Ess didn't even wake me for early Mass.

WILMA: She's got a lot on her mind, Thel.

THELMA: I don't care. I never want to come back here again.

WILMA: You must try to understand.

THELMA: There's murder gone on here and other things I've never heard about before. I don't belong here.

WILMA: You've just got to make the effort. This is where your mother is.

THELMA: Oh, she doesn't care about me. The way she went on last night, the things she said, she couldn't care.

WILMA: [*moving to place her arms about her*] Thel.

THELMA: [*moving away*] It's all right. I'm not going to cry or anything. I know she put me into that school up there because she couldn't be bothered with me. Even when she'd call to see me she never had anything important to say to me. It was all giving me things and putting on a show.

WILMA: Because she didn't understand that doesn't mean she doesn't love you.

WHITEY: You'll see it clearer when you get a bit older, Thel.

WILMA: No, White, she's got to see it now. This is the right time.

THELMA: All I know is I'm getting out of here and I'm never coming back.

ESSIE *enters from the hall.*

ESSIE: I got her settled down. [*To* THELMA] You needn't have got up yet, love. I was going to bring you breakfast in bed.

THELMA: I thought I asked you to wake me for early Mass, Auntie Ess.

ESSIE: Oh, well, you can go to a later one. It's not important which Mass you go to, is it?

THELMA: Yes. It's important to me.

WILMA: Thelma!

ESSIE: Heavens, she is overwrought this morning—

WILMA: She says she's going up to the convent to stay with the nuns.

ESSIE: Oh no, surely not, lovey. Your mother's going to need you today.

THELMA: What can I do?

ESSIE: You can stay and let her see you're sticking by her. After all she's done for you.

THELMA: What? Spent a lot of money?

ESSIE: What she feels about you can't be measured in money. And is that the sort of talk they're teaching you at school?

THELMA: No, I picked it up here.

ESSIE: You ungrateful little bitch, I don't want to hear another word from you. Go upstairs this instant.

THELMA: Yes, I will. To pack.

THELMA *exits into the hall and up the stairs.*

ESSIE: Did you hear her?! She sounded like Oola, digging her toes in. She's going to be all right. She's Oola's kid.

WHITEY: Come on, Wil. We'd better be going.

WILMA: Oh, glad you're ready at last. See you later, Ess.

ESSIE *throws* WILMA *a tablecloth she has been carrying over her arm. It is a casual gesture.*

ESSIE: Oh, wait a minute. I brought that down for youse. It's a wedding present. Just a little something.

WILMA: [*opening the cloth*] Oh, Ess, it's beautiful.

WHITEY: Thanks, Ess.

ESSIE: It's not new or anything, but it's never been used. It's been tucked away at the bottom of my hope chest.

WILMA: Oh, Ess, we can't take it.

ESSIE: Go on. I never found any occasion nice enough to use it. Maybe you will. It's all hand embroidered, see. Worked it myself when I was a girl of sixteen. I thought, then, things were going to turn out different to what they did. The colours have lasted real well, haven't they? All those years ago!

WILMA: I'll cherish it, Ess. Honest I will.

ESSIE: See you do. Now, off you go. Once the phone and the doorbell start ringing the less people I have 'round here the better.

WILMA: Okay. Ta ta.

WHITEY: Ta ta, Ess.

ESSIE: Goodbye.

> WILMA *and* WHITEY *exit into the hall. The front door slams.* ESSIE *moves to the statue of St Teresa and takes a rosary from her pocket. She prays for a moment, then the phone rings. She takes it up.*

Here we go. [*Putting on her phone voice*] Hello, Farrell's biscuit factory… Maguire's who…? I'm sorry, you must have the wrong number… That's all right, it was your sixpence. [*She replaces the phone and notices the rosary in her hands. She looks up to heaven.*] Well, I do. I make a lot of biscuits.

> OOLA *enters from the hall. Her hair is down and she wears a dressing gown.*

OOLA: Ess! Ess! I heard Thel coming up the stairs and I wanted to talk to her. But she's locked her door. She won't let me in.

ESSIE: She's got this silly idea about going to stay with the nuns up at the convent.

OOLA: Oh, is that all? Well, let her go. It's the best place for her.

ESSIE: How do you arrive at that conclusion?

OOLA: She told me yesterday it was what she wanted. She's planning to become a nun.

ESSIE: A nun! Well, what else has she known?

OOLA: I asked her about that too, but she said she didn't need to know anything else.

ESSIE: If that were true do you think she'd have fallen into Horrie's arms so easily last night?

OOLA: I don't know. Maybe not.

ESSIE: I'm telling you not. Now, you try and talk her out of going away. The chances are if she goes away now she'll never come back.

OOLA: Do you think so?

ESSIE: Let her see how much you need her. Maybe that'll do the trick.

OOLA: I'll try.

ESSIE: Here she comes now.

> THELMA *appears moving down the staircase, carrying her bags and dressed in her school tunic.* ESSIE *exits into the kitchen.*

OOLA: [*calling*] Thelma?

THELMA: [*offstage*] Yes?

OOLA: Will you come in here for a minute, love? I'd like to have a little talk with you.

> THELMA *enters the room, lingering by the door.*

Sit down.

THELMA: I don't want to be too long, Mum. I want to have a talk with the sisters too, before they go into meditation.

OOLA: You was going away without a word. No goodbyes?

THELMA: I decided I'd come down to see you again before I left tonight. I didn't know what I should say to you, what you could say to me.

OOLA: It's difficult, isn't it? But I would just like you to know how much I love you, how much I need you.

THELMA: You seem to have managed a good number of years without me.

OOLA: Because I had to, because I had other things to consider. Now I've got nothing.

THELMA: Well, that's not my fault.

OOLA: Maybe I have lied to you about the way I live, but last night I was being honest when I tried to protect you from Horrie.

THELMA: He was all right.

OOLA: No, you don't know—

THELMA: I know what he wanted from me. I'm old enough. But he wanted me. That makes a difference.

OOLA: Do you still want to be a nun? I haven't ruined that for you as well, have I?

THELMA: I don't know about that either. I'm all confused. Oh, Mum, can I go now?

OOLA: If you must.

THELMA: I'll come back and see you another time.

OOLA: Oh, Thel, kiss me. Say you understand. Forgive me.

THELMA: I'll kiss you if you like. But I don't think I'll ever understand.

OOLA: This is no way to leave me.

THELMA: You said you were being honest last night. Well, this morning this is the only way I can go and be honest.

OOLA: Then kiss me and mean that much.

> THELMA *moves to* OOLA *and kisses her on the cheek stiffly. She turns away to the door.*

THELMA: Goodbye, Mum.

OOLA: Goodbye, darling.

THELMA *moves to the door.*

Thelma?

THELMA *pauses.*

I also wanted to say to you you're not to regard this place, not to regard me as a good example of the world. We aren't, lovey. There are better places than this, better people than me. Just so's you know it.

THELMA: I know it, Mum. Goodbye.

OOLA *sits rigidly, waiting for the door to slam. When it does she breathes a great sigh.* ESSIE *enters.*

ESSIE: She's gone then?

OOLA: Yes. She's gone.

ESSIE: You got a match? We could light this lamp again.

OOLA: Will it make everything the same again?

ESSIE: Of course it will. Everything will be the same again. Oh.

She withdraws some matches from behind the votive lamp and lights it.

OOLA: There'll be a bit missing.

ESSIE: After a few hot showers and a dozen cups of tea you'll never know it was there.

OOLA *moves to Boxer's picture and straightens it again.*

OOLA: Well, some things remain. Is this straight?

ESSIE: You look at it too much. Things always look crooked when you look at them too much. Come on, I'm taking you back to bed.

OOLA: Okay. You will have to help me this time. All of a sudden I'm weak as a kitten.

They leave the room and move up the stairs.

Do you think she will come back, Ess? I mean, back of her own free will without thinking she has to?

ESSIE: She's your kid, Oola. That'll bring her back.

OOLA: I hope you're right.

ESSIE: Of course I'm right. I'm always right, aren't I?

They move out of sight. The telephone begins ringing; there is the sound of heavy knocking on the door.

THE END

Image in the Clay

David Ireland

David Ireland, born in Lakemba, NSW, first came to notice in 1958 when his play *Image in the Clay* shared third prize in a competition. After following a variety of occupations, he became a full-time writer in 1973. He has written another play, *The Virgin of Treadmill Street*, as well as poetry, but is best know for his novels *The Chantic Bird* (1968), *The Unknown Industrial Prisoner* (1971), *The Flesheaters* (1972), *Burn* (an adaptation of *Image in the Clay*, 1974), *The Glass Canoe* (1976), *A Woman of the Future* (1979, The *Age* Book of the Year Award in 1980), *City of Women* (1981), *Archimedes and the Seagle* (1984), *Bloodfather* (1987) and *The Chosen* (1997). He won the Miles Franklin Award on three occasions (1971, 1976 and 1979).

Maxine Miller as Joy and Hugh Richardson as Billy in the 1960 Pocket Playhouse production of IMAGE IN THE CLAY. *(Photo held in the Brendan Dunne papers, Mitchell Library. Courtesy of Norman McVicker)*

FIRST PERFORMANCE

Image in the Clay was first produced at the Pocket Playhouse, Terry Street, Sydenham, on 12 May 1960, with the following cast:

GUNNER	David Dickinson
JOY	Maxine Miller
MARY	Patricia Brownlee
SAWYER	Seamus Rothsey
BILLY	Hugh Richardson
GOROOH	Peter Potok
GORDON	David Brown
FIRST BOY	Kevin James
SECOND BOY	Robert Murphy
KINCAID	George McLaren
SONNY	Brendan Dunne
THIRD BOY	John Gully

Director, Norman McVicker
Settings, Brendan Dunne
Costumes, Elizabeth Hodge

AUTHOR'S PREFACE TO THE FIRST EDITION

Some say that every author wants to crowd into his first work all he knows, all he has ever experienced. This is not the case with *Image in the Clay*. The circumstances were these. Two of us had arranged to meet a third at his house in Darlington Point in June of 1947. The two of us got to the place: the third did not. We never did hear what happened to him—perhaps he'd gone back to gaol. He was going to get us 'in' with some timber-cutters who were on a good thing somewhere along the Murrumbidgee; ten bob a sleeper, bring your own axes. It was good money then.

We waited a couple of weeks; that was enough. In that time we lived on the south bank of the river. Across the way on the other bank was an Aboriginal camp, very quiet, minding its own business. The set lines were out every night. What the play doesn't mention is the number of hooks on the lines. Nor does it mention the bits of chicken wire patched together to make fish traps, and the rocks, when the river was down, moved over to dam the river where it was three or four feet across, and the traps placed so that only a very skinny fish could get past to the town. We were upstream from the town.

Those two weeks were enough of waiting. At the time I admired the dark boys for their football ability. There was a sharp, laughing boy there, under eleven stone, playing Rules on Saturday and on Sunday playing League as the nippiest five-eighth you'd see in a season. Of course, in that company he'd have no one with him when he opened the defence, but even that didn't break his heart.

I didn't see much of the women, only a few half- and quarter-caste children on the school bus—the High School bus to Griffith. The model for Joy was a white girl, anyway. At that time there were no coloured boys going to the city to try their luck: Gordon is imagination. Nor was there any talk of opening up land out that way. But of course it was only a matter of time. Neither did I hear of any white women living with native men. Mary, too, is imagination.

I find it hard to account for the sources of these characters and the events their personalities produced. People like Gunner and Billy and Joy live in your head for so long that they emerge on paper and onto a stage quite changed by their contact with the mass of ideas in a writer's head.

The effects of the heat, in the rise and fall of their attention, interest and activity; their jubilation over a caught fish; their loving interest in a fight, were all honestly come by. I was there. Their acts come from their characters; the 'rise and fall' atmosphere comes from the same source.

If there should be found in the play any attempt to move the reader or the playgoer to pity for the condition of these dark people—I deny any such intention—all I can find to say is that serenity and happiness and tough unconcern do not move us as much as misery. And, without knowing that they did, they knew misery.

People like these do not resolve difficulties, neither do they collapse under their weight. They hardly even put up a fight. It is as if they live outside themselves, things happen to them, but they themselves are hardly touched by things and events and situations that would dash others. Their apathy, their position outside the events that they see happening to each other, are their defence.

Yet they do have imagination. Each of them, in his mind's eye, can see his place in the world. How many of our neighbours can do that, even if they dare? I still doubt that these people would be different if their social circumstances were altered. Man is more, always more, than his circumstances.

There are no deaths in the play, yet it is a tragedy. Because it ends with no hope for these people. Nor are there misunderstandings; they understand each other perfectly. There is no bad luck: they are their misfortune. Something is missing in themselves which they cannot supply. Nothing can be done. They will be on their bottoms all their lives, living without alternatives. No opinions are presented: my interest in Aborigines is no more than anyone else's, except that they are people. That is my interest.

I find fascination, not only in the characters, but in the audience, which finds strange, alarming or amusing, the things and people around us all the time. They are there, twenty-four hours a day. I live with them. Apparently not everyone does. But the charm of being able to move people's feelings, when the living and breathing world does not!

Some things the playwright cannot learn from anyone. Only the writer knows when some lines are right and when what he is working on at the moment is good. You can't learn how to write from the *Sydney Morning Herald* critic any more than you can learn what to write from the theatre programs of the 'Elizabethan'.[1]

Since writing *Image in the Clay*, I am aware of many more things about my people, aware of many more things about them that I do not know, things I will to know. I need the answers to many questions, the sort of questions that probe more deeply than I probed into Gordon and Gunner. What are their spending habits? To whom do they use a different tone of voice and different words? Where is their particular serenity? What physical peculiarities do they have that were overlooked by the medical officers that examined them? What bores them? Do they have any nasty habits? What day of the week is their physical energy at its peak? What childhood ambition has persisted? What smells excite them? What diseases have they had? What desires are unrealised?

The list is a long one.

The man who looks only at the finished product does not see the process, the process which results in the play. What I have to say about any play of mine, or for that matter, about anyone else's, changes with time and feeling, changes with the time I am writing, changes with what I am writing, because for me, what I am doing at the moment is what counts.

I cannot conceal from the perceptive person the fact that I do not like writing about my own work, whether it is yesterday's, in which case it is dead and has ceased to influence me, or whether it is today's, in which case it is too close and too personal. And who am I to make comments and assertions on the work of others? I do not and cannot know the bundle of feelings and aims that have gone into another person's work. My concerns are not necessarily theirs, nor theirs mine.

When a writer is at the start of what he hopes will be a long career, if not a startling one, it is neither permissible nor tactful to begin by telling other people what to do or how to do it.

David Ireland
2 July 1962

---

[1] The Elizabethan Theatre in Newtown, Sydney, a former vaudeville house converted by the Australian Elizabethan Theatre in 1955 to house our first subsidised theatre.

CHARACTERS

GUNNER, a half-caste Aborigine
JOY, a half-caste girl
MARY, Gunner's white wife
SAWYER, Gunner's white father
BILLY, Gunner's elder son, a quarter-caste
GOROOH, an old man of the tribe
GORDON, Gunner's youngest son, a quarter-caste
FIRST BOY, from the town
SECOND BOY, from the town
KINCAID, a sergeant of police
SONNY, Gordon's city mate
THIRD BOY, from the town

SETTING

The action takes place in the same clearing throughout. The different times of day and the varying shadows cast by the shack and the surrounding trees and by the fire at night, mark off the separate scenes.

INTRODUCTION TO THE MAIN CHARACTERS

GUNNER: The half-caste son of the white-bearded old Sawyer, who is a white man. Gunner's age is around forty-two; he is crude, insensitive, tough. A sniper in the AIF in the Second War, he got on well with his white mates; he saw no colour problem, and there was none. His curly black hair is cut in the style he wore twenty years ago, and which is labelled 'bodgie' when worn now by a white boy. He wears dark trousers frayed at the cuffs; no socks, grey sandshoes. His pipe stays in his mouth except when replaced by food, a wine bottle or the need to shout louder than usual.

JOY: A barefoot half-caste girl sheltered by Gunner when her people deserted her. His one good deed: perhaps it has to last a lifetime. She is about to bloom into an exciting young-womanhood; already she has the regular, attractive features with which many half-bloods are blessed. Her age: fifteen. She will not reach the exciting young-womanhood; it will turn into a wine-sodden sluttishness.

BILLY: A superficially more ferocious quarter-blood than his brother, Gordon. Billy cannot hold his liquor.

GORDON: Outstanding in a tiny township, he finds himself one of thousands of bright youngsters in the city. If you questioned him closely enough, you would find that his wish to appear considerable wherever he is—fostered during his childhood—has led him to hate the city because of obvious comparisons he is smart enough to draw. He has the external good manners, intelligence and healthy appearance of a fortunate young man of the suburbs. Under his veneer is the entirely self-seeking image of the success he has seen around him. If he has conscience or humanity or anything but the most formal regard for the rights of family or neighbour, it is because less than this would retard his progress towards that inner image.

SAWYER: Gunner's father, a man with one idea: to have his own son work beside him in his struggling sawmill. He cannot see that Gunner resents the idea of working for him and going back to a dependent relationship to the old man.

MARY: Gunner's white wife, who lives for her son Gordon, now that she has nothing else. Her sacrifices to get the money to send him to a good school have, in her mind, justified the means she used.

GOROOH: The last of his tribe. Despises the white man and the half-bloods that surround him. This leaves him no world but that inside his head. He hangs about Gunner's shack because the Gunner is a man he can understand; by virtue of his War experience, the Gunner is almost a warrior.

SCENE ONE

The action of the play takes place a quarter of a mile outside Goolagong township, in what would be a shady clearing if a few tall, ragged eucalypts cast even a decent shade. An aggressive glare of sun hits the partly tin, partly patched-up roof of shaggy boards with strips of bark still clinging, striking a corner of a rough log 'verandah' and dazzling the dust of the patch of ground in front of the shaky shanty. In the verandah shade, with his legs in the sun, sits GUNNER.

You cannot see any other shanties, but they are there, stumbled almost into line along the banks of the Murrumbidgee, above steep banks eroded to a depth of perhaps twenty feet. Neither can you see the township itself, which has one pub, a shop or two, and three churches. Part of the river is used as a swimming hole.

The part of the river we are concerned with is upstream from the swimming hole. There is a set line attached to a thin but firmly embedded stick in the ground. The river bank dips sharply, partly towards the audience and partly towards the left side of the stage. It is six o'clock in the morning.

Now and again you can hear the mad cries of parakeet playing on the other bank of the river, where the trees are more plentiful. The town, across the bridge which carries the main road down towards Jerilderie in the south, is not stirring. The town resembles a small growth on the long, thin branch of the road—last year's seed-pod on a bottlebrush twig. The shanties are hidden from the road by a small stand of timber, mercifully left by the timber-cutters and now protected by the local council.

GUNNER*'s shack is supported on round log sections and irregular rocks. There are sparse weeds growing where they are protected by a pile of dead marines— empty wine bottles tucked under the house—and more plentifully around a couple of kerosene tins, one for washing and one for drinking water. There is a certain place on the verandah where, every time you rest your weight, there is a rattling of bottles against empty tins underneath.*

GUNNER *is a five-feet-nine half-caste, broad of shoulder, ferocious of temper and disgustingly lazy. His mouth is never without its pipe, even when it's not alight. It is a short pipe, entirely lacking the portentous dignity of the newspaper advertisements; it appears to have been gnawed to its present length. He served in the Second World War with the AIF, first in the Middle East, then in New Guinea. He has a Returned Man's badge and a Seidlitz Powder tin of medals in his shack. Unlike many of his white mates of those years, who have thrown out their medals long since, he keeps them, perhaps as a reminder to his wife, Mary, that once upon a time he was not entirely useless. Or perhaps as a symbol of his deeper desire for equal footing with those wartime mates whose equal he was, but only while the guns were going off. Meantime, he sits in the shade, inhaling the 'injurious resins and tars' present in the blue-white smoke of his pipe. One end of his shanty leans against the grey-pink flank of a river red-gum.*

All around Australia you can see these shanties in pitiful clusters around country towns; outside the town, of course, halfway between the white-man's world and their own native haunts, in a twilight of hopelessness and decay and violence; lost in that vast hinterland between the tribe and the Committee.

Inside the shanty someone bumps into something heavy. JOY *comes out, brushing hair out of her eyes with the back of her hand, rubbing her eyes and yawning loudly.*

JOY: Where's my little daddy 'smorning?

GUNNER: Aaaah, be quiet an' go'way.

> JOY *jingles the bangles on her bare brown arms, puts her hands up in the air and lets the bangles slide down to her elbows, then reverses the trick and catches them with her fingers spread.*

JOY: You had 'im last, I know. Where is he?

GUNNER: Why you always pester around me? Do I look as if I have 'im?

> *He draws deeply on his pipe, coughs violently and spits a brown slime on the ground. He grinds it with his heel.*

JOY: [*considering*] You never look like anything… but you're always something different.

GUNNER: You're an idiot. Beat it! Get out of here and stop muckin' up the fishin'. I got the biggest old cod you ever seen, lookin' at my line. How can he start bitin' and workin' up his appetite with you howlin' and screamin' on the river bank?

> JOY, *over at the river bank, is looking down, hitching at her dress and scratching. She is barefoot, wearing a sleeveless dirty-white dress which should have a belt at the waist. Buttons are missing and there is a tear in the dress; she looks as if she has slept in it.*

JOY: Any fish was there woulda been on your line hours now.

GUNNER: Never you mind woulda been. I tell you there's bigger fish in there than we've ever seen all landed up nice and ready for the fire.

JOY: [*impressed, in spite of herself*] You really think there's a big fish in the river?

GUNNER: There's always someone bigger than you are, just round the corner—there's always a bigger fish in the river.

JOY: Can I have some if you catch him?

GUNNER: You'll make a proper guts of yourself if I don't watch you, won'tcher?

JOY: [*with a lightning flash of bad temper*] Keep your dirty old fish, and you're a lousy, stinkin' old...

> *Her mouth forms the word 'bastard' as* MARY *rides over her words. She speaks from behind a rough wooden shutter in the wall of the shack.* MARY *is not seen.*

MARY: Keep your tongue off your father, you!

GUNNER: [*sucking and spitting*] I'm not her father. That's one thing you can't blame me for.

> JOY, *a little girl again, drops to the dust in a paddy.*

MARY: And don't think you're gunna start on me, you dirty, lazy old nuisance.

GUNNER: Old, you say? [*Comfortably from his position on the verandah, but still shouting*] Look in your bits of broken mirror and see who's old, you miserable old goat.

> JOY *is blubbering in the dirt. She stops her noise, grabs a handful of powdery dust and flings it at* GUNNER. *He springs off his seat with the agility of a scrum-half and hits her a backhander on the side of the face. She sprawls in the dust.* MARY *appears.*

MARY: [*into the silence*] I saw that.

> JOY *does not get up.*

GUNNER: [*wiping his face and spluttering*] She's always asking for it. Now she got it.

> *Silence inside.*

[*To* JOY] Get up, you. I know you're not hurt. [*To* MARY] See, in there? Look at 'er. You can tell she's puttin' it over. I don't see how she can take you in all the time. She don't fool me. Here.

> *He goes over and gives* JOY *a very mild kick in the ribs.*

Get up and get out of here. Have I got to have trouble with everyone?

> *He picks her up by one limp arm and hoists her to the other side of the clearing away from the river bank, as you would a half-empty sack. She falls flat.*

MARY: Get that girl fixed up, you. She's only a kid. And give her back her little toys. I saw you take 'em last night. Why you got to be on her back all the time I don't know. One day you'll hurt her bad and then you won't be able to fix it up without a lot of money.

GUNNER: [*very quickly and definitely*] I got no money for doctors.

MARY: You got more money than anyone round here. You're the only one went to the War.

GUNNER: My pension I got for myself. Shut up about it; it's mine.

MARY: If I'd had me hands on some of that money I wouldn't have had to skimp and scrape to get enough to send Gordon to school in the city.

GUNNER: For Chrissake, don't keep reminding me of that. Have you got to throw it up at a bloke all the time... I didn't go to any High Schools.

MARY: With him coming home today, and maybe Billy too, it's time you were reminded of some things. [*Sharply*] Now get and do something about that girl.

GUNNER: There's nothing the matter with her. She's right as rain.

MARY: [*her voice quiet, confident in its menace*] You've got something hidden away in here, haven't you? Something you won't ever let anyone see. You look at it every night when you think we're asleep, except when you're drunk, don't you...? Now get an' do as I say, or I'll tell the policeman.

GUNNER: [*equally determined*] You tell anyone anything that's none of your business and you'll go down in a screamin' heap, 'cause I'll clobber you for sure.

MARY: [*not at all daunted by his violent tone*] Like to be hung, would you?

GUNNER: They don't hang a man, now.

MARY: [*with great feeling*] Then cooped up inside four walls for the rest of your life until you rot away and die and they plant you inside the gaol, instead of our little cemetery out there behind the church with the trees shading you that were there before you were born, and the river with the soft-woods hangin' over into the water and the kids playin' and the men drinkin' and the birds makin' their noise nice and cheerful not half a mile away. That what you want?

GUNNER: Struth! You sound as if you like this place.

MARY: If you don't, why don't you go somewhere else?

> GUNNER *goes over to* JOY, *hesitates, spits, then bends down to touch her, gently.*

GUNNER: [*roughly*] Come on. Up you get. I suppose I did hit you too hard. Come on.

MARY: Tell her a story, why don't you?

> JOY *gets up, suspiciously.*

GUNNER: Come over here. You sit on the edge. I got to be near the line, 'case we get a bite.

> JOY *sits on the verandah.* GUNNER *squats in the dust near his set line. She moves around while he tells the story; standing, squatting like him, or lolling on the verandah.*

Long time ago, way back before old Gorooh was a little boy...

JOY: [*letting herself be interested*] Before Gorooh?

GUNNER: Long time 'fore him. There was a woman with long hair and skin dark and shiny like she could walk in bushfire country amongst the black stumps and a man not know she was there. Quiet she walked, so's you couldn't hear the old feet steppin' on the ground between the grey twigs and the hot stones. An' she carried her little old daddy, a bit in each hand.

JOY: He was broken?

GUNNER: In two pieces.

JOY: Where was he broken?

GUNNER: Right across his belly-button he was. She had 'im in two bits, taking him on the long walk up north to the warm country away from the frost and the cold wind.

JOY: But what broke him?

GUNNER: Will you stop butting in? The cold broke him. He froze out straight like a skinny stick and snapped across the middle.

JOY: What was he made of?

GUNNER: The whitest clay you ever picked out of the river bank.

JOY: Just like the ones you made me?

GUNNER: Like that, only better. She took him way up there in the hot north so's he might melt, and stick back together again.

JOY: And did he stick?

GUNNER: Wait while I get to it, can't you? No. There was no sticking together. She lost the top piece.

JOY: The head.

GUNNER: The head. All she had left was the legs. So she reached a deep gully up there where it was warm all the year, and planted him alongside a blackboy spear and went off, and while she was away the rains came and the wet winds of the hot country, and with the first green shoots of the spring up he grew, straight as the spear beside him. And he was the father of the dark man who started on walking round the land. Never did he settle down in any place, but always staying a bit, then off, off to new game and fresh berries, and he fought a bit and had his family and they all grew up to walk about the land. Walk, walk, walk. And when the wind blew the ashes from their fire, there was little to tell they had been that way...

A long silence.

JOY: Maybe it's my little man's been broken in two... What happened to the other part, the head? Did she ever find it? Did it ever grow up and be a man?

GUNNER: No one ever found him. The black man's never found his top piece. If he did, he might grow up to stay in one place and build something that'll last after him and be kind of his own. He's got nothing; but he could have something if he used his head and got away from his sorrow at not being able to walk free about the land. [*Expansively*] Wherever he liked.

MARY: [*listening at the round shutter of the window*] You're a fine one to talk, you are, about using your head. You don't walk about the land and you don't use your head either.

JOY: But you like the walking one better, don't you, Gunner?

GUNNER: I've told yer a story. It's finished. That's all I'm gunna say.

JOY: [*not put out*] You like Billy the best, even though he's gone away on walkabout, and Gordon's got brains, and he's workin' in the city.

GUNNER: I didn't say I liked any of 'em. Stop twisting my words.

JOY: [*not having any of it*] Your stories always mean something and I know what that one means. You broke my little man up and threw the pieces away. I'm gunna look and look. I'll get 'em, you'll see. Both of 'em. I don't care if you never make me any more little men or if all the clay in the river gets washed away. I'll have them two bits.

GUNNER: Have it your own way. [*Getting up*] I'm goin' down to see if there's any tucker on the line. He might be just lying there without a move. [*He goes left to the river, taking out a murderous knife.*] I'll get that big feller some day.

JOY: [*to* MARY, *through the window*] See. I can get 'im doing things for me any time I like. I know how.

MARY: Come in here and help me this minute or you get nothin' to eat.

JOY: Garn. Always bellyachin' about doing things. You got nothing to do. I could do all you do with one hand.

MARY: That's all you'll have if I catch you pinchin' any more of the food.

JOY: You shut up. You pinch more than food. Your old man ought to be woken up to some of the things that go on round here.

MARY: Don't speak of your father like that.

JOY: [*disdainful and shrewd*] He's not me father. I know that. But you're prob'ly me mother, if the truth's told.

MARY: You speak a word of lies to him or anyone else about things you don't understand and you'll wake up maybe in the river, belly full of water and the dogs pickin' at your fanny.

JOY: [*daunted at last*] Everyone round here knows what they knows.

Browbeaten by the threats, JOY *goes off.*

Something slams inside the shack, dogs barking, fowls crowing, birds screeching, pots and pans rattling, people stirring in the shacks around about, a truck starting up in the township and the smell of gumleaves burning. The comparative quiet is shattered by shouts from the river bank.

GUNNER *comes running back, waving his fish and extracting the hook.*

GUNNER: I've got 'im! Got 'im! The biggest! Get outa yer doors, you lousy loafers! Look what I been up an' got. The biggest cod you'll ever see out of this piddling stream. [*In the grand manner*] Who'll cook me the prize of this sneaking river that creeps past our doors?

A couple of half-caste NEIGHBOURS *appear.*

NEIGHBOURS: We'll cook it for you, Gunner. Give it to us, Gunner. My old woman's a beaut cookin' fish.

GUNNER: Whaddya mean, give it to you? Get away, you bludgers! Your old woman'll never see this fish. It's mine. You got Buckley's chance.

NEIGHBOURS: But don't you want us to cook it for you, Mister Gunner, you miserable, rotten old cow. [*Starting back just in case*] Tight as a fish's ears, you are.

GUNNER: Garn, get out of it, before I let fly with a goolie. [*He bends as if to pick one up.*] Go and catch a fish yourselves.

They go.

Go an' catch fifty and they'll never be the equal of this. [*He pats the fish.*] He's a bottler! You don't even know how to set a line, do yer? Takes something to get Mister Big Fish on yer hook. Cook it fer me! Just as soon give it to the mangy dogs that come yelpin' round me naked shins at tea-time. Hey, in there! Look what I got. [*Just for a moment he is a small boy showing off his catch to his mum.*] Now there's something for those useless two if they come home today.

MARY: [*appearing*] Gordon said today: he'll be home.

GUNNER: Now they can see what their old man can catch with his two hands.

MARY: A poor old fish that's tired of living.

GUNNER: One fresh from the city streets and Billy back from wandering the open land that's not open anymore. [*Shortly*] Here, cook it for 'em.

MARY: Cook the damn thing yourself. Don't try and tell me what to do.

GUNNER: [*genuinely surprised*] What's wrong with it? It's a good fish. I'll clean it fer yer.

MARY *doesn't answer.*

[*Roaring*] Whatsamatter with it? Any other time you'd be glad to get your hands on it.

MARY: He's not big, he's just swollen; anyway I got something special for 'em today.

GUNNER: Special! [*With disgust*] What could you have special? Eh?

Old, white-bearded SAWYER *comes in. Red face, grey flannel shirt and black trousers. A rough old codger, but fairly clean. A white man, but he fits into the general picture. On his feet are scuffed boots from which the colour has long since gone; no socks.*

SAWYER: I'll cook it f'ya.

GUNNER: What are you creepin' round the place for?

SAWYER: I know a good way to cook fish. That's a pretty fair fish.

GUNNER: Whatsamatter, isn't there any more trees you can take from the birds and the possums to hack about in your clatterin' old mill? Have you come to the end of all the timber in the bush?

SAWYER: Give us it, son. Y'only see a fish like that once in a blue moon.

MARY: You'd be a great one to worry about timber. All you'd know'd be what the dogs know about timber, you drongo.

GUNNER: Will you get off me back for just one minute?

MARY: Why should I? You're always on someone else's back.

SAWYER: I'll clean him.

> SAWYER *goes to take the fish.* GUNNER *crowns him with it.*

GUNNER: You'll clean him when I'm ready to give 'im to you.

SAWYER: [*quite used to this, with queer dignity*] What time the boys getting back, son?

GUNNER: Don't keep callin' me that.

SAWYER: It's true, ain't it?

GUNNER: I'd be the one to know, wouldn't I? It's a wise son knows his own father, they reckon.

SAWYER: There's a train gets in this morning at the town. Shouldn't take Gordon long to bludge a ride out. Be here midday, I s'pose. What about Billy?

> GUNNER *doesn't answer, but throws the fish over near the ashes of many fires, then goes inside.* SAWYER *shrugs and picks it up, dusts it down on the side of his trousers and lays it on the rock of the fireplace. He goes to the trees for some kindling and dry leaves and lays them in the rough grate.*

JOY: [*coming back into the clearing*] Where's he gone?

SAWYER: Hullo there, little Joy.

JOY: Where is he? He hit me. And she screamed at me.

SAWYER: Never mind, the boys'll be home today. No one'll take any notice of you.

> JOY *looks doubtful at his last words.*

You like fish?

> JOY *picks it up, examining it, looking into its eyes, making swimming movements with it in the air.*

JOY: He swims just like a plane flies. B-r-r-r-r-r, up and down, r-r-r-r-r-r turning round and round, r-r-r-r-r. [*Walking around with it*] Can I clean him, Fisho?

SAWYER: You know I'm not the Fisho any longer. I gave up the drinkin'.

JOY: The Gunner says you was the biggest drinker this side of Queensland.

SAWYER: The Gunner was pretty good himself. If you can call it good. If only he'd come and work in the mill. This is no life for a man that killed as many Japs as he did. It'd give him something to take his mind off himself.

JOY: [*couldn't care less*] Why should he do that? Give us your big knife. Ta. [*She squats and begins to clean the fish.*] Now off with his head.

SAWYER: I'll go inside a minute.

> SAWYER *goes in.*

JOY: Now, Mister Fish, we'll put you where you can see what's going on. This is your big day. When you was swimming in the river you used to look out an' see us watching, I bet. Well, we weren't praisin' you up for the clever way you swam in an' out them rocks. [*She suits the fish's action to the words.*] We didn't have our eyes on the smart flip of your tail, either. No, sir. We was thinkin' of what's inside you. An' here it is.

She draws the fish.

GUNNER *has come around the back of the house with an old shotgun.*

GUNNER: An' who let you muck about with me fish? That old goat that can't mind his own business again?

JOY: [*seeing the gun, terrified*] You wouldn't want to do that, Gunner. You wouldn't want to make a mess over the nice clean ground, now, would you?

GUNNER: [*with the gun pointing at the ground*] Who's making a mess?

JOY: Not you. I suppose I am. [*Holding up the giblets, she laughs foolishly.*] Look at me. I'm a silly girl. I can't even gut a fish without a mess. I know I aren't anything wonderful, but I aren't that bad. Am I?

GUNNER *is dumbfounded, but looks terrifying.*

I don't mind about you not being my father, Gunner. You been better than my father. Why, I don't even know him! You done everything for me. Let me go to school…

GUNNER: You gotta go to school. Nothing to do with me. What in the name of fortune is all this about?

JOY: You got me spending money when I had none. Let me come with you when they chuck us out of here…

GUNNER: I told you not to mention… [*shouting*] those dirty, rotten, stinking farmers; gunna take us away from here, are they?

The squawk of galahs, then the thunder of the shotgun, coincide with JOY's *scream.*

We'll show 'em a thing or two before we're finished. Live herded on a filthy reservation—be a good boy—do what you're told; someone always watching you. Well, I won't have a bar of it!

SAWYER *comes pounding out, fearing bloody murder. The noise of the makeshift shutter being moved—*MARY *is watching.* JOY *has been squatting; now she has fallen backwards with the shock of the blast.* GUNNER *is off towards the birds he has shot.*

SAWYER: Gunner! Wait! [*Shouting—a threat, an entreaty*] Joy, Joy!

The red on her dress belongs to the late fish; its giblets are spread over her front. GUNNER *comes back with the two birds, held carelessly by the feet.*

GUNNER: What do you want, you old fool? The birds'll get more fright from your wailing voice than my poor old gun.

SAWYER: [*recovering*] Two nice birds, eh? I'll clean 'em for you.

GUNNER: Have you gotta be getting under my feet all the time? Fair Johnny, I'm sick and tired of you and your damned trying to... [*sneering*] help. Why don't you stick to your mill? And let me go me own way.

MARY: Your way'll have the police on us before long; first, we're not getting out when they tell us to and now you go shooting off guns to make things worse for us.

GUNNER: You can always get out if you don't like it here.

MARY: If I'd woke up to meself a bit earlier I would have, and that's gospel.

SAWYER: Have any of you decided what to do about moving? You'll have to move, there's no two ways about it.

GUNNER: Have you gotta be in everything?

SAWYER: They've cut up the land on this side of the river already, as far as they're concerned; I can see 'em having you shifted if you don't get out. The reservations are not such bad places for a man as lazy as you are.

GUNNER: Are you trying to put on a blue? I said don't talk about those things! Reservations! Sheep pens!

SAWYER: Then come and work at the mill with me, like I've asked you to for years.

GUNNER: Blast the mill.

SAWYER: But why?

MARY: Yes, why?

GUNNER: I just don't wanta work in your screaming old mill. Drive me crazy. I'll live me own life.

SAWYER: Think what it'd be like to have the extra money.

GUNNER: What about me pension from the Gov'ment? I'm a wounded soldier, remember?

SAWYER: That was years ago. You don't get any headaches now. [*Looking for it on his temple*] You can hardly see where it was.

MARY: He's damn lucky it was in the head.

　　　JOY, *who has come back, laughs at this.*

GUNNER: [*to* JOY] You shut up!

　　　She shuts up quick.

SAWYER: They won't take your pension off you. Think what a fuss there'd be in the papers. Why, an ex-serviceman is practically holy.

MARY: And so he should be.

GUNNER: What do you want?

MARY: Nothing from you. Nothing's too good for a soldier. But a man that sits up in the trees, picking off men while they're having a bite to eat or having a bit of a shave out of a little tin mug or reading a letter from their kids back home—that's the lowest...

GUNNER: That was the most bloody dangerous job there was! And I only got it because I could shoot. I didn't ask for it.

MARY: And because you could sit on your fat bottom for hours and hours like you do here.

GUNNER: Fair dinkum, I don't know why I put up with your tongue.

He kicks the house; the corrugated iron rattles and his foot hurts.

MARY: Kick the place down, why don't you? And get that gun away before the copper comes over on his bike.

> GUNNER *takes out a pull-through, drops the weight through the broken gun, and pulls-through several times, squinting through the barrel at the sky. He pulls the hammer back and dummies a shot over the heads of the audience. The gun clicks on the empty breech. He goes inside to stow the gun.* MARY *comes to the shutter, which is opened wide.*

SAWYER: Mary, will the boys be here for lunch?

MARY: Well, I can't say they're gunna turn up. But Gordon said today, and I'm hoping he comes here straight from the town.

SAWYER: He'll be here, then. How about Billy?

MARY: Him? He just sent word he'd be here this week. I don't have to get anything special for him. Any boy that listens to old Gorooh and wastes his time making spears out of bits of wood and then going off as quiet as you please, with hardly a word to anyone, on some silly 'walkabout' and stays away months at a time, he isn't the sort you'd take extra trouble with when he comes home. But, Gordon...

SAWYER: [*settling down to roll a smoke*] Wouldn't you call going to the city a sort of walkabout for Gordon? It's in the blood, remember.

MARY: [*firmly*] Gordon's got brains; everyone knows that. Didn't they pick him out of everyone else to go to a High School in the city, and hasn't he been there working now for... for...?

SAWYER: For three years. Been away eight altogether. Must be a man now.

MARY: Well, it isn't his fault if he hasn't had time... if he's been too busy to come up and see us. He wants to do it right; he wants to get more money together—I had a letter from him only the other day...

SAWYER: [*gently*] When was that?

MARY: Not long ago. He's busy, I tell you. He doesn't loaf around all day like us; he's tearing around working...

SAWYER: Where's he working now?

MARY: He doesn't tell me that. The name wouldn't mean anything to me. But... [*this is big business*] he's getting experience all the time.

SAWYER: Why is he coming home just now?

MARY: Isn't it time he came to see his mother? Eight years! How many days is that? My little Gordon. The youngest. I remember when he was a small brown bundle in a white shawl, laughing and smiling like you'd think he was a little bit of the sunshine itself, his shiny little face and little bits of teeth poking through, and curling up his toes when he laughed. Ah, he was different...

SAWYER: Was he that different from Billy?

MARY: You liked him calling you Granpa, didn't you? Just like a little white boy. They were better days, then. He… [*with a sneer and a thumb in the direction of Gunner*] was away at the War and I had the money coming in nice and regular from his allotment an' there was plenty to talk about to the other girls and all the men away and we were younger, then. The whole lot of us. Now look at 'em. Old as me. Nothing to talk about anymore. They stick in their places and I stick in here. Ashamed to go over to the town, now. Might as well not be alive. Except that Gordon's coming back today. 'Course he won't want his old mother making a fuss around him, you know what boys are like when they're men. Fancy him… twenty-one.

> JOY *reappears.*

SAWYER: Did you write and tell him about having to get out? Is that why he's coming back?

MARY: [*righteously*] He's coming back to see his mother. He was born in this house.

SAWYER: So he was. But did you tell him?

MARY: Oh, I don't know.

JOY: If she doesn't want to tell you, she won't.

MARY: [*irritated*] I don't know if I told him or not. I suppose I must have.

SAWYER: [*not believing a word of it*] Well, it's not many women forget what they write in letters.

> SAWYER *is obviously determined to assert his own view at the first opportunity.* GUNNER *comes in lighting his pipe, from which he blows a huge cloud of smoke.*

GUNNER: When are you going to cut out yer jawing, and get us something to eat?

SCENE TWO

A frightening bath of unrelieved sunlight; noon in the little clearing, and a silence explained by the sleeping form of GUNNER *on the uncomfortable-looking verandah in the shade. There is the slow whine of a truck in the distance; you can hear it slow down and move off without coming to a stop.*

JOY: [*squealing*] Ooooooh! Eeeeeeeh!

> *She comes from the river dangling a dead blue-tongue lizard from her thin, bangled wrists. She looks about for something to do with it, decides on putting it on* GUNNER's *chest, with its head facing his. To do this, she creeps around the front of the shack, tip-toeing up to* GUNNER, *straightening the lizard's body, then moving around near* GUNNER's

head to look at the lizard as he will see it. She goes off a little distance, picks up a stone, ready to hurl it at the shack wall and wake GUNNER— *far enough away to be able to get a flying start, and near enough to get a dress circle seat at the fun.*

BILLY: [*stumbling in the bush, offstage*] Arrh, butter the muddy king!

JOY *looks away, stone still raised, and recognises* BILLY. *He stands there, shoes without socks; trousers too short, tied up with string; grey-white shirt not quite tucked in all around, open at the front, no buttons, dark patches under the armpits. A surly, primitive face covered with dust from fights and the ride, and blood on his face and spattered down the front of his shirt. He sways slightly, not only from a recent drink, but from the exhaustion of defeat upon defeat. He throws his sugar-bag onto the verandah.*

JOY: [*pitching a stone into the river, screaming*] Billy!

She runs to him.

GUNNER: [*waking suddenly*] Aaarrrgh! [*Roaring at the top of his voice and jumping sideways*] Get it off me! [*He sees* BILLY.] You dirty, sneaking little cow!

BILLY: What you talking of, you old useless?

GUNNER: You know damn well what I'm talking of, you poor, beaten, dirty little boy!

BILLY: [*badly affected by being called a boy*] I'll learn you to keep your trap shut if I got to spear you through!

MARY: [*calling from inside*] Billy! Leave your father alone.

BILLY: Is that what you say when I been away so long? Places I been to, the mothers make a fuss over their oldest sons, not like here.

MARY: Come here, then... come on.

He goes to her. Still unseen, she goes to kiss his cheek behind the shutter.

Ugh! Smell that plonk! Hey, he reeks of plonk. That's the way he went away and that's the way he comes back. [*She knew she would have this excuse for her absence of affection.*] My boy Billy. A fine boy. He never changes. Just like his old man—stinks of it.

BILLY: [*used to it*] That sissy young brother of mine not back, eh? Probably afraid to show his face here, I bet.

GUNNER: Ah, well. He might not be no oil painting, but we oughta welcome him back.

JOY: Welcome back, Billy.

GUNNER: [*throwing him a bottle of wine*] Here, son. Have a swig of this. Do yer good. Then yer can clean up a bit.

The 'plonk!' as the bottle is opened is resounding.

JOY: Let's have a look at your cuts, Billy.

BILLY: [*not too gruffly, suspected of liking the attention to his wounds*] They'll
  be all right.

JOY: Ooh! Where did you get this one? Over your eye?

MARY: [*sarcastically*] You should see the other feller.

GUNNER: [*much more interested now there is evidence of action*] There's some
  fine cuts here. Here's one almost healed up. [*Taking back the bottle*] Where
  did you get a cut like that? Right over the eyebrow. Musta bled like a pig.

BILLY: She bled all right. [*Expanding*] Give us the bottle. That was las' week
  at the back of a pub. Out in the yard, there was this fight, see, a few of 'em
  against me, an' I dropped some of 'em, and this rat, I had him in a corner
  and he picked up a bottle and knocked off the top of it on a corner of the
  brick wall and up at me eyes in one sweep. [*He pauses for effect.*] I saw
  the gaping mouth of it coming up at me face and got out of the way just in
  time. Almost. One edge of it just caught me going away and opened me
  forehead here.

MARY: You're as good as your old man with your likely yarns. I s'pose what
  really happened was you got slung out for trying to cadge a beer, or getting
  some city visitor that don't know the ropes to buy 'em for you.

JOY: Why do you have to keep picking on your own son? Anyone'd think he
  was some dirty stranger the way you treat him.

BILLY: How about you taking your chattering somewhere else? Go on, I can
  look after meself without help from some raggedy sheila.

JOY: [*hurt*] Don't you want me on your side?

GUNNER: [*taking the bottle*] Leave the boy alone. He don't need women
  sobbin' round him.

MARY: Yeh. Let him stew in his own juice. He can take care of himself, just
  look at his face.

BILLY: Chrissake, will you get off me back? I come home to listen to you bash
  my ear? [*He goes to the shack and apparently talks to it.*] You look out, you
  get me mad too much I'll get my spear and take to you.

  He punches the wall, a vicious one-two.

GUNNER: [*throwing the bottle*] Here, have a guzzle.

BILLY: Strikes me this is a good place to get out of, anyway. What does a man
  want to stay here for?

GUNNER: There's plenty worse places than this.

BILLY: Do you reckon they'll really put us out?

GUNNER: The land's sold. We can't do anything about it.

BILLY: I can't see 'em making farms out here. I just can't imagine it.

GUNNER: That's why it's them making the farms. They can imagine it. And
  they'll do it, what's more. I've seen places you wouldn't give tuppence
  for, with a bit of building and tractors and fences and things, turn out into
  decent little farms, with a bit of wheat or some sheep, or rice like on the

irrigation area. Your trouble is you can't sit back and picture it: a little weatherboard house and a bit of garden, a few shade trees, a pump for the water and fences going miles and miles. [*Sitting back*] I can see it.

BILLY: Well, it hasn't got you a farm.

GUNNER: Me? I don't want no farm! I'm happy. She's apples with me, whatever happens.

BILLY: Then you don't care if you gotta go?

GUNNER: 'Course not. I'm gunna sit pat. Then let 'em see what they'll do. They'll end up begging me to take some other place. The Gov'ment has to find some place for us. Just sit it out, that's what I'm doing.

MARY: You'll beat the whole world at sitting, you will.

BILLY: Then what? Where can we go?

> JOY *comes back with something in her hand.*

JOY: [*the rebuffs apparently forgotten*] I found 'im! Here he is. My liddle daddy again! Look, Billy. He was lost before. But I found him.

> GUNNER *groans and turns away as if by so doing he can dismiss the whole affair.*

BILLY: What are you gibbering about, you little ape? Just a coupla bitsa clay?

JOY: They weren't together. [*To* GUNNER] You threw them away, didn't you? Well, I don't care now.

BILLY: [*handling them*] Whose face has it got?

GUNNER: No one's face.

JOY: It's my little man's face, that's what it is.

BILLY: Looks a bit like that useless brother a' mine.

GUNNER: Throw the damn things away, can't you?

JOY: I thought he looked a bit like you, Billy.

BILLY: Don't like to be caught mucking around making faces out of bits of clay, do yer? She dobbed you in, good and proper.

JOY: I'm not throwing him away for no one. He's mine, an' I'll keep him. You couldn't have lost the top piece like you told me in the story.

BILLY: Are you still telling those mocked-up stories? Why don't you leave that to old Gorooh?

GUNNER: I can tell a better yarn than that old, half-dead bag of bones. He's not in the same street as me.

BILLY: Maybe. But you got no right to be telling them. His father was the old man of his tribe…

GUNNER: He tell you that?

BILLY: … and you just make 'em up in your head.

JOY: Do you, Gunner?

GUNNER: What if I do? Anyone can do it. All you gotta do is string words together.

JOY: Was my story just a made-up one?

GUNNER: [*wriggling*] Every story has to be made up sometime or other.

BILLY: Yeh. Depends on who makes it up. You never even seen a tribe.

GUNNER: [*rising*] Don't tell me what I've seen and what I haven't seen.

JOY: Anyway my little daddy's here. He can tell me stories all day when there's no one else to.

GUNNER: [*worked up over something*] I told you not to call that thing your… [*spitting the word*] 'daddy'. Why do you keep having to call something your father? [*Holding out his hand*] Give us it.

JOY: [*in terror*] No!

> GUNNER *lunges for the pieces clutched in her hand. A swipe knocks one to the ground. He grinds it into the dust.* BILLY *throws aside his bottle, which he has been sucking like a contented baby, and rises to his feet scowling.*

GUNNER: Now give us the other one!

JOY: No! Not my little man! Billy! Don't let him get me! Billy!

BILLY: Leave the kid alone, you old bastard! [*Attacking from behind*] Get away from her, or I'll drop yer!

> *They fight.* JOY *draws away to one side, holding her precious little image and watching. Gradually she becomes absorbed in the battle and forgets the ground-to-dust piece.* BILLY *bores in like a windmill.*

JOY: Come on, Billy! Go it! Get round the other side of him. His left arm's no good. I saw him, the other week, that fight outside the pub, he can't hit with it, get round him, go on, quick, his left side, hit him in the nose, he bleeds easy, he's getting old, go on, hit him. Oh, no!

> GUNNER *steps inside one of* BILLY*'s rushes and clips him as he goes past.* BILLY *falls in a tangled heap, the father of the rush-artist.*

Billy, you fool, you couldn't fight your way out of a paper bag. [*Bending over him*] Oh, I think I could fight better than you. [*Patting him in pity*] You have to be all worked up to fight; why can't you just stand back and pick him off, without getting excited, like he does?

> GUNNER *comes near, to grab the remaining piece.*

You won't get 'im!

> *She deftly kicks him in the shins.*

That's for you!

> *She dodges him.*

Now I'm going to plant 'im, like in the story. Plant my little daddy and maybe get a little boy all joined together. [*Running off*] Just like in the story.

GUNNER: [*puffing, to* BILLY] Sure, I'm gettin' old. My guts are shot to hell with cheap plonk, but if you ever know half the tricks I know, you'll be a hard man to beat… Here, have a drink.

He throws the bottle to the now sitting BILLY, *and rubs his shin.*

BILLY: [*sitting and drinking*] Huh... that's better. That was a lucky one; just lucky. That's all.

SAWYER *has come back with* GOROOH.

SAWYER: Don't kid yourself.

BILLY: Who brung you? And who the hell do you think you're talking to? Why don't you crawl off and die somewhere, under one of your rotten logs that you're always cuttin' up and destroyin'? What would you know about fighting?

He tosses the bottle to GUNNER.

GOROOH's *old eyes have no fire. There is a quality of stillness even in his movements. His voice is weak with age and defeat. Sometimes you get the feeling that his words would not have shown the least breath-weight on a fine scale. Then he surprises you with a down-to-earth quality which seems strange issuing from his legendary head.*

GOROOH: The old man with the white hair like the God of the Sunday School would punch you into the middle of next week.

BILLY *catches the bottle from* GUNNER.

BILLY: Arrr, ses you.

GOROOH: I have seen it.

SAWYER: Forget it. I'm just an old dog, with old tricks.

GOROOH: Old tricks have the longest history. [*To* GUNNER] He would also put you in the dust, Stanley.

GUNNER: Don't call me that!

SAWYER: Lay off, Gorooh. I'm an old man.

MARY: You keep callin' him Stanley, Gorooh. That'll really get his goat.

GOROOH: Stanley is your name; Stanley you are to me. Gunner is not a name I like to hear. Your fathers fought with the weapons of a man, not crouched in trees a mile away, with telescopes to set the crosshairs over a man's heart.

GUNNER: They had the grooved stick to throw the spear and the boomerang to strike from far off, and their stray shots came back. They weren't such beauties. Anyway, what did you come hanging around for? We can do without you.

GOROOH: I came to welcome back the other young man from his long walking.

GUNNER: Walking? He went to the city.

GOROOH: Walking. It was walkabout; it is in the blood.

GUNNER: We can welcome him back without you. Beat it. He's not here yet.

GOROOH: The welcome I had was not your welcome. [*Pointing to* BILLY *still on the ground*] Why do you bash the man who tries to make a proper walkabout?

MARY: Man! Show me a man among you lot.

GUNNER: Keep your face shut, you!

GOROOH: [*sadly*] Your woman does not speak to a man the way a woman should.

GUNNER: She never did.

> GUNNER *goes out into the trees.*

GOROOH: That fault is at your door. My welcome to the young man here is my ear ready for his story.

BILLY: Yeah… I haven't been able to get a word in edgeways. [*Through the fog of wine he has remembered the custom.*] Siddown, all you, and get ready to listen.

> *The others dispose themselves around the clearing.*

Here, old Gorooh. Have a swig. Do yer good.

> *He throws the bottle to the old man, who catches it cleverly. There is silence, and they all watch as the old man drains the bottle. A general sigh greets the disappearance of the last drops.*

GOROOH: [*seating himself near the fireplace, cross-legged*] Now the story.

SAWYER: [*pointing to the old Aborigine*] And there sits a man who could drink the likes of you… [*to* GUNNER *and* BILLY] under the table.

MARY: Well, that is a help. He can do something, then, except sit around all day and hand out advice to everyone for nought.

BILLY: First, I went north, since the cold season was on us. I climbed through a lot of fences, up there. I jumped the rattler for a long way and dodged the narks that were after me for tickets. Once I hid in a food truck on a long spell with nothing but a bottle of steam and got through a tin of biscuits. All sweet ones, like we pinched off the town kids in school. Where the Dorrigo is, I started my walking and fighting. Everywhere I went there was someone to fight.

MARY: Bet I can tell 'em your score, too.

BILLY: [*not noticing the interruption*] By and by I come on a cocky farmer and got some chickens from his coop and oranges from his trees. I stayed with him for a bit and got my tucker and a sleep in the feed shed with the rats—big, shiny-eyed rats they were—and one sleep, on the night I went from there, with the girl of the place.

MARY: I bet you had to put some plonk into her.

BILLY: When I left he was still wondering where those chickens went to.

GUNNER: [*derisively*] I bet he was.

BILLY: [*his honour questioned*] His dog didn't have a chance of hearing me.

MARY: What does that make you but a sneaking thief?

BILLY: [*righteously*] There's an art in it.

MARY: I bet you cleared out like a scalded cat, and that's one of the fastest of God's creatures.

GUNNER: Was it his daughter?

BILLY: No. Just the one helped in the house. [*Putting on a brave show*] I could have had the missus too, if I wanted her. They go for lean men, nippy on their feet.

GUNNER: [*raising his voice and directing it towards the window*] Yeh, and fat ones, thin ones, tall and short, bald and hairy. Anyone but the bloke that brings in the money for 'em.

MARY: If you're talking to me, I haven't seen a man for many a long day, let alone spoken to one.

BILLY: Just let me get on with it, will yer...? Anyway, there I was out alone in the middle of nowhere and nothing to set my fanny on but big, snaky logs and red-hot rocks and the bare dirt. I had a knife...

GOROOH: You took a knife on walkabout?

BILLY: I took it, all right. Half-inched it from the cocky farmer. If you'd had one, I bet you'd have taken it on your walks. See, there was this sheep. I caught the sheep and cut its throat...

GOROOH: Sooner bite out its throat than use a knife.

MARY: Why didn't you just talk it blue in the face?

BILLY: Why don't you come out here and talk, 'stead of hiding in there?

MARY: I'll get out when my Gordon takes me to the city.

SAWYER: He may not want to go back...

GUNNER: She'd have a bellyful of the city in a week.

MARY: Least I'd have the pictures to go to, different one every day.

GUNNER: [*spitting*] Pictures!

MARY: I'll get back there one day, if I get to be a cleaner woman.

GOROOH: [*quietly, but with definite contempt*] I think you could be happy in the city.

BILLY: Doesn't anyone wanta listen?

GUNNER: What are you trying to do, you old devil? Get her out of the place?

MARY: [*to* GUNNER] Who'll get your food then, and throw a blanket over you when you come home full?

GOROOH: The wine has made a mess of you, Stanley.

GUNNER: [*brandishing the bottle*] And the bottle will make a mess of you, if you don't look out.

BILLY: I haven't finished, yet!

GOROOH: I will not stay here. I will watch for the boy myself.

  He goes.

GUNNER: Old goat wants to see Gordon. Wonder why?

SAWYER: Perhaps to talk of going to the reservation. His mother is only waiting for the boy to come.

GOROOH: [*coming back*] I will not go to reservations. I am not a chicken to be cooped up. They will carry me when I go.

  GOROOH *goes again.*

BILLY: I wish they'd carry you now!

A moody silence as the others poke about in the dust. BILLY *goes on into the silence but nobody is listening.*

I killed the old sheep, musta been a stray, and made a fire to cook his chops, just like old Gorooh showed me. Lucky I had that meat inside me, 'cause there was the travelling rodeo at the next town. All the boys lairy in big hats and check shirts. I was getting pretty ragged by then. I had a go at the horses, rough riding like we used to do in the yards when we worked for old Smith's. I won a coupla quid and the mob gimme a cheer... Say, ain't any of you listening to me?

GUNNER: [*to* MARY] Chuck us out that other packet of weed, will yer?

He tosses his empty packet away.

SAWYER: [*to* GUNNER] I don't know what you're going to do. It beats me.

GUNNER: We'll get out of it. Forget it.

He gets up to retrieve the tobacco which has been tossed out of the window.

BILLY: And then I got a game of football with a team just finishing up their season with some picnic games, and I scored.

GUNNER: Snuck over at half time?

BILLY: That night I was trying to get something to drink and there was a fight. Too many of 'em. They all picked on me. You can't win all the time.

MARY: Some people can't win anytime.

BILLY: Then I got a beaut ride through to Darwin...

GUNNER: Ride! What sort of a walkabout is it that gets you rides on your fat bum? [*On his feet*] Can't you see, you little idiot, that the time for walkabout is gone? Didn't old Gorooh walk out on you? Why? Because you weren't doing what he told you! And because you're not all dark blood. You haven't got it in you! Walk! Walk! Walk! Bare feet! Get your shoes off!

BILLY does so.

Take off that filthy shirt! Go on, take it off! Now those pants! Go on! Go on!

BILLY: You can't do that here! The cop'll come over here and run me in.

GUNNER: You know damn well that cop won't come over this side of the river unless it's a damn sight more important than this. Go on, take 'em off!

BILLY: I don't want to!

GUNNER: [*mimicking*] He don't want to! Hear that. While you got dark skin underneath, those whites don't think you're naked without clothes. They expect a dark man to have no clothes. They grow up to it in school. They suck it in at Sunday School. It's a black man in clothes they think is funny. When I got back from New Guinea, I got around Sydney in a double-breasted, pin-stripe, grey suit. On me deferred pay. People looked at me 'cause they expected me to have no clothes on. You're caught in the middle of that, you poor fish, and right now you don't look like coming out of it as well as I have. I got me medals in there, and a souvenir or two, and a beaut time for six, seven years, into the bargain.

It's too late for walkabouts; you gotta get a lift in a truck. And it's too early for trying to dress up like your brother and mix with the whites. You're not one of them. You're something to gape at.

And I'll tell you something else.

He lifts BILLY*'s hand and points to his skin.*

You think that's the sun and the colour of your skin; but, sonny, it's not. I'll tell you what it is: it's dirt! Grimed-in, smelly, lousy, stinkin' dirt! That's how they look at it. They don't want to touch you or stand near you. They can deny it, but it don't do no good. If you don't believe me, ask her! [*Pointing with his thumb at the house*] We try to think their skin is wishy-washy and soft like the skin of a festered sore, or like the naked, helpless skin of a skinned rabbit, but it doesn't work for long. There's always the feeling that—well—they're on top, maybe they're better than us; maybe white is the only colour to be. What does that make us…? I'll tell you what it makes us! It makes us not quite men. Maybe we're a sort of animal, only different from kangaroo and snake and birds. Since we're not the colour men ought to be, they give us a fenced-in place, a reservation… [*sneering at the word*] and by and by they come to look at us. [*Imitating a barker*] Real native! Aborigines! Almost human. Watch them throw a boomerang. They eat grubs; there's roots and berries out there and no one but the Abos know which to eat.

The others flinch at the word 'Abos'.

Have you ever thrown a boomerang? Do you know how to live off the scrub? Have you ever swallowed a grub? No! Not on yer sweet life yer haven't. And then they drive off in their big cars, all shiny and pretty with lovely colours, and they tell others and more to come and gape. That's what the reservations is!

Don't you get it? You don't fit in there either. I might; the women don't care. Gorooh doesn't realise it, but in a reserve he'd grow fat. He's got as sweet a line of bull as ever I've seen. Those city people'd lap it up. He'd make some spears, take off his clothes and creak around on his rusty old pins like they expect the old man of the tribe to do. They wouldn't know the difference in the spears.

Your young brother might be all right in the city; I doubt it. But you, haven't I tried to learn you to fight, to be a dark man? You don't have to go to city schools; you don't have to dig for grubs: just stay alive and keep out of their way if you can…

MARY: [*this is the nearest to admiration of* GUNNER *that she has come in many years*] Well! I didn't know you had enough brains in your head to make speeches. You oughta get elected for Parliament.

SAWYER: This is the time for making speeches. You've gotta do something about moving and if talkin'll make you do it, then keep talking.

MARY: I'm right: Gordon'll fix everything for me.

GUNNER: [*back to earth*] Ar, so it's 'dew ett mon droitt': hang you, Jack, I'm all right.

SAWYER: [*the only one he wants at the mill is* GUNNER, *his son*] It's good for a mother to love her son; she wants to have him with her. He is a lucky boy; we'll see if he deserves it.

MARY: He doesn't have to deserve it. And who's talking about 'love'…? He's all I've got.

BILLY: Mummy's boy… Who's that little squirt? What's he ever done? Cleared out and gone to some fancy school. Who paid for it? You did. And there was me working for a man's wage and getting me two quid a week to keep the place going.

GUNNER: Get out. It was me kept the place goin'.

MARY: And what would you say if it was me kept the place going?

GUNNER: I'd say where did you get the cash, and don't answer me if it's where I think you did.

SAWYER: All this was a long time ago, and you were away at the War.

MARY: I bet what he did up in the islands wouldn't bear repeating. What were the little fuzzy-wuzzy girls like, eh?

BILLY: Has he sent you any money, now he's working in Sydney? What does he do for a crust? You never say anything about the wet-mouth little bugger. How old is he, now?

> BILLY *goes out into the trees.*

MARY: He's twenty-one in the New Year.

SAWYER: Must be grown up a bit by now.

GUNNER: Prob'ly just about your size, Billy.

BILLY: [*offstage*] Well, you haven't said anything yet.

MARY: He has a good job. He told me so in his letters.

BILLY: [*offstage*] But what does he do?

MARY: Never you mind… Anyway, he does send me some money…

GUNNER: Why in hell haven't I seen it?

> JOY *springs from nowhere with Billy's spear in hand.*

JOY: I got no clothes to wear.

BILLY: [*coming back*] I can't see that mingy little cow parting up with too much.

GUNNER: So that's why all those trips to the post office every week.

JOY: The other girls all laugh at me. Look at these rags.

GUNNER: Not just letters. And no one over there ever mentioned it to me.

MARY: Post office business is secret.

> *The others laugh derisively.*

GUNNER: Secret, me fat foot!

JOY: With all those old stickybeaks talking to the postman...

GUNNER: ... in his office...

JOY: ... and out on his run...

BILLY: ... and him the biggest stickybeak of them all...

MARY: ... and them women standing round trying to get a look at the papers. But I fixed him. And them. I told him if a word of my business got around you'd all come over and fix him.

SAWYER: So he thinks the rest of you know all about it. Very clever, Mary.

GUNNER: Clever, is it? It's a great thing when there's money coming into the house and the man of the house knows nothing about it.

MARY: Who said it's coming into the house?

BILLY: Where else would you have it?

MARY: You never hear of banks in your life?

GUNNER: Banks!

BILLY: Banks?

MARY: Yeh. [*Mimicking*] Banks! You know well as I do there's one pub and three different banks in the town.

GUNNER: Yeh. All in the one shop.

JOY: [*reasonably*] All I need is some summer dresses; I'll make do with what's underneath.

BILLY: [*laughing*] You'll make do with that all right if I know you.

JOY: They'd change their tune if I had some real pretty ones. And some things to hold me up, here. And some nice shoes. Gold shoes for the dances. Ooh, Mary, I'd do anything for that. I'll sweep and empty the rubbish and clean up...

BILLY: You'd do a lot more for a lot less than that. I heard about you at the town, what you been doing while I was away.

JOY: And what business is it of yours, Billy...? I'm not your wife that you can tell me what to do.

BILLY: Okay. Go and find someone else to play with. I don't want you... Hey, what's that you got there? My spear!

She starts to chase him with it.

Hey! Get her away from me! She'll spear me!

GUNNER: You were gunna spear me a while ago. See how you like it.

JOY: I'll spear the breath right out of your lousy body. I'll make you pray through your rotten teeth!

GUNNER *trips her up as she goes past.*

GUNNER: [*retrieving the spear*] Look out, you'll kill him.

BILLY *takes the spear—he made it himself.*

MARY: He's probably half-dead of fright as it is.

GUNNER: [*in a much more pleasant voice*] How much money you get?

MARY: Never mind. [*Boasting*] Plenty.

JOY: Where you keep the bank book? I had a bank book once. They got it for us at school. You got me to take out the money. Ten and nine, a penny a time, and threepence still in it to keep it going. And all to go and get drunk.

BILLY: Those were the days.

> BILLY *has his spear; he looks all over it with pride of making, examines the barbs and the fine point and tests the resilience and hardness of the five-foot weapon. He sits down and lays it between his knees.*
>
> *In the following, they all gradually recline, drowsy in the heat of the day.*

GUNNER: We could start up something with a bit of money…

JOY: Get out of this place with their women that think theirselves a bit good…

SAWYER: Blow it all in a couple of drunks' sprees…

BILLY: Let's go north…

JOY: We can buy clothes and things…

GUNNER: Maybe a small business…

SAWYER: Business, my foot…

BILLY: A small farm, be cockies…

JOY: Gee, it's nice to sit here and talk about what could happen, with no yelling an' all that…

GUNNER: There's a lot of money in pigs, they used to reckon at the pub…

SAWYER: So there is. And in pubs too…

JOY: [*near* BILLY, *belly-down in the dust, watching him*] We could get married and go away from here to a nice town where everything is clean and have a little house like those over the river, with a little white fence, and flowers in the garden and cement for the path, and curtains, and everything painted and bright, and shiny taps in the kitchen and 'lectric stoves like in the *Women's Weekly*…

BILLY: Whaddya have to say that for, about getting married? We could go and do something to make our money grow…

SAWYER: Such as bury it in the backyard…?

MARY: With all that dough the Gunner could go into Parliament: he seems to have plenty to say on everything without actually saying a damn thing that matters.

GUNNER: And I could afford to get rid of a woman that'll be the death of me with her nag! nag! nag…!

JOY: It'd be like starting a new life over again…

SAWYER: All you need now is the mazuma, the dough, the gelt, the loot, the spondulicks…

> *As their ambitions soar, so their bodies relax back to earth, flaccid at noon in the sunglare, under the hypnosis of the sun's burning eye.*

They do not notice the visitors: two YOUNG LOUTS *with long hair and plunging side-levers; tight, uncomfortable trousers of dull black to show every spot; and short-sleeved t-shirts. They move quietly from behind the town side of the house and stand still a moment. Only* SAWYER *sees them. He smiles broadly, anticipating trouble, and maliciously turning its possible effects over in his mind.*

FIRST BOY: Ay, Joy!

As no one moves, they advance to JOY, *stirring her with a foot.*

SECOND BOY: C'mon on, kid. Sat'day afternoon. C'mon. Let's go. Leave these squares snore their heads off.

FIRST BOY: Well, c'mon!

JOY: I'm not going to town today.

BILLY: Where you going with them?

FIRST BOY: [*to* BILLY] Keep out of this, blackface.

JOY: You should never have come here. I told you not to.

BILLY: Oh, so you meet 'em on Saturdays, do you?

SECOND BOY: [*to* BILLY] You heard, dark man. Shut your dirty trap.

GUNNER: [*on his feet, now—it was done very quietly*] Well, gentlemen.

GUNNER *rubs his hands—they don't bother to face him.*

FIRST BOY: Yeh. We've taken a fall for this little skirt. Now git a move-on. Go in and get some beauty on, and let's go.

MARY: Wow! I've seen phonier Yanks than that at the pitchers on a Satidy night, but they're not doing too bad for kids.

SECOND BOY: Shut up in there, 'less you want some split gizzards.

He draws out a ponderous great hunting knife—on sale at all sports stores.

GUNNER: [*smiling*] Boys!

They flinch at the word 'boys'.

If there's one think I like, it's men of spirit. There's too little of it these days. Specially round here. That's pretty nice knives you got there, men. [*Coming closer, still with an almost ecstatic grin*] Can I see one?

FIRST BOY: Keep your distance. [*To* SAWYER] You, too.

SAWYER *has lumbered to his feet on the other side of the two.*

SAWYER: [*his voice slipping back into something coarser and more masculine than his usual paternal voice*] I'm old enough to be your grandfather, young feller me lad. Look. You're not going to let an old man worry yer, are you?

GUNNER: Go on, give us a look. A solider knife I never seen… well, almost never.

SAWYER: I can only think of a couple that big. Say, Mary!

FIRST BOY: What are you trying to pull?

MARY: What now?

GUNNER: You ever seen two knives big as these?

MARY: No! You mustn't do it! Gunner! Don't hurt them! They're only kids. They don't mean it. They just picked it up from the pictures. Whatever you do, don't go fighting them, or you'll be sorry.

SECOND BOY: I'll say you'll be sorry.

MARY: Oh no, sonny. Not like that at all. You've never seen beef carved the way the Gunner can do it.

> *The team-spirit in this whole operation is very evident.*

He was in the War, you know, trapped in Jap territory. He cut his way through a platoon, a whole platoon of men, with his knife that he had in the War...

> GUNNER *looks at the shutter to see if she is ready with the knife.*

... made out of a filed-down bayonet. Split 'em from ear to ear, like their heads was hanging on a thin thread of blood, and then finished 'em off by giving 'em a hara-kiri cut in the belly and didn't stop until all their what-you-call-its fell out.

SAWYER: [*enjoying this despite his tally of winters*] Now, Mary. Musn't frighten the boys.

FIRST BOY: [*not exactly wavering*] You don't frighten us. Do they?

SECOND BOY: [*spitting, said too emphatically*] No. Me neither.

FIRST BOY: [*to* JOY] Are you coming with us, or do we have some fun with the old geezers here?

MARY: Catch!

> *A large knife comes from the window near* GUNNER. *He catches it by the handle.*

GUNNER: Don't go, men. Take a look at this, men. You have to keep a knife like this very sharp. Best way is on a flat rock with spit. Or someone's rich, red blood. [*He chuckles redly.*] Do you boys really know how to fight with these things? 'Course you do. Well, I'll just see how well you've learned. Just call this an exam. Final exam!

> *He roars with laughter at his own joke.*

> GUNNER *advances in a crouch; the* FIRST BOY *imitates.* GUNNER *flicks the knife from one hand to the other. He feints with one hand, changes from one hand to the other a few times, and thrusts suddenly. The* FIRST BOY *steps back.*

You sure you know what to do with that thing? Cripes, don't throw 'im at me; I bleed easy. [*To* BILLY, *who is still lying back at his ease*] Hey, Billy! Shouldn't you be lookin' after your own girl? She's not mine.

BILLY: [*casually*] No good trying to stop you when you're havin' a bit of fun.

GUNNER: Listen to him. Isn't he a card? He thinks I make a joke of everything. Now I ask you, do I look the type?

The business of feinting and thrusting goes on all the time.

Why, me dear old mother, resting over in the field outside the town there— in the dark section, o' course—God rest her soul, she'd have a fit if she thought I'd laugh at anything so serious as spilling a man's heart down the front of his shirt.

FIRST BOY: [*sweating and wiping his hands on his trousers*] Stop talking, for Chrissake!

GUNNER: [*sweetly*] Does it bother you? My apologies, friends.

As the FIRST BOY *is changing his knife from one hand to the other—he would never have done this had not* GUNNER *done it first—*GUNNER *flicks out and up and the* BOY*'s knife is spun out of his hand.* GUNNER *advances the point to the* BOY*'s throat.*

[*His old self*] Get back in the family circle, mug. Go on, back there.

As the BOY *goes,* GUNNER *chops him at the side of the neck; he drops.*

Well, that's that.

He gives the knife to MARY *at the window.*

[*Turning to the* SECOND BOY] Your turn.

SECOND BOY: [*about to leave*] Get outa the way, old man.

SAWYER: I can't hurt you, son. Look, no knife.

He sweeps his hands out in a gesture of innocence, then down across the SECOND BOY*'s wrists. The knife clatters to the ground. The* SECOND BOY *stoops after it, but* BILLY *has risen and has the point of his spear behind the* SECOND BOY*'s neck.*

BILLY: Pick your mate up and throw him in the river, boy.

The SECOND BOY *hesitates, receives a prick with the spear, and bolts for it.*

Presently there is a splash and a gasping yell. The Murrumbidgee is cold as ice. A floundering in the water, and the delinquent struggles up the opposite bank.

The home side is already sitting down or lying in the shade. BILLY *is choosing which knife he will have.*

MARY: I hope you didn't hurt those boys.

SAWYER: We didn't. No harm done.

GUNNER: Billy, get him out of here before yer mother starts raising Cain.

GOROOH comes in, squats in the shade, looking in the direction of town. BILLY *goes in and appears with rope, tying the* FIRST BOY*'s feet together and pulling him offstage like a bull after a bullfight.*

JOY: Gee, have you got to come back just when things are going nice and even again? Here we are, all friends now. With you about there'll soon be an argument.

GOROOH: [*unseeing her, with his loftiest tribal stare*] I will wait for the young boy to come home.

MARY: Anyone'd think he was your boy.

GUNNER: [*yawning*] Never can tell, can you?

> *There's a man's scream from the direction Billy took—no one notices.*

MARY: There's no reason at all for filthy cracks like that from you or anyone else. I put up with far too much of that, what with one thing and another. There's plenty of nasty things could be said about all of you, even old nose-in-the-air Gorooh. He likes the young girls…

SCENE THREE

Into the clearing in which the exhausted bodies of GUNNER *and* BILLY *are lying and in which* SAWYER *and* GOROOH *are sitting and squatting respectively, comes the sound of a fast car in the distance, howling down the long and lonely stretch of road to the outskirts of the town. The sound diminishes to the gear-change growl associated with coming to a halt. After a few seconds the car starts, turns, and heads back the way it came.*

A whistling, a crushing of leaves and sticks, a brushing of the dry undergrowth, steadily growing nearer. The whistler breaks into a few ravaged bars of 'Home Sweet Home', breaking off in a chuckle; the sleepers stir to smack insects and slap ants; and the two old men watch steadily the approaching figure of GORDON.

Just as he comes into the clearing, we are struck by the young man's size. This is not the skinny little runt that BILLY *has led us to expect. This is not a scrawny, lathe-like actor, all wrists and Adam's apple—*GORDON *is a man. He carries a brave array of cheap ports and packages. He is not the weary traveller borne down under a load of tiredness, but a young man in whose hands the luggage and trappings of a homecoming, well-heeled city man are light as feathers.*

GORDON: [*softly with not a trace of bitterness, only a gentle malice*] Well… well. All flaked out. Welcome home, boy. God, the place is small.

> *Before the old men have time to say anything wise,* JOY *jumps out of the shack like an excited rabbit, and with a flurry of arms and legs and clean linen, darts at* GORDON *and jumps him from at least six feet away.* JOY *and* GORDON, *parcels and bags, descend with a splendid crash to the ground.*

GUNNER: [*on his feet*] What the hell's up?

JOY: [*still on top*] Look at 'im! He's home!

GORDON: [*from the ground*] If you can just spare the time from your snooze and booze you might give me a hand to get her off me.

> GORDON *holds out his hand.* GUNNER *takes it reluctantly and in helping him to his feet is pulled violently forward.*

You've lost a bit of weight?

> *He kicks parcels to one side.*

JOY: How did you get down from town?

GORDON: Taxi, kid.

JOY: Gee. Billy had to bludge a ride on top of a truck. You must have tons of money, Gordon.

GORDON: Billy? How're you doing, Billy? All right? [*Unconscious of any strain*] Gee, it's hard to imagine you're my big brother.

BILLY: [*grudgingly, an enemy as only a brother can be*] You've grown a bit.

GORDON: Seems like it. The old place looks pretty small. I thought of it as much bigger than this. Looks pretty lousy after the big smoke... Well, I suppose, if you can't afford anything better...

SAWYER: Not much money up this way, boy.

GORDON: Grandad! How are you, champ? How're the lot of you...? Where is she?

SAWYER: Inside, boy. She'll be out in a sec, I expect.

GUNNER: When the right moment's come, so's she can douse the lot of us with cold water.

GORDON: I don't hear her slinging off at you; why poke crap at her?

GOROOH: The city has not taken away his belief in a fair go.

GORDON: Heh! Not on your sweet life; back there you gotta keep a fair go in mind. Not for someone else; for yourself. You don't keep kicking and hitting out trying to get a fair go for yourself, you won't get any sort of a go at all.

GUNNER: That's all right about that. Just stick around, you'll hear how she picks on me.

GORDON: Poor old Daddy-oh! [*Ruffling his hair*] Does the little woman keep him under the big thumb?

GUNNER: Arrrh, take your hands off me!

> *He pushes at* GORDON, *but he is not there.* GORDON *is busy with his portable radio, which he gives to* JOY, *who takes it over to one side to listen.*

GORDON: Well, isn't anyone going to ask me things about where I been?

MARY: Yes.

> *She comes from the shack for the first time.*

Your mother has questions for you, Gordon.

> *She sweeps tragically out, clad in the meanest of the rags she uses to do her housework in.*

JOY: Gee, what a bag you look out here in the light.

BILLY: Look out, she'll smell your breath first.

MARY: [*so worked up that it is not funny*] Gordon. Little Gordon. You're all I've got in the world now. The others are cruel to me, and I work so hard for them all. It's so wonderful to have you home here again.

> *She kisses him, pulling him down to do it. He shows a large amount of distaste and embarrassment.*

Thank goodness you haven't been drinking, anyway. You have no idea what it's been like here amongst all this drinking and dirtiness and none of them wanting to do any work. Not even about the house. Oh, Gordon, when I think what a good little child you were, and how you used to come in and comfort your poor mother when the others had ill-treated me, it makes everything a little worthwhile. And to have you, with all those brains, going to a high school in the city, and then getting a good job there. I'm so proud of you. How you must have worked! And did you think of your poor old mother when you were down there amongst all the bright lights and the nice people, where everything's decent and there's lino on the floor and the water comes out of a tap over the sink and they have the sewer on, and where you can see all the lines full of nice, clean washing for miles and miles…? [*Clinging to him*] Oh, my little boy, you are glad to be back with your mother now, aren't you? Just say it. Tell me that you did it all for me. Oh!

> *She bursts into tears—a nasty, sobbing sound.* GORDON *stands awkwardly, giving her a pat or two.*

GORDON: Who's been upsetting her? What's she all miserable about?

JOY: What an act!

BILLY: You're Little Boy Blue; you calm her down.

SAWYER: She thinks you're still a kid in bib and braces, Gordon. It's hard for her to realise that you've grown up almost out of sight. I hardly recognised you meself.

GOROOH: The years have made you look like a man.

GORDON: [*almost convincing*] That's the good food and plenty of places to go; fun and games, thousands of girls, wonderful place.

MARY: [*quickly*] Take me away there. Oh, we'll all be so much happier there…

GORDON: Sure. Sure. We'll all be all right, Mum. How about something to eat? Eh? C'mon! Don't go to any trouble, just a bit of bread and scrape'll do me.

GUNNER: That's all you'll get round here.

BILLY: Maybe he'll do better than us. He's the white-haired boy.

He laughs foolishly. No one else laughs. GORDON *leads* MARY *back to the shanty.*

GOROOH: [*to* GUNNER] Your woman needs better clothes; she will be giving less whingeing then.

JOY: Pigs she does! She got dressed up in those old rags on purpose.

BILLY: Just so's you'd see her like that. She never gets round like that other times.

GORDON: Get off her back, you lot.

MARY: [*sweetly*] I just don't take any notice of them anymore. If I did I'd go stark staring, raving mad…

GORDON: See, you make her life a misery, all of you.

SAWYER: She's put it over you, I can see that.

GORDON: Go on, Mum.

He senses traces of the old feeling which must have aroused derision in past years amongst the rest of the family. He feels uneasy at this reminder of younger days.

Go in, I've got a surprise for you.

MARY *goes in.*

Here, where's that bag of mine? Not that one. No, in the parcel. Shoot it over, will you, Billy…? Thanks.

He rips open the package, disclosing a summer dress and a warm coat.

Hey, open the window. There y'are, what do you think of that?

MARY: Oh, my boy! Oh, thank you. I'll put them on now. But why didn't you leave them in the paper? It's more exciting when they're wrapped up.

MARY *busily admires herself in her makeshift mirror.*

GUNNER: There you are. Never satisfied. [*Speaking away from the shack*] They're all alike. Coupla minutes time, after she's thanked you about fifty times over for our benefit, she'll be letting drop something about it's not her colour, or she wishes they'd made it bigger here and smaller there, or with a belt, or she'd rather have a pair of shoes. You wait and see.

GORDON: That's okay. Don't bother me any. She's just a woman. You expect that sort of thing from a woman.

BILLY: Oh, boy. Big lover. He knows all the women now. [*To* JOY] Git away from them things. Nothing there for you.

GOROOH: There is something there for the girl.

BILLY: How do you know?

GOROOH: There is something for everyone in his parcels.

GORDON: Almost right, Goroh. The only one who misses out is you.

He laughs the heartless laugh proper to a young man.

SAWYER: Give the old man some little thing, Gordon.

GUNNER: [*nodding to* SAWYER] Watch him when he gets friendly, Gorooh. He's after something, betcha life.

GOROOH: There are times when the old must stay together.

GUNNER: All right, be mysterious. But you missed out, didn't you?

GOROOH: [*sadly, it's not a bit of good talking*] When the tribe was, no young one would speak to me that way.

SAWYER: No need to be rude to the old man.

GORDON: [*old loyalties don't matter to a young man fit and well*] Who's calling who old? Anyway, what's it matter? It's not a criminal offence to be rude, so the cops aren't in it. It's just him and me. I can't see he has any friends here to back him up, so it's still him and me. He wouldn't last thirty seconds with me, so who's going to make me polite to him? Or anyone here for that matter? If I feel like it, I'll call him any name under the sun. If I don't feel like it, I won't. And that's all there is to it. Any objections?

JOY: Yes. Come and help me get this bag undone.

GORDON: [*his mood gone in a flash*] You little nuisance!

> *He lifts her up and away from the port.*

Soon as my back's turned, you've ratted my bags! If that isn't like a woman!

JOY: [*a youthful siren*] You're pretty good on women, aren't you? [*Holding a gaudy shirt over her body*] I s'pose this isn't for me? Shows you thought of me. Remember the times I used to come and watch you when you were reading all them books, 'fore you went away to school? Remember you called me your little sister? [*Forcing him to look at her*] Well, I'm no sister now, and what do you say to that?

GORDON: Chicken, will you marry me?

JOY: Not on your sweet life, I won't. Billy'd give me hell. He wants me.

GORDON: Then I can't have you, can I?

BILLY: Who says I want you?

JOY: You did. The way you're not taking any notice of me. We were going on like we'd have to get married, just before you went away. You wouldn't have had much luck away amongst strangers, so it's not natural for you not to want me now. I'm the only girl around... You can't go chasing after the girls from the town, can you? Unless you wash off that colour? So it's still me. [*To* GORDON] Unless you want to take me back to the city?

GORDON: C'mon, that's not yours. Billy, I brought that shirt for you. Looks like you'll have to get it off her.

BILLY: I don't want your shirts.

JOY: Good. Then it's mine.

> *She starts to put it on.*

BILLY: Yeh? What if I change me mind? C'mere, gimme that. [*Chasing her*] Cut it out. Gimme it.

BILLY *catches her, and she manages to fall underneath him. She pulls him down to her, but he is intent on getting the shirt. She tries again, with the others looking casually on. He gets up with the shirt.*

JOY: I give up. There's something on your mind. I can't tell if you want me when there's something on your mind.

BILLY *puts on the shirt.*

GORDON: Here's a new pipe for you, Granpa. [*To* SAWYER] And a parcel of foreign tobacco. Got it in a little shop in Pitt Street. Special wayside mixture. [*Laughing immoderately at the old joke*] A carton of cigarettes for you, Dad. Coffin nails. Ear-rings for Joy. Try these on, kid.

There is no sound for a while but the tearing open of packets and the trying on of clothes and examining of presents. GORDON *goes around watching each one and seems to get a kick out of giving something away. It feels good to come home bigger than when he left.*

GUNNER: Hey, Mary! Shoot out a couple of bottles, will you?

MARY: You come and get 'em yourself. I'm busy.

GORDON: I'll get 'em.

GORDON *goes inside.*

GOROOH: Your son has his heart set on the city, Gunner.

SAWYER: His mother will be happy if he keeps that up.

GUNNER: If she's going back to the city with him, they're going without me. The city's no place for me. 'S all right when a man's young, but there's no room for a man my age. What could I do?

BILLY: Don't tell me you're thinking of going back to work? That pension you're getting for a little scratch in the head, that'll make you think twice before you get so low as to do a bit of work.

SAWYER: You can always come over to the mill.

GOROOH: How long is the mill going to last? You are one man. There are big men coming out to cover these little corners of the world with branches of their big mills.

SAWYER: I'll get along.

BILLY: You'll go broke if you're gonna wait around till he... [*pointing to* GUNNER] makes up his mind to help you over there.

SAWYER: All of you are welcome to have a go at working there. It won't hurt you to try. If I fold up you can work with the big men, as you call them.

GUNNER: [*with bitter finality*] We'll end up on the reservations.

GOROOH: Half your family there and the rest scattered and broken.

SAWYER: If you help me you could show 'em you can earn as much money as any white man. You could live in a little house over the back of the town, maybe save up and buy a little old bomb to get to the mill in, or the boys could get married...

BILLY: There's not much talent around here…

SAWYER: … and take their kids to the city for the Show, all things like that. Like everyone else does.

BILLY: [*derisively, but unconvincing*] Show!

GOROOH: They are not white men. The town will not have them, and the city is too big…

GUNNER: How would you know?

GOROOH: I hear men talking. I see pictures in the papers. I listen to the radio at the pub.

BILLY: How can you get near the pub?

GOROOH: There is the kitchen at the back and a window. I sit in the shade outside and hear things.

GUNNER: They'll hoy you outa there if they find you.

GOROOH: The fat woman there leaves it on for me.

SAWYER: That'll be the old Irish cook. You must pick up a bit of tucker there, too.

GORDON: [*from inside*] You had it well hidden. Catch!

> *He throws a few bottles out. Co-operation is remarkable in this operation.* GORDON *comes out.*

SAWYER: We wondered if you were gunna stay here or go back to the city, Gordon. When you've had a bit of a holiday.

GORDON: Oh, I'll get about a bit, I reckon. Still pretty young.

GOROOH: That is not an answer to the question.

GORDON: You seem to have a lot to say, old feller.

GOROOH: I am used to the way young men talk to old men.

GORDON: Not like the good old days, is it? You can't have things all your own way now. With young boys doing what they like and going off in all directions, Billy to the bush, me to the city…

GOROOH: Both walkabouts.

GORDON: Have it your own way. But I bet he did a hell of a lot more walking that I did.

BILLY: In the city you walk on your belly, not your legs, trying to get the nod from some big-gutted boss.

GUNNER: You leave big bellies out of this. This cost me quids.

GORDON: Who says I walk on my belly? You, you little squirt? My big brudder! Get on your feet and we'll see who's a crawling maggot. C'mon, and let go of that bottle. Bare hands.

SAWYER: Stop it, you young idiots. You won't prove a thing by fighting.

> *They are circling.*

GORDON: Oh, yeh? While I'm socking his nasty little face into the dirt he can remember the time he batted me over the head with that cricket bat at school and all the times he got the others to sneak up behind me and got on to me all together. I don't forget easy.

BILLY: You sneaking, snivelling mother's pet! I'll cut you down to size.

GOROOH: The young have long memories.

He settles down comfortably to watch.

SAWYER: This is stupid! Call 'em off, Gunner!

GUNNER: Not on your sweet life! Garn, you like a good fight as much as I do. Well, stop dancing around and get stuck into it!

GUNNER gives GORDON a push into the arms of BILLY.

GORDON: Quit pushing!

GORDON cannons into BILLY who gets in a shrewd one and misses with a wild swing. BILLY charges in. He is not at ease standing off. GORDON pulls him and swings him over an outstretched leg.

BILLY: What sort of fighting d'you call that?

Emboldened by the absence of punches so far, BILLY charges again. This time GORDON goes down with him and the action stops with GORDON taking him in a wrist lock on the ground.

GORDON: Give in?

BILLY: Yeh.

GORDON releases him and gets to his feet. BILLY starts in again.

GORDON: Hey, you lost! You gave in!

BILLY: Like hell I lost. That was then. This is now.

GORDON: You're supposed to stop...

GORDON goes to meet him centre stage, sweeps his leg up in the air, and drops him back to the ground, moves around, grasps his legs and rolls him over in a 'Boston Crab'.

Now you've had it. Submit. Go on, tap the ground. That's the finish.

BILLY taps and they get up. BILLY wades in again, this time going a little better. GORDON forgets science and mixes it, giving and taking resounding blows on head and body. Both miss frequently with wild swings.

SAWYER: That's better. Mix in with it!

GOROOH: Get in close to him! Go for his head!

GUNNER: Just keep fighting. That's all I ask.

MARY: [*joining in with savage relish*] Close his eyes, Gordon. Get him in the shins. He's weak there.

JOY: [*drinking from the bottle*] Go it! Go it! Both of you!

MARY: Stop that drinking, you little slut!

GORDON: [*pulling himself up, this is not good fighting*] This is a stupid way to fight.

GUNNER: Good enough for a man. Don't try that other stuff. There's no kick in that.

GOROOH: Those other tricks are not fighting a man can understand.

GORDON: No? Well, watch this.

> *He keeps off from* BILLY. BILLY *becomes bolder, advancing. For once* GORDON *does not retreat, but somehow, as* BILLY *strikes at his middle, brings his two arms down, one on either side of* BILLY*'s neck, the outside edge of his hands making contact.* BILLY *drops like a stone.*

Hey, gimme that bottle.

> GORDON *drinks.* BILLY *is still down.*

JOY: The champ!

> *She rushes over to kiss* BILLY.

Oh, pooh! Smell that lovely wine! Give the dead 'un a drink, too.

> *She pours wine sideways into* BILLY*'s mouth.*

GORDON: What's that?

> *He looks in alarm at* BILLY *who has not moved.*

[*To* JOY] Get out of it.

> *He goes over to* BILLY, *turns him on his stomach and pressures his lower ribs with a steady rhythm.* BILLY *stirs.* GORDON *rolls him onto his back and slaps his face fairly hard.* BILLY *wakes.*

BILLY: Aaaarrrrgh!

> *Half rising, he remembers what has happened and flops down again.*

GOROOH: What have you done to the boy?

SAWYER: Doesn't look like fair dinkum fighting to me.

GUNNER: What do you call that?

GORDON: He'll be okay now. [*To* GUNNER] That's like your gut. It cost me quids to learn, and a couple of years of being a chopping block for the fellers who knew a bit more than me.

MARY: I knew you'd beat him, Gordon.

GORDON: You didn't know at all. I'm always a little nice boy to you. I'll have you know I earned a few quid taking it on the chin. But you always hoped I couldn't fight my way out of a paper bag, so I'd still be a mother's boy. [*Pointing to* BILLY] He was right. I was. But that's all changed now. I can take care of myself.

MARY: Gordon! [*It's a shriek.*] Don't ever say things like that…!

GORDON: [*interrupting glibly, his voice back to normal*] Didn't mean a word of it, Mum. [*An obvious lie*] Take no notice of me. Hello! What's this?

> *A hidden cache of* GUNNER*'s clay figures has been disturbed during the fight.*

GUNNER: [*coming over*] Never mind them. It's nothing. Get away from them.

JOY: That's his little men. He makes all sorts.

> SAWYER *has gone over to* BILLY *and propped him up. No one else has taken any notice of the fallen hero.*

BILLY: When you're down, there's no one on your side.

JOY: [*turning around to sneer*] Stop your crying, can't you?

GORDON: Say, these are good.

GUNNER: How the hell would you know? C'mon, give 'em to me. Give 'em to me, I tell you!

GORDON: [*giving him a push*] Shut up! And keep your shouting for them you can push around. They all look like Billy.

SAWYER: I didn't know you still did this sort of thing, Gunner. When you were a lad—

GUNNER: Never mind when I was a lad.

MARY: It's a wonder you didn't know, you're over here often enough.

JOY: He hides them from people. He's ashamed of them.

SAWYER: This is my family, just as much as yours. I'm his father, aren't I?

JOY: Don't ask us, aren't you sure?

GORDON: I've seen a lot worse than this in the city.

JOY: He made me a little man, then broke it on me! Then he told me a story about an old dark woman who took 'im up to the hot country and planted him and he grew up to be a big man.

SAWYER: The Gunner told you that?

JOY: Didn't I just tell you? And when he broke my little daddy, I went and planted him, but I only had the top half, 'cause he was broken in two.

SAWYER: [*sentimentally*] I told him that story when he was a kid...

JOY: [*matter of fact*] Then it ain't a real story?

SAWYER: Sure it is.

JOY: Couldn't be if a white man made it up. Must be a phoney.

SAWYER: I got it off Gorooh's father...

GOROOH: How did you come...?

SAWYER: He was the best teller of dream stories in all the tribes.

>*The lie is passed over, because it is palatable.*

GOROOH: He was the best. The best of great men.

SAWYER: See?

BILLY: Well, what an idiot. Fancy taking notice of a man with stories like that.

JOY: I planted him, and it's Gordon'll come up, not you! So don't you dare call them that! Gordon, hit him again, and make him shut up!

GORDON: [*at the he top of his voice*] Shut you yourself, and don't keep bothering me!

JOY: All right both of you! [*She picks up jewellery, jingling the bangles defiantly on her shiny brown arms.*] I'm sick of the lot of you. There's no men here, and not having a man with you is like being undressed... Those boys that were over here like me, anyway. I'll find someone real easy, you'll see. I don't have to go on my hands and knees to them. They burn holes in my clothes with their eyes when I walk past. At least they appreciate me. Goodbye!

JOY *goes out.*

BILLY: Good riddance!

GORDON: [*to* BILLY] Well, how're you feeling now, kid?

BILLY: None the better for your asking.

GORDON: Here, have a drink.

>   GORDON *tosses* BILLY *the bottle.* BILLY *drinks.*

BILLY: [*diffidently*] What was that you done before?

GORDON: Tell you some day. Come on, don't drink all the damn stuff.

GUNNER: [*pleased, in some corner of his heart, that his boys are drinking together*] Here's another bottle. Let him keep that one. It'll take the sting out of his bruises.

MARY: Gordon, your food's ready. [*Sharply*] Come on, you others, get a move on, it's on the table. I'm not waiting for anyone, if you don't come now it'll be cold and it'll be your own fault, you can't say I didn't tell you, come on! Gordon, there's something special for you.

BILLY: Any bacon?

MARY: You know we can't afford bacon.

>   *They all disappear inside, except* GOROOH *and* SAWYER.

>   *The others come out presently with thick slices of bread and butter and jam, and with a piece of what looks like meat. It could be fish.* GORDON *has an extra large piece and something on a plate. This is the only plate on show. They squat down in silence, as befits men weary from long battles,* GUNNER *on the verandah edge,* BILLY *on the ground.* GORDON *stands up.*

[*To* SAWYER] Come on, you! We didn't ask you to come here, but I can't see you go without while those hungry-gutted devils eat. Here, get off your bum and come and get it.

SAWYER: [*going*] How about Gorooh?

>   GOROOH *says nothing but looks down at his crossed legs.*

MARY: He's got his own place to go to. [*To* GOROOH] What's the matter? Don't they feed you down there? I can't be expected to go feeding every stray that wanders in. I'd have nothing over if I was doing that all the time. What do you think it is? A grocer's shop or something?

>   *The others, with the exception of* GORDON, *who gives him a curious glance without pity or blame, take no notice of the old man.*

Ar, come on, then. You make me miserable, looking like that. But I'm not coming out serving anyone. You want this, you come and get it yourself, and then perhaps I can have something to eat, after dishing up for everyone else first. Come on...! Arrrh, you stubborn old nuisance.

>   *She goes in and comes out with a small ration.*

Here, grab it! Haven't you got any hands?

> GOROOH *makes no move to take it. She plonks it down in front of him and goes back. She stops short of the door, watching him take the food and eat. He eats slowly, chewing many times, like a man who has been often hungry.*

You ought to be in pictures, fair dinkum! What an act! You're not too proud to eat it, are you? Just too lazy to save my legs. Arrrh, people like you make me sick!

GUNNER: [*without looking up*] Why don't you have your dinner, Mary? That oughta keep you quiet for a while.

GORDON: [*without looking up*] Good fish, Ma.

GUNNER: I caught 'im.

GORDON: Musta been a big 'un.

GUNNER: Biggest in the river. [*To* MARY] Hit us in the eye with the salt, will yer?

MARY: You told the kid there's always a bigger one round the corner, so this can't be the biggest.

BILLY: This could do with some more salt, too.

GUNNER: Eat it and be satisfied, can't you?

> *The salt comes through the door.* GUNNER *catches it expertly.*

MARY: Still can't be the biggest.

GUNNER: Shut up and let me eat in peace!

> *He tosses the salt to* BILLY.

GORDON: You shut up, too.

> GUNNER *hasn't got used to being less than top dog, yet.* GORDON *will have trouble with him.*

MARY: Don't you like what I made for you?

GORDON: Oh, that? 'Course I like it... [*Holding it up*] What is it?

GUNNER: You better tell her it's good. It's some foreign recipe she got out of the *Women's Weekly*.

MARY: The picture of it looked lovely. I only made it for you... And I still think... [*to* GUNNER *as the curtain falls*] there's much bigger fish left in the river, I don't care what you say...

SCENE FOUR

The sunset is red as hell. Midsummer insects are loud in the clearing and down at the river. Frogs croak lazily and the air is thick with mosquitoes. Birds cry only occasionally; a circling crow is disturbed by the sight of some scrap on the ground and cries 'Caa-ah'.

GUNNER *is propped against the house.* GORDON *and* BILLY *are lying full-length in the dust. These two now wear the same sort of rough clothes.* GORDON *is back home. The slaps of their battle against the mosquito are resounding in the cooling air. There is the murmur of a voice inside the shack*—MARY*'s voice humming and singing in snatches. Suddenly a flock of galahs shriek and race to another tree.* GUNNER *sits up quickly, looking towards the sound.*

GUNNER: [*quietly*] Shut up in there.

> *There is silence for a while. No sound from the trees.* GUNNER *slides off the verandah, prods the prone two in the ribs with the toe of his shoe, and signs to them to be quiet. They move into the shadow cast by the shack and wait. More birds cry—this time, smaller birds. At a sign from* GUNNER, BILLY *sneaks off in the direction of the other shacks, to warn the others. As he gets back, the attack begins. The attackers make no more attempt to conceal their presence. Stones land on the house. The rush begins.*

> *The clearing is filled with men fighting each other in a vicious home-made manner—few expert fighters are there. Reinforcements from the other shacks mix it with the attackers, men fresh from the pub. As the women scream,* GUNNER *manages to call to his lieutenants.*

Get them away from the houses! Draw 'em away! Billy, you hear me. Go on! Gordon, take 'em away over that side!

> *The boys do as they are told, and gradually the fighting moves away, to the river and to the other direction, towards the main road. As they go,* GUNNER *comes back quickly towards the house.*

MARY: [*at the door*] Is that what you came back for?

> *She holds up a beautiful rifle, such as a marksman might prize.*

GUNNER: How the hell did you know where it was?

MARY: You'd be an idiot, wouldn't you? Do you think anything goes on here that I don't find out about? Who are they out there, anyway?

GUNNER: [*just wanting to be out there*] Search me.

MARY: Those agents for the people that are gunna buy the place are behind it. [*A sudden tone of responsibility in her voice*] We were supposed to be out of here a week ago, that letter said.

GUNNER: I don't care what the letter said.

> GUNNER *works the action of the rifle, disposing of the shells about his pockets. He adjusts the sights and goes off.*

MARY: [*coming out*] What dopes they are! Fancy trying to protect me! I had enough hot water in there to give 'em a billycan at a time in the face. That would have driven the whole lot off quick smart... [*Busy clearing stones away and setting to rights everything that has been knocked over*] God alone knows what they're fighting for now. I don't. If they didn't give each other an excuse for a bit of a stoush, they'd have one just for the fun of it… If I thought those fellers from over there were fair dinkum enough, I'd go out and give them a hand myself. And it's not as if things are any different when they're finished with fighting—things are always the same afterwards. They just have to have their fun. [*She straightens up, the tidying finished.*] There's nothing much else here for any of us… When I get to the city, it'll be different…

> *She goes back inside. There is the crack of a high-powered rifle. Repeated again and again. There is a joyousness in the quick-fire of the shots—* GUNNER *is back in the New Guinea jungles. The yells and curses take on a new and startled urgency, then start to die away—it is a rout.*

GUNNER: [*coming back quickly, calling to* MARY] Quick, Mary. Get the rest of the shells. Kincaid'll be over now I've fired the gun at last.
MARY: Sure, Gunner.

> MARY *appears with the rest of the shells in several cardboard boxes with red labels.* GUNNER *breaks the gun, using a pull-through on the barrel and wrapping it lovingly in the cloth and canvas she brings out.*

GUNNER: Now take 'em, love. They go in the old red-gum. There's a dead branch—Billy knows it—he can get up there with the rope the kids use for climbing. Tell him to be sure and cut the rope down.
MARY: [*incredulous*] You mean you're gunna let me carry it? You'll have me gettin' snively next… Or maybe I'll come over all lovey-dovey. How does that strike you?

> *She ruffles his hair.*

GUNNER: Strewth, Mary! You're as mad as a meat-axe!
MARY: He calls me by me name, too! Must be turning over a new leaf.
GUNNER: Just get it out of here, quick. He'll be here any minute. He's been waiting to pinch me for this. Wants to get his hands on her.

> *He pats the rifle affectionately.*

MARY: I might be a bit more use to you if you'd pat me like that, sometimes.
GUNNER: Go on, Mary. Beat it! That rifle's worth quids! Find Billy. Or Gordon'll do. And tell him to stuff some twigs in after it. Keep out any wet.
MARY: Only thing in the world he likes better than a bottle of steam, and that's that gun…

> *She goes.*

GUNNER: Ah, well. Now everyone'll know about it. Can't expect to keep it dark forever, I s'pose. [*He sits down in deepening shadows.*] First, the biggest fish ever to come outa the river; now I've let 'em see the rifle. [*Laughing suddenly*] Now there's nothing to stay in this place for. That'll be him, now.

A stealthy crunching of twigs. No close approach to their camp can be silent. This is, of course, no accident.

KINCAID *enters, dressed in uniform trousers and braces and boots. That is as far as he resembles a policeman.*

KINCAID: All right, Gunner, where is it? And don't say 'what?'. You could hear it for miles on a night like this.

GUNNER: Hear what? The mossies?

He slaps one.

KINCAID: Arrrh! Don't give me that. You've got a three-o-three in the camp, and you know you're not allowed to have it. Where did you get it? Souvenir it when you got out of the army?

GUNNER: Souvenir what?

KINCAID: We all know...

BILLY *and* GORDON *are back now;* MARY *too.*

... what you did in the War. You can shoot. It's just possible that you hit someone today, although I doubt it. I doubt it very much.

GORDON: Yeh? He can shoot the buttons off your shirt when it's too far way to see 'em.

KINCAID: [*shrugging*] I've had no complaints. No bods on the ground.

GORDON: No. That's because he was aiming about one inch from their backsides. 'Course he didn't want to hit anyone. All they felt was the wind of the shots.

KINCAID: So you did use the gun? I know that old shotgun you bring out whenever I try to do a little detecting is just a cover-up. Now I've got you. Your own son gave you away. [*Looking* GORDON *over*] Fresh from the big smoke, too. Learn anything in the city?

GORDON *has met the police in the city, and doesn't realise you can talk with a country policeman. He stays dumb.*

GUNNER: But the old shotgun is all I've got. You can have a look inside.

KINCAID: I know a shotgun when I hear one. All right. It's getting too dark to look. And I'll bet there's only the shotgun inside. But you and me and all of us know that was no shotgun. And you were firing at or near people from over the river. That's the finish for you. I wash my hands of you. You're supposed to be out of the place. The owners want me to do their dirty work for them ...

BILLY: They're not game to come and get us out themselves...

KINCAID: All right, they're not game. But it's their land, and they want to use it. They want to make a start on their water pumps. The pipeline's going to come somewhere round here. Now you've done this, you've made it easy for me. I didn't like the job of putting you off here. But I feel a lot easier now; if I come across that gun you'll all be in the reservation so quick it'll make you giddy... You've really had the sword this time... If I

don't find it, you've got a choice; there's plenty of places you can go to—
I wouldn't suggest coming over the river—but there's little towns, all
over the country, where you can settle down. None of you are stupid;
there's things all of you can do...

BILLY: Plenty of jobs, too?

KINCAID: Well, maybe not plenty. But you've got to make a big effort...

BILLY: Now, you're telling me, there's not plenty. There's not enough jobs to
go round in the town...

GORDON: What was that all about? Have you been getting the housewives in
trouble?

GUNNER: That's not funny...

KINCAID: I did hear tell that two of the kids from the town were... ah—
assaulted here. They reckon you all set on 'em like a pack of wild beasts.
And one of 'em was found strung up by the heels to the fork of a sapling
over there, with a bit or rope. We haven't got any sense out of him yet. He
nearly went off his head. There was some ants in that tree.

MARY: They came for us with knives.

KINCAID: They had no knives when they got back home.

MARY: That's because we—Oh, no you don't. That's what you did to Gordon.
You're not going to get away with the detective stuff all the time. We
know you're in the saloon on Sunday mornings over at the pub; now you
make accusations about guns, and you can't prove 'em; oh no, you're not
so smart... They must've lost their knives on the way back. They went
faster than they came, and with their tails well and truly between their
legs, and us tossin' gibbers and goolies after 'em.

KINCAID: Okay, but let it sink in. Be out of here... New Year's in the morning;
make a clean start to it. I don't know where you can go, but you've got to
get out of here.

GORDON: Keep moving...?

KINCAID: It's not my problem. I can't help you.

GUNNER: Never mind your charity... We'll be out of here by morning.

SCENE FIVE

Towards midnight on New Year's Eve, around the tiny fire. From time to time
GUNNER *or* SAWYER *or* BILLY *puts some kindling on the fire; and now and
then someone makes for the trees for a minute.* SAWYER *is on the old log
drawn up at an angle.* GUNNER *is on the verandah.* MARY *is on a chair brought
from inside.* BILLY *and* GORDON *squat or stand, restless.* GOROOH *squats
nearest the fire as if his old bones need the fire.*

GOROOH: If the men have all become firm in their wish to leave tonight, then before sleep stretches you out flat on your backs, you had better decide where to go.

GORDON: Yeh... I know it's hard for the rest of you when you've been here so long, but you've gotta have something cut and dried before you start setting out for the ends of the earth. Think of the—

BILLY: You know where you're going? How about letting us in on the secret?

GOROOH: First, I can speak for the others of my family. They will go where I go.

GORDON: All rush downhill together?

SAWYER: Fair go there. Give him a hearing; then we can take it in turns, and all have a go.

GOROOH: My people want to stay. But I can see that will not be. Some want to keep moving west. They are not fit to find food. They have lost the ways of hunting the goanna and digging for food in the earth. We have been near the town men too long, and admire only the ways of getting food from the government or killing birds with guns or bludging on women from the little town over there. We set lines for the fish, knowing that there are better fish in the river away from the towns.

BILLY: Get to it, get to it. Is that all you got to say?

MARY: Yeh, we know all that, just as well as you.

GUNNER: Bet you haven't seen a fish round here like the cod you had for tea.

MARY: He caught himself, he was tired of living.

SAWYER: Come on, let's get back to it. Strike me pink, one word and you're all off the track to billy-oh!

GOROOH: None of you wants to hear me. Such things would not have happened in the days of the tribe.

SAWYER: Too bad, Gorooh. Your trouble is you're too long-winded. My idea is that you, Gunner, bring Mary over and start work in the mill. We'll be putting out as much as we can handle for a few years yet. My lease is still healthy. Billy can go up north, not to move around, but get a job with the cattle. Riding'll always suit him, and they need stockmen, and... [*turning to* BILLY] if you're single you've got all your cash to yourself. You can even get 'em to bank it for you. So... [*with the air of having settled it*] that means the Territory, or Queensland in the west.

BILLY: Two quid a week!

   He spits.

SAWYER: And all found! And they pay a bit more in some of the better stations. Three quid. Spend one and save two. A hundred quid a year! Think of that. You'd have your own money then, and if you wanted to get married...

BILLY: I don't want to get married. I'll catch mine on the hoof...

SAWYER: If so, you've got dough. Look round. How many blokes your age...

BILLY: ... and colour...

SAWYER: ... have any dough at all? None of 'em.

GUNNER: It's no use. We just can't save dough. We gotta spend it.

SAWYER: Bull! If you got someone to save it for you, you're right.

BILLY: I want my dough in my own hand.

SAWYER: Wake up to yourself! You're not on a picnic. Look at you, you're living on the city people. They pay tax so you can go along to the post office to pick it up. Don't be a bludger all your life! Get a grip on yourself.

MARY: I know the only grip he gets on himself.

SAWYER: You do what you want. But the main problem is the Gunner and Mary. The only thing to do is split up. It's gotta happen sometime, so you might as well make up your minds to do it now.

GORDON: Nothing in mind for me?

SAWYER: You left here—how many years ago—with better marks in your examinations than any of the kids around here; everyone thought you were a bit of a genius. So far the only one who's had news of you since then is your ma, and now you're back we haven't heard just what the score is. I'd say you could look after yourself.

MARY: Never you mind about Gordon. We'll work that out, won't we?

GORDON: [*by no means sure*] Sure. Sure.

SAWYER: Well, that's it. That's my idea.

GOROOH: You have nothing to say about us?

SAWYER: A man as wise as an old man of your tribe does not need words from me. Besides, what the hell do I care about you? I'm interested in my own family. The Gunner's my only son still living.

BILLY: Maybe your idea's not so bad for me. Only it seems I'm to beat it, off by meself, just out of the way of everyone. Orright, if that's the way you want it, maybe I will. Then... [*to* GUNNER] you'll have to work or just hang around with no one to spin your yarns to but your old man or her. Suits me.

GUNNER: [*thoughtfully*] I've got me pension from the War. I could beat it by meself, except that I'm not getting any younger. I could go to the reservation...

MARY: Not on your sweet life!

GUNNER: I could build another humpy somewhere else, where there was no farms to be started. Or maybe I could go with you... [*to* SAWYER] for a while and see what happens.

SAWYER: Now you're talking...

MARY: There's only one thing I've wanted to see. And that's Gordon come back to his mother. And now he's come. I've waited for this day for years now. He's been away in the city working and getting plenty of knowledge under his haircut and the time's just about ripe. Gordon, I don't care about the others. You're my baby, and you're the only one I care what happens to. There's just one thing I want, and it'll fix all our troubles. You others go where you like, but I've scraped and saved all this time for this; Gordon, you must take me back to the city!

GORDON *is struck dumb, literally.* MARY *looks at him as he tries to cope with his reactions.*

[*Pleased*] See? You didn't think I'd be so pleased to get back there, did you? [*She prattles happily on.*] But all this time, I've wanted nothing better than to be where you are. That's been the main trouble with me. I thought when we sent you to school that it was best I stay back here, but now I'd rather be there with you. So take me back, Gordon…

She advances to him and takes him by the hands.

GORDON: No! No!

As GORDON *frees his hands with a gesture,* MARY *clutches his shirt.*

MARY: I'll be no trouble. It'll be a pleasure to get back there; I can get a job in a factory—or a shop. [*Speaking very quickly*] I won't be in the way…

GORDON: Oh, no… oh, no… not there… I'm not going back there. I'm keeping out of that damn place as long as I can.

BILLY: [*alert for the first sign of weakness*] Hullo, the boy's not the big man we thought. What's the matter, sonny, didn't you do so well there?

MARY: You shut your yap. He's forgotten more than you ever knew…

GORDON: And there's a lot I learned that I wish I'd forgotten. They thought I was good when I was a kid. They taught me a lot of things. I was better than the other kids. Where are those dead-heads now? On their fathers' properties, getting about in brand-new Holdens to round up the sheep when they've had a few in. All the money in the world. They've got brains in their bank books and that's a damn sight more important than me knowing a few facts they've never heard of. Sure I had jobs. They let me in, working with the others. I wasn't too bad, I think. When I was at school, I learned something new every day; but in those city jobs I did the same damned thing every day, day after day. I worked in a white collar, but I soon changed to grey shirts and blue shirts. You know why? Those kids I worked with slaved all the weekends to get a suntan… [*with derision*] but, brother, do you think they ever got one as good as mine? And I didn't have to go out in the sun to get it! With a white shirt I looked like the apes in the zoo, like a zombie among the white girls. How clean they looked! Scrubbed clean every morning, and they all smelled good, boys and girls. And their houses! Clean as the District Hospital!

GUNNER: Yeah? Well, I wasn't born in a hospital, and I won't die in one. So why should my shack look like one?

GORDON: They looked at me and they didn't see a better suntan than they had, though that's what they said sometimes. What they saw was dirt! I saw it in their faces! Look! It's black; so it's dirt. You don't believe me, you try going there and working up next to 'em. In the train, in the bus, in the taxi, that look: 'Why don't they wash?' I scrubbed and scrubbed and sweated in hot baths until my skin was stiff with soap and my hands and feet pink like a baby's bottom, and I changed jobs time and again, out in the suburbs and back in the middle of the city. I could tell those numbskulls three things for every one they could tell me, but that made no difference... If only I could sing, or something.

SAWYER: Join the choir at the church. They'd never know it was you.

GORDON: Face it! I haven't got the brains to carry on with those things I was good at when I was at school; I got so far, but no further. I can't get myself a profession. Who'd go to a black doctor?

SAWYER: [*kindly, without being patronising*] Not black, son. Your skin's only brown.

GORDON: It's black alongside theirs... And would I get any promotion in those jobs I had? Not on your bloody life! They think I'm just a little bit simple. Ought to be home playing a didgeridoo. I've never seen a didgeridoo. I couldn't throw a boomerang. I couldn't stand still for two hours on a rock and spear a fish. I've only ever heard about corroborees. They think I'm straight from the dead heart of the country. Primitive man! Keep him away from the women and kids! I'll tell you where the dead heart of Australia is! It's right back there in the city! Not out in the sand and the mulga and the stones burning hot under the sun and smoke going straight up into the sky like a spear at sunset. It's in the big blackness under the neon signs. It's back there in the forest of elbows—elbows shoving you out of the way and pressing on your ribs so you can't breathe, and the nice polished shoes to kick if you get in the way. [*Speaking in parentheses*] But you oughta see what happens when the cop points to 'em crossing the road; they sneak across like kids coming late for school... and their eyes that go through you in a split second! Not to see inside your heart and tell if this one's a man or a liar or a good bloke or a thief. No. Those eyes tell in a moment where you come from, what sort of job you've got, how much a week you get and how much your clothes cost, right down to your socks, and where you live and how much rent you pay. And on top of that look is another look that says they wouldn't be surprised what sort of filthy things you did when you got in off the streets. And don't catch anyone watching you look at any of the little kids that play in the streets or walk through the city with their... [*sneering*] mummies. I did at first—there were some lovely children there, all done up in beautiful clothes—I did, and once I had three men walk over and ask me what sort of bastard I was, and if they caught me looking at kids like that they'd put my face out through the back of my head... Aaaah, forget it.

Anyway, they wouldn't have me working as a boss over white boys; I'd just be the crap round the place. I couldn't even ask anyone out for a beer, let alone stop by on Friday nights with the boys. All I could do was take a bit of grog 'home'—and get tossed out for drinking on the premises. The landladies always used to go through my things; I'd see 'em disturbed, every place I went. I dunno if they thought I was a crook, or if they expected to find bugs and silverfish in my clothes. I don't know. But, brother, was I sick of it all! Billy, you were right. I'm not a big man, not by a long chalk. And I'm a damn sight smaller for spending those years in the city. I tried. I didn't want to come home and say I was beat. But it was no good... And now you've got to move too. You take my advice, all of you, and go with the old bloke. Go and work in the mill; work somewhere, because you're either going to work or get put in pens for foreigners and city people to come and look at like animals in a cage—'the most primitive aboriginals on earth, watch them eat witchetty grubs'. The only other thing you can do is let 'em keep you on the move. Today here, tomorrow a bit further west, and next year further still. West all the time. What happens at the end? Are you going to wait until they push you clear across the country and into the sea? And all because there's no room for us in our own country? We're just like New Australians here. But there's the point. It's not our own country anymore.

SAWYER: Don't forget you're part white; part of you was one of the people that put old Gorooh out of date.

GORDON: That part doesn't count at all, as long as I've got dark blood, and it's their country. They walked in and took it.

GUNNER: What can we do? Take it back?

BILLY: That's a laugh.

GORDON: We can either let ourselves be penned up, or driven out until we're gone right off the face of the earth, or we can find a few things they'll let us work at.

GOROOH: They'll *let* us!

GORDON: Yes. We can't do anything they won't let us do. Simple as that.

SAWYER: You sound as if you've got something in mind.

GORDON: Maybe. But that's what all of us have to do. We can't like 'em, so we'll join 'em. And that's the only hope I can see.

GUNNER: But if you don't get on in the city, how then?

GORDON: There are things I could do there if I looked round more. But I'm staying out in the country towns. Well, that's the story. And, what with money for this and that, I wasn't able to send any—

MARY: Never mind, Gordon.

BILLY: Wasn't able to send what?

GUNNER: Yeh. What was that?

BILLY: He was gunna say money.

GUNNER: What about all the dough you said he sent you?

GORDON: I sent?

Pause.

MARY: Well, don't speak, whatever you do! You all got your ideas where I got it! Well, why don't you say it? Go on, why don't you? You've got to make a mouthful of it just as he comes home! [*Crying*] Haven't any of you got enough sense to shut up about it when he's back home…? Gordon, you're still my little boy! All of it's for you…! And the rest of you, you always knew I was doing it. And some of it's gone on keeping the food in your bellies when… [*pointing to* GUNNER] he's been rotten with grog and lost all his money on the dogs or the horses or the football. Or his women. Don't deny it! I know just as much about you as you know about me! You rotten hypocrites! As long as you think you're getting the benefit, it's all right. As soon as my boy comes home you've got to let him know…!

She sobs.

GORDON: Now, Ma. Come on. Cut it out. It's not as bad as all that.

MARY: Well, what did they expect? There's no money coming in from him, but what he spends on himself. And when you didn't send me any, I knew it was because you couldn't. So I just had to get some together.

More crying from MARY.

GORDON: It's done now. Stop crying, Ma. Go on, there's a good girl. I know the money came from you to send me to high school.

GUNNER: What? More money? Why, you dirty rotten—

He strikes MARY, *a back-handed slap across the jaw-line. She falls, perhaps for effect, but she hits the ground all the same.*

I didn't know it was going on then!

SAWYER: [*in a low voice*] Yes, he did.

MARY: And I suppose you don't remember what you said time and time again while you were drunk, about your fine experiences in the War, up in the islands and in the cities. You were a great one for boasting; what a great one you are to be slinging off at me!

GORDON: Get away from her.

GUNNER: Don't you talk back to your father like that, you soft-bellied, mealy-mouthed, gutless wonder!

GORDON: Get away from her, where I can get at you. I reckon you got it coming, Daddy.

They circle. The others move back. BILLY *jumps* GORDON *from behind.* GORDON *holds his arm, so that* BILLY *is lifted up on* GORDON's *back, and he swings* BILLY *into* GUNNER's *punch.* BILLY *collects it in the ribs and drops.*

Your offsider didn't get the best of that. He always was a fighter from behind. Did you teach him that, too?

Each feint's an advance. They do it again, then on the third time GORDON *makes a double-feint and comes in on the second one.* GUNNER *is off-balance and* GORDON *hooks a leg behind him and sits him down with the momentum of his advance.*

Well, get up. Why take it easy when there's work to be done?

Instead of getting to his feet, GUNNER *springs from a crouch.* GORDON *neatly sidesteps and brings the edge of his hand down in the classical chop on* GUNNER*'s neck.* GUNNER *drops and stays down.*

SAWYER: There's still one to go, young 'un. It's not decent I should sit down while my son gets knocked about.

GORDON: Go to hell, Grandaddy. You're not fit to be fighting. I won't fight a lame man.

SAWYER: [*patting both legs*] I'm not lame.

GORDON: No? Well, that other leg is dragging awful heavy in the grave.

He laughs at his own joke.

SAWYER: Joke, is it? I'll wipe the smile off your face. See if I don't.

GORDON: Go away, Methuselah.

He gives SAWYER *what appears to be a shove, but withdraws the arm before* SAWYER *has a chance to grab it. He gives a simple trip and the old man is down.*

Now no one is on my side. I've just pushed over the old, old man. Now I can't trust any of you. [*To himself*] Never trust a man you've beaten. [*To* MARY] What do you think of your little boy now? Pushing over old grey-beards?

MARY: Who cares about him? I'm only thinking of you, Gordon. Can't you really see it'd be best for us to go back to the city?

GORDON: Arrh, give up, Ma. I told you before, I'm not going back. Anyway, aren't you sick of living with us Abos yet? You might get on better if you did clear out to the city. [*He stops at the rising horror in her face.*] You're always quarrelling with him. As long as I can remember you've been at each other's throats.

MARY: There's been good times. We've had good times together. We talk a lot rougher than we mean, sometimes… [*She looks at* GUNNER *lying in a heap.*] He's not such a bad stick, you know. Or maybe I'm just as bad as him, so I don't notice it in him so much.

SONNY *appears on the scene—a well-built, very fair-haired young man of* GORDON*'s age. Well-dressed appearance, smart shoes, well-creased trousers and spotless white shirt. All other pretences at white in the dress of the others fade into morbid greys in the presence of this shirt. He wears his hair short.*

SONNY: What's this, a massacre?

SONNY*'s ebullient tone contrasts strangely with the others.*

GORDON: Sonny! Where'd you spring from?

SONNY: You said you'd be back before midnight. I got tired of waiting, so I asked the way over at the pub. They said I was taking my life into my hands to come over here... I flaked out this afternoon in my room, I was all tuckered out from the train ride. They said there was a little fuss over here earlier. I didn't hear it.

GORDON: An attack on the old homestead, no less, Sonny boy.

SONNY: Still keeping the old spirit alive, eh? Keep in nick, I say. [*Pointing to the three men*] Who are the crocks?

GORDON: Jim, meet my mother. Brother, that one. Father. Granpa. The entire family is on my back. Except Ma.

SONNY: [*with practised ease*] I've heard such a lot about you from Gordon. He always says he owes you all he has. Whenever he speaks of his family, it's always his mother he praises right up to the sky.

MARY: [*vastly pleased*] Well... thank you, Jim... thank you very much. Heavens, I must look a sight... I'm sorry Gordon couldn't have brought his friend over when... we... when I had a... I mean if I'd known, I'd have tidied up... and things. You know.

SONNY: Don't give it a thought. Say, you couldn't be mistaken for anyone else but Gordon's mother. I've never seen such a resemblance. And your hands. [*Holding her hand up*] See?

MARY: Oooh, I don't know... Do you think so? Ah, no. [*She draws them away.*] These hands are all swollen and... they used to be small, though. Very dainty; I thought, anyway.

SONNY: No one who saw them could possibly think otherwise.

> *He shakes hands with the others.* SAWYER *is standing, and mumbles.* GUNNER, *on the verandah, shakes surlily.* BILLY, *rising, shakes. He gasps a little at the pressure, pressure which probably was not applied to the hands of the others.*

Now I've met you all. [*To* GOROOH] Except you, sir.

GOROOH: I am an old man of a tribe which is no longer a tribe. I have seen many young men. Beware not of other tongues, but of your own tongue. It is the one most likely to lead you astray. [*To the others*] It is settled, then. We leave tonight.

> GOROOH *goes. The others will not miss him.*

SONNY: Say, what's he talking about?... Well, Gordon, you coming, or waiting to see the New Year in with your folks?

MARY: What do you mean? Where are you going?

GORDON: [*treading softly*] Well, we were only coming back for a day or two, then we were going to shoot through.

MARY: You weren't going to leave me? *Gordon*! Say you weren't leaving me!

SONNY: [*jumping into the breach*] That's all right. Of course he's not leaving
   you.

BILLY: Don't believe him. I wouldn't trust a word he says.

SONNY: [*smoothly*] No?

GORDON: Don't you start.

SONNY: [*watching* BILLY] I can see why you have to keep in training here.
   You'd have a stoush every second sentence.

MARY: [*she knows*] Gordon, don't let me grow old here. Stay with me.

GORDON: Sure. Sure. Cheer up.

SONNY: [*lying glibly*] He's not going anywhere. Just a misunderstanding.

MARY: Well… I hope so. I don't know, though.

   After a burst of cracked twigs and scuffling, JOY *and a* BOY *from the
   town enter the clearing. She has had close to a skinful.*

JOY: Oh, brother! Look at all the men! Who are you, boy? It's Gordon! Well…
   [*to* MARY] don't just stand there! It's the wandering boy back again…!
   Ooooooh, and who's his handsome friend? [*Making for* SONNY] You beaut!
   [*Pulling at his shirt*] Daddy, buy me this one!

GORDON: Get away from him! What a sweet little thing you've turned out to
   be!

JOY: That's right, darl… Didn't you get back this afternoon?

GORDON: You know I did, what of it?

JOY: Well, what's happened since then? I wouldn't know! [*She laughs and
   falls to the ground.*] Last thing I remember I was sitting by a stretch of the
   road, catching the wind of the fast cars, out there in the heat, to cool me
   down. What came after that…?

GORDON: Hadn't you better be off with your friend? He doesn't seem to be
   enjoying himself.

JOY: He's just a… [*her voice changing*] a darl. Aren't you? What's your
   name again? [*She laughs.*] He's the poetic type. He said—what was that
   again? He said my skin smelt of boronia. Is that good?

BILLY: He just meant you smell… You don't take a pull on yourself the way
   you're going you'll end up in a humpy like this, rotten with metho.

   BILLY *is really affected by the sight of his playmate drunk.*

JOY: Speak for yourself, square! [*She laughs at the smartness of it.*] Anyway,
   where are you going, if you're not staying in a humpy like this? You
   gunna build a high-class one out of kerosene tins? And paper the walls
   with lottery tickets?

   Fresh peals of laughter from her.

BILLY: We're all going off to the old boy's for a start, and we'll see what happens
   after that.

SAWYER: That's real good sense, Billy.

MARY: Well, I'm staying. I've got friends in town. [*To the* BOY, *who doesn't answer*] Haven't I?

BOY: I've had enough of this...

He goes off.

JOY: [*noticing him going*] Come back! I want to tell... [*attempting urgent intimacy*] you something! Come back! I've got something for you!

While shouting this, she is stumbling off after him through the bush.

Oh hell! [*A half sob, half curse*] Come back!

GORDON: Well, what with things the way they are, Sonny, how about coming over to Granpa's with us, until we all get straightened out.

GUNNER: So we're all good pals again, eh?

BILLY: Ah, come on! Can't you see those two are going to fix everything up, with their own lily-white hands.

SONNY: [*conciliating*] Don't get us wrong. I bet you can show us points when it comes to working with your hands. We're not too used to it, you know. City blokes, and all that.

BILLY: Well... I'll show you points all right.

GUNNER: Gees, don't let 'em bull you. Let them lead you on and you'll be working like a navvy 'fore you know where you are.

MARY: Doesn't sound much like him, or you either.

GUNNER: Me? I'm saving me energy for a crisis.

GORDON: [*to* SONNY] Granpa has the sawmill a few miles out of town.

SONNY: Why, you old capitalist! I bet you coin the dough. Look at the price of timber now! Way up!

SAWYER: There is a good living for us in it. That's if you really work.

MARY: No need to start preaching. [*To* GORDON, *very tired and much older*] What are you going to do? I mean when you clear out... I know you're going to... I knew I couldn't really have you any longer.

GUNNER: Don't mind her.

GORDON: I'm a big boy now, Ma. I can wash my own face. You see, when I found I wasn't as big up there in the city as I looked in a little bush township, I looked for something I could do, and I found it.

SONNY: We're getting the franchise on a service station.

GUNNER: A garage!

MARY: What's a franchise?

GORDON: Just a sort of license... But we've saved a bit and we're partners. He's got the most of the money, from his old man. Sonny was my mate at school. We played football together.

SONNY: Brother, what a combination! Well, we just stuck together. And soon we'll be in business.

BILLY: I thought you said you had no money.

GUNNER: Ar, don't bring that up now. We've had enough strife for one day. Let it ride. Looks like we got rid of the girl, and we won't have that old, skinny bone-pointer nagging at us, where we're goin'.

SONNY: [*cheerfully cynical; they don't notice it*] All set for a new deal, eh?

> *The church bells start up for midnight. The little town's tiny celebrations make a distant din, with car horns and garbage tins and people yelling and singing.*

SAWYER: C'mon, get your clothes and whatever you want to take, and off we go.

> *They start bustling about, routing out things they want in the firelight.*

GUNNER: Gordon!

> GUNNER *whispers to* GORDON, *who then goes off with* SONNY.

MARY: What was that about?

GUNNER: Nothing to fret about.

MARY: Ah, I know... You'd better wrap it in a couple of sugar bags. Kincaid'll be watching when we go through the town.

> *They assemble their belongings, ransacking the shanty, until they are ready to leave.*

GUNNER: Goodbye, house!

> GUNNER *gives it a kick in the verandah post. The roof sags down. They move off.*
>
> *Silence.*
>
> *Two shadowy figures creep back, on either side of the clearing.*

SAWYER: Who's that?

GORDON: [*stepping out*] Who're you?

SAWYER: Gordon! What d'you come back for?

GORDON: Don't kid me, Granpa. Same reason as you.

SAWYER: Right. Let's get to work, then...

> *They savagely demolish the humpy until all is flat. They stop and straighten up now and again as they speak the following.*

GORDON: Do you believe it? All this stuff about starting out fresh? For the lot of us, I mean?

SAWYER: Do you?

GORDON: Not a chance... For myself, yes. For the rest of 'em: I'll believe it when I see it... Five years from now, they'll still be the same... Me...? I'll have a new car... then a house... then see if I'm not getting whiter all the time!

SAWYER: You've got to be white, haven't you?

> SAWYER *is an old man, not really concerned about those who will inherit his earth. He does not sound interested in* GORDON's *problems.*

GORDON: If there was a choice, which would you have?

SAWYER: Yeh.

GORDON: Brand new car and a brick house. With that I'll soon get a wife. My kids'll be whiter than I am, and their kids won't be any different from whites. Then this dirt'll... [*looking at his hands*] be cleaned off for good.

SAWYER: You know it's not dirt... No point in bashing yourself over the head with words.

GORDON: I know it's not dirt. So do you, perhaps. But while they look on it as dirt, to me it's dirt. And I'm going to get rid of it. Getting the poison out of my family, in the future, will be just like getting white myself. That's the only way to win this little game.

Pause.

SAWYER: That's all. You coming?

GORDON: You go on. I'm not finished.

He grabs bits and carries them to the river bank.

SAWYER: They can't live in it, now... You're not going to start a fire, are you?

GORDON: No.

SAWYER: [*going*] Well, it takes a blackbutt wedge to split the blackbutt. I been at 'em for years. It took you half a day to get 'em out.

GORDON: They had to get out.

SAWYER: Now they're really gone. Can't quite believe it, myself. Lock, stock and barrel, to a fresh start...

SAWYER *wanders off.*

GORDON: [*aloud, to himself*] Start up again! They're too old for that. They'll never do it. I wouldn't give twopence for their chances. They don't know what they're up against.

The iron from the roof and the main supports go over the riverbank.

I reckon I'll be the only one out of us lot to get through... [*He picks up some of the broken clay figures doubtfully.*] The old man could make it all right. [*Disgusted*] But he doesn't want to. The others've had it... I'll be the only one that's going to make it.

He walks to one side, then looks back at the empty space. Behind his back the great darkness begins, and only a short distance further on, rapidly becomes impenetrable.

And I'm the only one that's going to make it.

SONNY *appears.*

SONNY: Ready to shove off? I told 'em to keep going. [*Cheerfully malicious*] Said we'd be along later.

They light up cigarettes.

GORDON: Good man. Well, I'm finished here. We can get one of the locals to run back. Sleep in the car. Should be a train out in the morning.

SONNY: Beats me why you came back here.

He looks with frank disfavour at the rubbish.

GORDON: [*judiciously*] I think I owed 'em a visit. Poor old Ma. She saved up her pennies for me. How about that?

SONNY: Yeh. How about that?

After they go off, the township sounds have faded, the fire damps down and a few crickets start to sing, hesitantly at first, then louder and more confidently. Far away in the town a rooster is disturbed, and crows. There is an early morning breeze in the eucalypts. The bush noises, too, fade. At last there is dead silence... and the curtain.

THE END

The Life of the Party

Ray Mathew

Ray Mathew (1929–2003) was born in Sydney. Initially training as a teacher, he worked as a journalist, lecturer, art critic and editor, as well as poet and playwright. He moved to London in 1960 and settled in New York in 1968, where he remained until his death. His plays include *Church Sunday* (1950), *Sing for St Ned* (1951), *We Find the Bunyip* (1955), *The Life of the Party* (1957), *The Bones of My Toe* (1957) and *A Spring Song* (1958). *The Life of the Party* was a finalist in the 1957 London *Observer* International Play Competition, as a result of which he received a Commonwealth Literary Fund grant in 1958.

Ray Mathew in Italy, February 1960. (Ray Mathew papers, National Library of Australia, MS 5634, folder 11. By permission of the National Library of Australia)

FIRST PERFORMANCE

The Life of the Party was first produced at the Lyric Opera House, Hammersmith, London, on 22 November 1960, with the following cast:

JACK	Anthony Booth
MOIRA	Olive McFarland
ALEX	Alan Badel
MARINA	Davina Dundas
BERT	Charles Rea
TANYA	Martina Mayne
PEG	June Ellis
LORNA	Jill Melford
SYLVIE	Dorothy White

Director, Frith Banbury
Settings, Loudon Sainthill
Lighting, William Lorraine

Jack Bedson and Julian Croft (*The Campbell Howard Annotated Index of Australian Plays 1920–55*) suggest *The Life of the Party* was 'performed in 1958 or 1959 at the Independent Theatre in Sydney' (and also dates the script c.1959). No evidence, however, of such a production has come to light; certainly it is not mentioned in the Independent Theatre production list in Doris Fitton's autobiography *Not Without Dust or Heat*.

CHARACTERS

JACK, in his early thirties
MOIRA, his wife
ALEX, his friend, a radio actor and scriptwriter
MARINA, a young girl (in love with Alex)
BERT, a bookmaker, in his thirties
TANYA, a European
PEG, Jack's landlady, in her fifties (in love with Alex)
LORNA, in her late twenties (in love with Alex)
SYLVIE, Lorna's ally, aged twenty-five

SCENES

Act One   Jack's flat, Saturday night
Act Two
  Scene One The same, Sunday night
  Scene Two The same, later
Act Three   Peg's flat, Monday night

ACKNOWLEDGEMENTS

'How Fay Morgana' is an adaptation from d'Annunzio
'What Thinks the Rose' is by R.W. Tracey
'The Shell' is by James Stephens

ACT ONE

It is a living room in a flat at the Cross, the Bohemian section of Sydney. There are three doors: one to the bedroom, one to the kitchenette, one to the hall outside of the flat. The apron of the stage is a balcony.

The room has a divan, some makeshift armchairs, a standard lamp, a small table. A calendar with notes written on it hangs on the wall. There is a clock in the room and a few obviously feminine ornaments. There are books but no pictures. The room is neat and tidy. The set need not be realistic.

MOIRA *is sitting on stage. She also is neat and tidy.* JACK *enters, defeated. He wears careless clothes, an open-necked shirt. There is a Turf Guide in his hip-pocket. He flings his coat on a chair, lights a cigarette and flips the match wearily across the room, then takes out the paper to read. While they are speaking,* MOIRA *puts his coat away, then picks up the match.*

MOIRA: You're home early. Couldn't you get a girl?
JACK: I lost.
MOIRA: No one wins.
JACK: Are you glad?
MOIRA: You are funny, Jack.
JACK: Are you laughing?
MOIRA: What have I got to laugh about?
JACK: This is how you want me. Beaten. A baby. You'd like me to cry. [*Violently*] You'd like me to cry. Wouldn't you? Wouldn't you?
MOIRA: Yes.
JACK: [*sadly*] You don't want me to win.
MOIRA: I want you happy.
JACK: What you call happy.
MOIRA: Oh, darling, it would be good. We'd have a house. I'd keep it nice. You'd come home in the evening—
JACK: [*almost crying*] God damn you, God damn you! I don't want a nice house!
MOIRA: [*triumphantly*] What do you want?
JACK: I just want to win. I just want, I just want.
MOIRA: [*gently*] Now don't be cross, don't get in a temper—
JACK: I'm not cross—
MOIRA: Come here. Let me hold you.

> *He looks at her. She goes to him.*

JACK: Leave me alone.
MOIRA: I'm not as attractive as I used to be.

JACK: [*tired of this line*] Yes, yes, you are. You're just the same. We're married.

MOIRA: I didn't ask you to marry me.

JACK: You cried. I can't stand it when you—

MOIRA: You say that, but you make me cry. [*Pause.*] You should get a job. You'd feel better. You could still gamble. I don't mind. But then it would be gambling—something for Saturdays, a bit of fun, not losing everything and nothing to go on with. You could still have other girls—I understand that—if you wanted them.

JACK: If I had time.

MOIRA: I only want you to be sensible, to have something behind you—

JACK: Why do you make it hard? Why do you make it hard for yourself? You know you want more, more than I can give—a house with a man next door and a lawnmower. And if I can't give you that then you want me sick, and weak; losing, giving in, for you to baby.

MOIRA: You used to like me to call you bubba and boy and baby—

JACK: Well, I don't like it now, see. See, see this. [*Lifting a clock*] This is how I don't like it now.

He throws the clock against the wall.

MOIRA: You're controlled. You don't care enough to throw it at me.

JACK: [*picking up an ornament*] Don't I? Don't I?

There is a very light knock at the door.

MOIRA: [*over him*] I don't know. How could I know?

The door opens and ALEX *comes in. He switches on the main light. He is plump to fat, carelessly but expensively dressed. He talks quickly and acts all the time. He mimes his adjectives and stories. It is difficult to know when he is sincere. His sincerities are followed instantly by flippancies and reverses. It is they, perhaps, that are his sincerities. The truth is that he cannot face what he is or what he might become. He acts for* JACK, *and* JACK's *silences are important to him.*

ALEX: Moving house?

JACK grins and puts down his weapon.

Enter, attendant imps!

MARINA and BERT *come in.* MARINA *is dressed like a typist ready for work, but she has been wearing these clothes for two days. She is annoyed about* TANYA *who follows.* BERT *wears a respectable suit. He carries some bottles of beer.*

Friends of mine. Tanya's the important one.

TANYA is interesting; ALEX *sees something in her. She is memorable because of either her striking dress or striking features. She does not speak because she is death; she has decided what has to be done.*

[*To* JACK] How are you, Mix-Nasty?

JACK: [*smiling*] Hi.

ALEX: Shh! Shh! No noise. No shouting. Think of the landlady.

JACK: You think of the landlady.

ALEX: These walls are like paper. [*He shuffles Japanese-fashion to the wall and listens.*] We live in Japan, and say that it's Sydney. [*With a great cry*] Oh, for the bush! Shh! Shh! But I need to shout. Open the bottles. Not only have I won at the races— Have some money.

> *He holds out a roll of notes. No one takes it.*

No, I thought not; almost counted on it. You don't want money. Not only have I won but I have also taken part in—back in employment!—in a radio play. Was it by Shakespeare? Oh, no. It was by me, ho-ho! If only I were really drunk. If it were possible. I had to say—my own lines, I tell you! 'Marcia, don't go!', and 'I'll wait, Marcia. My God, I'll wait!' Who's waiter here? And I've been commissioned—commissioned like the laureate... [*bowing to the laureate*] to engage on a serial. And to play the lead, Dr Fix-It. I'm going to be not just filthy rich. I'm going to be filthy and rich. Won't you have some money? Give us a drink. Let me drown my joy. Life's a filthy mess.

> MOIRA *has brought glasses and an opener from the kitchen.* JACK *opens some bottles and pours.* MOIRA *serves drinks.* JACK *gives a glass to* BERT.

JACK: [*to* BERT] Why are you sad? You're not successful.

ALEX: [*to* JACK] You've spoken on the phone. [*He points to the calendar.*] His number's up there.

BERT: [*to* JACK] I'm Bert—

ALEX: [*to* JACK] The bookie.

JACK: [*to* BERT] You cleaned me today.

> BERT *grins miserably.*

ALEX: [*to* JACK] And Miss Prim-and-Not-So-Proper on his arm is happily called Marina. I've loved her for her name, at least a month. No, a fortnight. I could run away to sea and be a cabin boy, if I were the sort of person who did anything drastic. I mentioned your name. She has vowed never to love anyone who isn't called Jack.

JACK: [*to* MARINA] I'm Jack.

ALEX: And this Marina is his wife.

MOIRA: [*to* MARINA] How do you do?

MARINA: [*to* JACK] I met you once, for a minute, at the races.

ALEX: Jack doesn't notice women at the races.

MARINA: Alex says you're a genius, but never what at.

ALEX: At being indifferent. [*He picks up the clock. To* JACK] Why so glum?

JACK: I'm running true to form. I lost.

ALEX: We are all lost. Think.

> *He suddenly strikes an attitude and declaims dramatically.*

> What thinks the rose
> That grows
> Where men and maids
> In passion's throes
> Have lived,
> And loved,
> And vowed—
> In vain?
> What
> Thinks the rose?

JACK: [*acting up to him*]

> What thinks the flea
> That cannot be
> Where men and maids
> On passion's sea
> Expose,
> And pose,
> Their chub—
> by toes?
> What
> Thinks the flea?

> JACK *and* ALEX *laugh companionably.* BERT *guffaws.* MARINA *smiles.*

ALEX: What is there to think? I think about Tanya? Look at her legs. But you're not a leg man. And then you're married.

MOIRA: [*to* ALEX] He's not tied down.

MARINA: [*looking at* JACK] I like people with a modern attitude.

> ALEX *seizes a shell from the mantelpiece. He holds it to his ear and recites, wonder-struck, as though improvising.*

ALEX:

> And then I pressed the shell
> Close to my ear
> And listened well,
> And straightway like a bell
> Came low and clear
> The slow, sad murmur of far distant seas...

BERT: That's beautiful, Alex.

MARINA: The act. I thought it was his own the first time that he did it.

JACK: [*to* MARINA] When did you first hear it?

MARINA: A long time ago. A month.

MOIRA: [*to* MARINA] Are you in love with him?

MARINA: Don't be silly.

ALEX: [*speaking over the top of her, to* JACK, *tragically*] They all love me.

JACK: [*to* MARINA] What's love got to do with it?

MARINA: Nothing.

ALEX: [*talking to* JACK, *looking at* TANYA] Look at her legs. Don't you want to bite them?

MARINA: Oddly enough, I don't.

BERT: I'm married. I've got four kids. I don't bite legs.

MARINA: You look married.

MOIRA: [*quietly*] Four.

ALEX: [*to* BERT, *speaking over the others*] Thank you. It was—manly of you to tell me. Tanya's not—?

BERT: [*to* ALEX] No, she—

ALEX: [*to* BERT] Don't explain. Life's too short. Let's keep it clean, shall we? [*He turns to* TANYA.] Speak to me in Russian—

BERT: [*to* ALEX] I met her in the pub.

MARINA: I'm sure you did.

BERT: [*to* MARINA] It's where I run my business.

MARINA: Where she runs hers?

MOIRA: [*to* BERT, *speaking over* MARINA] What about your wife?

BERT: [*defensively*] What about her? She's all right.

MARINA: Doesn't she mind?

BERT: She doesn't complain. I never go home on Saturday nights. We get on real well on Sunday mornings. There's no need to laugh; it's a way of life.

MARINA: [*to* JACK] Do you always stare?

JACK: When it's worth staring.

ALEX: [*looking at* TANYA] The perfect woman. Life made quiet. [*To her*] Look at me. Your eyes. Your troubled, troubling eyes—

> TANYA *turns her head from him.*

MARINA: Alex!

ALEX: Call me Alexander; I'm looking for new worlds. Tanya. Tatyana. She only needs dusting. You've made her dirty, Bert.

BERT: I haven't touched her.

ALEX: Lack of initiative; the modern disease. I touch.

> *He gently moves her head around.*

Are you unhappy? Do you want money? Here. [*He holds out his roll.*] Just for one smile. Smile. No? No, there's nothing to buy. Have it anyway.

MARINA: He gets caught in his acts.

ALEX: No one wants it! I've sold my soul for what no one wants.

MARINA: It's a wonderful chance. The serial's for fifty-two episodes.

ALEX: A thousand if I like! If the listeners like! The sponsors like! A thousand.

A life sentence.

> *He throws the money in the air. The notes flutter down.* TANYA *jumps up, grabs some of them and throws them up again. Then she collects them all, rather frightened, rolls them and gives them back to him.*

Thank you; I exist.

> *She sits down again.*

There's a bedroom here. We're sophisticated people.

BERT: [*uneasily*] What a line.

MARINA: The same line.

JACK: [*to* MARINA] You need a change.

ALEX: Tanya, Tatyana—

> PEG *enters. She is over fifty. She is very skilfully made up, and very well dressed.* ALEX *looks affronted at her intrusion.* MARINA *is annoyed.*

PEG: [*to* JACK] I couldn't help hearing you'd a party and it sounded so very like the old days when there was some point in staying young and gay that—

JACK: The landlady.

BERT: [*to* PEG] We didn't mean to be noisy.

PEG: I'm sure you did. You had to let me know that you were here. Call me Peg. Alex! You here! What a surprise! You may call me Margaret.

ALEX: [*to* PEG] You've been listening.

JACK: Good on you, Peg.

PEG: [*over* JACK] Really, Alex! I was given ears to hear with, sense to feel with. I heard a party. In my own house, too.

ALEX: You knew I was here.

PEG: What were you playing? We live in Japan... Really, Alex is a silly man.

ALEX: I'm just a boy.

MARINA: [*looking at* PEG] Comparatively.

BERT: [*laughing*] A big boy.

MARINA: [*to* PEG, *interrupting* ALEX *before he can speak*] Darling Alex! He mentions you such a lot.

PEG: Really? He never mentions you.

BERT: [*to* PEG] I'm his bookmaker.

JACK: [*to* PEG] You know me.

PEG: But we hardly meet. It's extraordinary the way the Landlord-and-Tenant Act has split the human family. We have such a lot in common really— Alex. I know how you turn his head with army days and party days and pick-up days and gay-dog days and never-be-sober-till-Monday days.

> ALEX *is imitating these days.* BERT *and* JACK *are laughing at him.*

Moira, I'm not drinking. There used to be glasses; they went with the room. I would like this to be a never-be-sober-till-Monday Saturday night. It's my birthday.

MOIRA *gets her a drink.*

BERT: Many happy returns.

PEG: Not so many.

ALEX: Peg's always having birthdays; it's how she gets her way.

PEG: I could never count—drinks, money, lovers, anything. But it is my birthday. Come and kiss me.

MOIRA *kisses her.*

Thank you, dear. All of you— [*To* MARINA] No, not the women. I'm not a gentleman, I'd tell.

BERT: My name's Bert. [*Kissing her cheek*] Well, this is celebrating.

PEG: How gallant, Bert.

She looks at ALEX.

JACK: You're not... [*kissing her*] my type, Peg. But I'll play.

He kisses her again.

PEG: How very honest. Alex is neither gallant nor honest. Alex.

ALEX *goes towards her facetiously for a kiss, but she turns away. He stands there pouting. The others laugh at him.*

Make a toast, somebody.

BERT: [*brightly*] Many happy returns.

PEG: [*facetiously*] Dare I say to us? No, I dare not. Bottoms up! [*Seriously*] No. Wait. Let us drink to the spring. When everything is born and all the world is young.

ALEX: [*with a sorrowful, continental accent*] If only I had brought my violin.

MARINA: [*to* PEG] Do you sing, too?

ALEX: [*playing the violin in* TANYA*'s ear*] Ah, Tanya, Tanya. Listen to my music. Here is the throbbing, the voice of the spring—

PEG: I've started him off.

ALEX: When love and everything is born, and the gypsy blood sings in the veins—

MARINA: Oh, stop being childish!

PEG: So young, Alex.

BERT: [*to* PEG, *a little drunk*] You know, you're still an attractive woman.

MARINA: [*to* JACK] And you stop looking up my skirt.

BERT *laughs.*

JACK: Then why are you wearing such a frilly, looking-at-me slip?

MARINA: Alex, we ought to be going—

JACK: [*to* MARINA] And such pretty, pink—

MARINA: They're not pink!

JACK: [*triumphantly*] Ah!

BERT *laughs again.*

ALEX: Oh, God, I'm bored!

PEG: You mustn't talk; you mustn't live; you must listen to Alex. Go on, Alex dear.

ALEX: Somebody sing.

MARINA: [*imploringly*] Alex.

PEG: Yes. You sing, Alex.

JACK: [*singing*]

> Chase me, Charlie,
> Round the barley,
> Up the leg of my drawers—

Seeing that ALEX *will not leave,* MARINA *sits down again.*

MARINA: Well, we might as well stay if you're going to be amusing.

BERT *laughs.*

BERT: Sing 'The Good Ship Venus', by cripes you should have seen us—

ALEX: You're drunk, Bert; you're laughing. He's drunk, Tanya. He's no good to you.

BERT: [*over* ALEX, *half-singing*]

> The figure-head
> Was a whore in bed
> and the mast was an upright—

What's the rest of it?

PEG: Bookmaker, darling! I don't really know.

JACK: [*over* PEG, *singing to* MARINA]

> The admiral's pretty daughter
> Went swimming in the water.
> Delighted squeals
> Reveal the eels
> Have found her ticklish quarter.

He looks up and sees MOIRA *standing with a bottle.*

Why don't you sing? Sing 'Home, Sweet Home'. Sing something.

He takes the bottle.

I'm starting to drink.

He flings himself at MARINA*'s feet.*

They're blue.

MARINA: [*contemptuously*] You can't see.

JACK: [*pleading*] Can't I? Please.

MOIRA: [*reflectively, while they are talking*] When everything is born...

PEG: [*kindly, to her*] And all the world is young...

ALEX: [*to* TANYA] My God, your eyes... [*To* MOIRA] Fill up my glass. 'Let me be always drunk and never reason.' [*To* TANYA] I could drink your eyes and be forever drunk.

MARINA: The old line.

PEG: The very old line.

JACK: [*to* MARINA] Try a new one.

BERT: [*over* JACK, *to* PEG] You know, I'm not as young as you might think. I'm thirty.

PEG: Oh, dear. Oh, dear. Thirty.

BERT: I've got four kids.

PEG: I should be too frightened.

JACK: [*singing*]

> When Tristram loved Isolda
> He offered her some wine-a,
> And while she danced the polka...

BERT *and* MARINA *sing with him.*

> He slipped on her va—
> Foot suck-boo, foot suck-oo,
> Foot suck-oo-la-la.

MOIRA *has hummed the chorus, watching* JACK. PEG *has watched* ALEX. *Suddenly* ALEX *leaps among the singers, who are sitting in a circle.*

ALEX: [*passionately sincere*] Depraved! Animals! Filth! Now, listen. Listen, and I'll tell you what reality meant, how things once happened.

He declaims.

> How Fay Morgana, that confusing fairy,
> Foretold it all, the story of their love,
> Good Tristram and Isolda of the flowers,
> How it should come between that white-skinned girl
> And him the least suspicious in the world;
> And how Isolda and her Tristram drank
> The poisoned drink for them and not for them;
> And how so perfect was this act of love
> It led two persons to one only death.

He recites. BERT *begins to beat the rhythm with his glass.* JACK *and then the others take it up.* MOIRA, *alone, does not participate.* TANYA *beats time, almost unconsciously.*

> The moon was up before the sun
> Had touched the western sea,
> But Tristram to his sailors called,
> 'Go let the sails hang free'.
> The ship sailed west, a night a day,
> They called it ship of hate,
> And Tristram cursed the unseen girl
> Who gave to him this fate.

> The land is good, the land is safe,
> The wine flows white and free,
> But for this girl that King Mark loves
> I sail upon the sea.

LORNA *appears in the doorway and stands there listening. She motions to someone behind her.* JACK, *seeing this other, slowly rises and stands staring.*

> Through black, black storm the ship sailed on,
> It came at last to land.
> Isolda came to meet the ship,
> Gave Tristram her white hand.
> No word they spoke, but their hands touched,
> They caught upon the breath,
> To go to Mark, to lose you now,
> That were a perfect death.
> 'Ah, better to drink', Isolda said,
> 'The poison of the vine'.
> Their lifted glasses held the light,
> It was not poisoned wine,
> It was a perfect drink of love.
> The potion brought them life.
> And lip to lip and hand to hand—

LORNA *runs silently behind* ALEX *and puts her hands over his eyes.*

LORNA: Darling, guess who?

ALEX: Lorna! My other love—

LORNA *is very fashionably dressed.*

LORNA: They told me you'd be here, because you'd won.

MOIRA: We don't see him much.

ALEX: [*to* LORNA] My hostess. Everyone, it's Lorna. Lorna, it's everyone.

MARINA: [*to* LORNA] How do you do?

LORNA: I do very frequently, and very pleasantly, thank you, ma'am. [*She kicks off her shoes.*] My shoes oppress me.

MARINA: Why not take them off?

PEG: [*to* LORNA] Alex has mentioned you.

SYLVIE *has come through the door.* JACK *is still standing, watching her. She is dressed simply and well. She carries gloves.*

SYLVIE: Will no one mention me?

LORNA: Sylvie.

ALEX: 'Who is Sylvia? What is she?'

LORNA: A friend.

SYLVIE: Sylvie, not Sylvia.

LORNA: We were in despair. One of these nights. Not a thought in our heads but why and what for. I thought of you. Have you married yet? Neither have I. [*To* MARINA] You're not his wife, by any chance?

MARINA: No.

LORNA: No. [*To* ALEX] And no children to speak of? Neither have I. You are more subdued.

ALEX: I'm watching the act. We are not amused.

LORNA: How Victorian. [*To* MOIRA] But I've met you before. You were with Jack. Hello, Jack. Still chasing girls? Oh, Alex. I could eat you.

ALEX: Save me, someone.

He bounds gracefully behind PEG. LORNA *follows him. She stands in front of him and smooths her hips.*

LORNA: I've improved, you know.

MARINA: With practice?

PEG: I can't save you, Alex.

ALEX *flings himself by* TANYA.

ALEX: [*with a Russian accent*] Oh, Tanya, Tanya. Save me.

LORNA: Tanya?

ALEX: [*definitely*] Tanya.

BERT: [*waving a bottle*] What a Saturday night! It's a party.

LORNA: Who is the enthusiast with the bottle?

BERT: I'm Bert.

LORNA: [*to* PEG] I've met everybody else?

PEG: The landlady. I pick up the pieces. You might call me Peggy.

LORNA: I've heard of you, Peg. [*Seductively*] Alex…

ALEX: Tanya. Or even Peg. Or even Marina.

MARINA: Exclude Marina. [*Cooingly*] Jack… [*Sharply*] Jack!

JACK: [*not looking at* MARINA] Yes. Sylvia—

SYLVIE *has been standing still and looking at him.*

SYLVIE: Not Sylvia. Me.

JACK: You.

PEG: 'Or even Peg'… Moira, my pet, we all need drinking.

MOIRA *goes on serving.*

I want soft lights.

She switches off the main light, leaving a standard lamp and the moonlight from the balcony.

And hard drinking. And let us have music, soft music, soft.

She puts on the wireless and fiddles with the dial.

LORNA: I'd love to dance. I feel— [*To* ALEX] Dance?

The wireless plays.

JACK: [*to* SYLVIE] Would you—?

SYLVIE: Jack.

> *They move together.*

ALEX: [*to* TANYA] Lend me your body for a while. It's all right, Moira, I only want her to dance.

> TANYA *shakes her head.*

BERT: [*over* ALEX, *to* PEG] Could I have the honour?

> ALEX *is watching* JACK.

ALEX: They move like professionals. Hardly at all.

PEG: [*to* BERT] I've passed dancing. Dancing's done.

MOIRA: [*to* PEG] Dance if you want to.

PEG: It would look absurd.

LORNA: [*to* MARINA] What elegant shoes, dear! Let me.

> LORNA *removes* MARINA's *shoes.*

BERT: [*to* PEG] You're never too old.

PEG: Shh! I'm hearing the music.

> *She leans back and watches* ALEX *caressing* TANYA. BERT *and* MOIRA *watch the dancers. They dance to the front of the stage, into the moonlight, onto the balcony. We see* MOIRA *serving drinks.*
>
> *The light on the stage fades into darkness.*
>
> *During this scene the wireless is switched off.* JACK *stops dancing. A gauze curtain may have fallen behind them.*

JACK: See. The moon.

SYLVIE: The moon on the balcony. Yes.

JACK: Do you want to go in?

SYLVIE: We're above the trees. They've got new leaves. It's spring. I suppose it's the spring, that's all.

JACK: That's all. Sylvia, Sylvie.

SYLVIE: John, Jack. Honest Jack.

JACK: God, how it happens, all the odds against!

SYLVIE: How has it happened? I feel shy.

JACK: Sylvie.

SYLVIE: Don't talk.

JACK: There's nothing to say.

SYLVIE: I know nothing about you. You know nothing about me. Do you—? Do you ever look at the stars and think they look like a river? You can't see, now; the moon's too bright.

JACK: I don't think much, what anything's like.

SYLVIE: I think all the time. No, that's a lie. I don't think at all. We've got everything in common! I think—no, I feel—I look at the stars—when they're there, and they're like a river; like the stones in the gibber creek at the back of the house, at home—all separate and apart. They shine in the water, you know. You can see them. When the river's in flood, you can't see them at all; they don't shine. It's the full of the moon. The moon's in flood. They move with the river. They rub and they break, get pushed here and there, touch one another and break. Why? Because the river's in flood? When the water goes down, when the creek's like glass again, a string of beads like glass, you can see them again and they shine like before, but they're in different positions; the whole thing's changed. I—I feel like a stranger. That—that's why I talk.

JACK: Hello, stranger.

SYLVIE: Don't look at me; the moon's too bright. Look at the street. I like balconies. I like to watch people, when you're not up close to them, when you don't have to talk. It's easier, isn't it, from a balcony—when you don't have to talk? There's a man and a woman. I suppose they're married. He'll beat her when he gets her home, and she'll put out the cat, and that's goodnight. Good night.

JACK: Where do you come from?

SYLVIE: You never ask that. It's where are you going. I come from the bush. I should be at home, the daughter at home. But I couldn't be, could I? I had to come here. And I'm not very useful; I get nothing done. Dad thinks he knows everything, knows what I'll do. Knows I'll come back. I'm always a failure. Look at me. No. Why don't you talk?

JACK: Sylvie—

SYLVIE: I'm cold.

JACK: You're trembling.

MOIRA: [*calling from the stage behind the gauze*] Jack. Jack.

SYLVIE: Coming.

JACK: Why did you say that?

SYLVIE: They want you.

JACK: Why did you say that?

SYLVIE: I'm trembling.

JACK: Do you want to go in? Do you want to?

SYLVIE: No.

JACK: Do you want to?

SYLVIE: No!

JACK *kneels and embraces her thighs. She springs away from him.*

Don't! Don't! We can't.

He stands and looks at her.

JACK: We have to.

SYLVIE: Oh, Jack. Jack… The others.

JACK: What have they got to do with it? We're on our own.

SYLVIE: Don't be angry.

JACK: You know we've got to.

SYLVIE: [*trying to laugh*] Don't be like father, bullying, telling me—

JACK: You do know. Don't you?

SYLVIE: Yes.

MOIRA: [*from the stage behind the gauze*] Jack.

JACK: Moira; calling the dog.

SYLVIE: [*frightened*] Who—who's Moira?

JACK: We're married.

SYLVIE: [*turning away*] This is a quiet street. Nobody—I didn't know you were married.

JACK: Does it make any difference? Are you married?

SYLVIE: I'm not wearing a ring.

JACK: I didn't look. I looked at you. Did you look at my hand? Did you say, is he married, is he—?

SYLVIE: [*interrupting*] No. But I looked at your hand.

> *She takes his hand and looks at it, caressing it with her fingers. Then she lets it go.*

JACK: What difference does it make? We've got to, haven't we?

SYLVIE: Yes. Yes, but it makes all the difference.

> *She turns to go in.*

JACK: Are you going?

SYLVIE: It's— [*Childishly*] It's not what I wanted.

JACK: You know what you want. You do know, don't you?

SYLVIE: Is she nice? Your—wife?

JACK: It doesn't affect her.

SYLVIE: Yes it does.

JACK: It hasn't happened to her.

SYLVIE: I'm going in. She's your wife. I'm—

JACK: A pebble in the creek.

SYLVIE: There are lots of pebbles in the creek.

JACK: There's you and me. You know that, don't you? You know there's you and me.

SYLVIE: I don't. I don't.

> *She turns from him.*

> *The gauze lifts. The voices sound clearly.*

JACK: Sylvie.

> SYLVIE *looks at him, then goes in. He lights a cigarette and leans against the arch, watching her.* PEG *is sitting on the floor.* BERT *is lying with his head in her lap.*

ALEX: [*to* JACK, *pointing to* TANYA] She's asleep, Jack. Gone to sleep on me. What a lover I am!

> ALEX *stares at* JACK *curiously.*

LORNA: Sylvie, where have you been? I hope you've done better than I have. But I borrowed some shoes. Look, aren't they smart! They belong to Marina.

> MARINA *glares at her.*

And I've danced and I've wriggled—

> MOIRA *goes near* JACK *while* LORNA *is talking. They talk over* LORNA.

MOIRA: Jack.

JACK: I'm here.

MOIRA: Jack, I'm sorry.

JACK: We're all sorry. There's something to be sorry for.

> PEG *continues a story while the others talk; eventually only she is talking.*

PEG: Yes, they were great days, Bert, before you were born, before you were even a twinkle in your father's eye. No, not quite so long ago. He has charming eyes! They were great days before any of you were born. There were poor people everywhere—poor from choice. Because that made them free from everything but—economic necessity. Painters, writers, actors… There was a boy I remember who used to go round saying: 'I'm a poet'. In such a tone, with such an air, that no one dreamt of offering him work.

> *She is describing the young* ALEX. *He goes to her.*

ALEX: [*nastily*] He wasn't any good.

PEG: [*to* ALEX] Was I talking for you, Alex? Or for my sleepy Bert?

BERT: Bert.

PEG: [*to* BERT] He wrote lots of things. None of them lasted. [*To* ALEX] You're right; he wasn't any good. But then—then, they seemed as bright as— flowers. I loved him for a while.

BERT: I wish I wrote flowers. I write down the odds.

ALEX: And after him, Peg? Who was after him? There's always another one.

PEG: A pianist, the landlord, a man in the street, a painter—I forget.

ALEX: The man in the street is a myth. You picked them odd.

PEG: Some of them very odd.

ALEX: I don't mean me. She was an actress, you know—on the stage. She was a model. A model, in the olden days, before you were born. It was *September Morn.* [*He poses.*] It was *Lady Godiva Rides Through Coventry.* [*He poses on an armchair and strokes his long, long hair.*] Tell them how you posed and what it led to.

BERT: [*to* PEG] I wish I'd been born then. When you were posing, I mean.

ALEX: Good for you, Bert!

SYLVIE: [*conscious always of* JACK's *eyes*] Talk to us, Peggy. Tell us about those days. Do you know, I haven't got a drink; I feel sober.

> MOIRA *serves her a drink.* SYLVIE *looks at her.*

I love stories. I love those days. I used to imagine I'd be like that. A model. Or a singer. With fierce, careless love affairs.

PEG: They didn't seem careless.

SYLVIE: Or a little lady, very rich and bullying and very nice, with white gloves, and terribly respectable. I suppose that's why I wear gloves now.

ALEX: [*to* PEG] And what did it lead to? Nothing.

PEG: To what I am now.

ALEX: In one bed and out the other. And in the morning pretending it was worth it.

PEG: Sometimes it was not pretending.

LORNA: It can be worth it, Alex. Be reasonable. Remember.

MARINA: [*to* LORNA] Perhaps he does remember.

SYLVIE: Alex. Is it worth it?

ALEX: There's nothing else, is there? Is there, Tanya? She must have something to say.

BERT: [*to* ALEX] Wake her with a kiss.

PEG: Let her sleep.

LORNA: I want to dance.

> *She puts on the radio. She dances over to* ALEX.

BERT: I don't want to dance. I'm tired. I'm tired of being a bookie. I don't even make money, not enough money—four kids, you know. I work through the week, too. I'm a clerk for a lawyer. It's all adding up things, all of my life.

MARINA: Some multiplication.

> *She goes to* JACK.

ALEX: One up, Marina!

MARINA: [*to* JACK] Are you shy, now?

JACK: Scratched.

BERT: Don't talk about the races. I'm tired of races.

ALEX: The human races.

> ALEX *goes to* LORNA *and kisses her.*

BERT: I just want to lie here. I don't want to move.

SYLVIE: Lorna's stupid.

PEG: [*to* SYLVIE] Perhaps she loves him.

SYLVIE: He's stupid too.

PEG: What has that to do with it?

MARINA: Alex.

> ALEX *disengages from* LORNA.

Come home. You've had enough to drink.

ALEX *goes to* TANYA.

ALEX: [*to* MARINA] I am home.

PEG: Are you frightened of her now, Alex?

> MARINA *goes and stands near* JACK. LORNA *sways to the music, in front of* ALEX.

LORNA: [*to* MARINA] Can't you dance, dear?

ALEX: [*to* MARINA] I might come if you danced.

MARINA: [*to* LORNA] Give me my shoes. Give them to me.

> LORNA *slips out of them and enjoys her stockinged feet.* MARINA *puts them on.*

I'm ready to dance.

ALEX: For me, not with me.

MARINA: Don't be ridiculous.

ALEX: You never loved me. Dance with me, slut! Dance for me!

> ALEX *and* MARINA *dance together.* LORNA *sways among them, laughing quietly.* ALEX *turns from one to the other.* BERT *laughs.* ALEX *stops and watches them.*

Bring me my hookah! I have immoral longings in me. The pasha in his harem! Look at them, Peg. Look at me, Peg. You won't see me like this in the serial, guaranteed unlike life. Look at me, at them. Animals. All of us. Animals.

> *They have stopped dancing.*

PEG: [*leaning over* BERT] And dear Bert has four children.

ALEX: Which will I choose for tonight, Peg? Look at me, Jack.

> MARINA *is looking at him.*

PEG: And Bert has a home he can go to, when he's tired.

BERT: [*interrupting her*] Have I got to go? Is the party over?

ALEX: The party's always over. We're the guests who stayed on.

MARINA: You're disgusting, Alex. It's you that's an animal. A bull with cows—

BERT: [*delighted*] Atta boy! Atta boy!

ALEX: [*miming, to* MARINA] Roars like a bull, moves like a bull, mounts like a—

> *He jumps at her and she throws her drink at him.*

MARINA: You don't even like women! [*To the others*] I'm sorry for the carpet.

LORNA: It will help it to grow.

ALEX: [*to* MARINA] That was unnecessary.

MARINA: It's all of it necessary. [*To* ALEX] It's the last time that you'll make me cry. My glass—seems to be empty.

ALEX: Don't fill it, anyone! [*He brandishes his glass.*] I've got you covered.

MARINA: Well, have him and welcome. Anyone, have him. Do you know, I feel better. He's not much of a lover.

PEG: Perhaps we know that.

MARINA: I don't know why anyone wants him.

ALEX: It's my charm, my fatal beauty.

BERT: He talks like a book.

> MARINA *stares at him.*

MARINA: What a happy fool!

> *She goes out.*

ALEX: [*imitating her*] 'What a happy fool.' [*He minces to the door.*] Have I lost your sympathy?

SYLVIE: She loves you.

ALEX: [*at the wireless*] Love! What's this muck?! [*He switches it off.*] What's love, Lorna?

PEG: Any display of genuine emotion, Alex, seems rather real in your company.

ALEX: 'Seems, madam.'

MOIRA: [*cleaning the carpet*] You shouldn't upset her, when she's so keen on you.

ALEX: Did I make her keen? Have I encouraged her? Have you once seen me be nice to her?

LORNA: [*sadly*] You are naughty, Alex.

ALEX: All have a go at me! All of you women. All except Tanya. And, of course, she's asleep.

PEG: Let her sleep if she needs to.

BERT: [*to* ALEX] You are a bit of an animal, mate.

ALEX: *Et tu*, Bert! All with your darts, your little pinpricks of pain—into the bull. Do you want a real bullfighter? [*He imitates one, using a coat for a cloak.*] The matador, entering the ring. The cape. The challenge. The *veronica*. The *farel*. The *reolera*. The *gaonera*. [*He seizes something for a sword.*] The *muletta natural*. The kill.

> *He lunges, drops the sword, swirls the cape in front of his face and stands still. He lowers it slowly. His face is filled with pain.*

The bull. [*He is looking towards* JACK.] How are you, mate?

JACK: I'll live.

SYLVIE: We're all dying.

PEG: What an unnecessary thing to say.

SYLVIE: It's true.

LORNA: You're drinking, darling.

SYLVIE: Bang! The world blows up.

> *They look at her.*

I'm not drunk. I'm telling you. There's nothing. There's no point. You've got to be like Alex, like us; make jokes—while you can. There isn't time for anything else, everything's too complicated for anything else. Your world blows up. All you can do is go on living, living like us. You don't want to think. You don't want to make anyone keen on you.

ALEX: No. Ever been loved by a natural man?

JACK: [*softly to* SYLVIE] The world has blown up.

LORNA: [*to* ALEX] It's what I've been saying, Alex; enjoy yourself.

    ALEX *looks at her in despair. He turns to* PEG.

ALEX: [*pleading*] Oh, Peggy. Peg!

PEG: You don't mean it, Alex; you don't mean that you need me.

BERT: [*to* PEG] I need you.

ALEX: The tryer! I'm sorry for Marina. But she tries too hard. She knew that I'd have to upset her. She wants too much.

PEG: But sometimes you can't help wanting. There's no one you can blame. I wish there were.

JACK: [*during* PEG's *speech, to* SYLVIE] Your glass is empty.

ALEX: [*sadly, turning from* PEG] Tanya. Come home, and be my love.

SYLVIE: She's been smiling in her sleep.

ALEX: [*waking her*] Tanya Tatyana… Eyes like a girl. Open them wide. The world! She's smiling.

BERT: Just like a baby. [*To* TANYA] You've been asleep, sound as a baby. You were dreaming.

    TANYA *laughs.*

ALEX: She laughs! Music!

    A violin plays. SYLVIE *and* JACK *grasp hands for a moment.*

My God, God!

MOIRA: It's the boy upstairs.

PEG: He plays the violin.

ALEX: [*shaking his head*] No God. [*Happily*] But the boy upstairs, he plays the violin. And Tanya laughs and miracles begin.

JACK: Oh, God help me, I can't bear it!

    He goes to the proscenium and bangs his feet against it.

SYLVIE: [*softly*] Jack…

ALEX: [*to* JACK] Don't throw the clock. I won't recite no more.

MOIRA: He's only joking.

    She watches SYLVIE.

JACK: [*banging his fist*] Beating time!

ALEX: [*watching* JACK] Can't someone stop that violin?

LORNA: 'It is not so sweet now as it was before.'

ALEX: [*to* LORNA] What a disgusting display of culture.

MOIRA: Sometimes he plays for hours.

PEG: The walls are made of paper, and the floors.

BERT: [*brilliantly*] We live in Japan!

ALEX: [*to* PEG] Is he young?

PEG: A boy.

ALEX: Bad luck. How young?

PEG: He has a moustache. But he doesn't shave every day.

SYLVIE: Lorna, I'm going. Are you coming now?

LORNA: But the party's just starting; I feel it.

SYLVIE: Goodnight, everyone.

JACK: I'll see you to the door, lady.

SYLVIE: It's open.

JACK: It's never locked.

> *She looks at him.*

SYLVIE: Goodnight.

> SYLVIE *goes out.* JACK *stands at the door.* ALEX *watches him, then turns to* LORNA.

ALEX: You should have gone, Lorna. You're wasting time, here.

LORNA: What makes you think so?

ALEX: I'm not having any.

LORNA: And why should you think that I am interested in you?

ALEX: [*pleasantly*] You're not interested in me, my dear, my natural girl; in me or anyone. You've an active mind in an active body. When you're hungry, you eat. When you're thirsty, you drink. And when your other appetites are engaged, you come to me—or someone. Our little friend upstairs has stopped!

LORNA: Always so frank and manly, Alex. You don't even like women.

ALEX: I like you, Lorna—in a twisted, unnatural way. Who was the blonde?

LORNA: Sylvie? An accident. We went to the same Ladies' College. We can't bear one another really, but we're very good friends. Bert should take me to coffee.

> *The violin plays again.*

BERT: [*sitting up, to* PEG] You're tired of holding me.

PEG: [*smiling delightfully*] Tired. Alex, isn't he beautiful?

ALEX: You're lost, Bert.

BERT: Gee!

LORNA: You will, won't you, Bert?

BERT: Yes, that's if—if everybody'll excuse us. It's been—it's been a party. [*To* PEG] Thanks.

PEG: Thank you.

ALEX: Second prize, Lorna.

LORNA: That remains to be seen.

ALEX: Exit Lorna, bearing sacrifice, to ancient gods.

BERT: See you.

ALEX: Like a lamb to the slaughter! Perhaps. [*Looking up*] That bloody violin!

LORNA: I'm glad, Alex, that your quiet friend has got her strength back.

ALEX: Get, blast you! Eh, Bert! Before you go. [*With a British accent*] I'm no good at speeches, old man; you know that, but—well, I just want to say—best of luck! Stiff upper-lip!

BERT: [*seriously enough*] Thanks, thanks.

ALEX: Remember that you're British!

LORNA: [*laughing*] Come on.

> *She drags* BERT *off.*

PEG: [*to* ALEX] You're not dropping into my place for coffee? No. An interesting night. A re-shuffle. I'll help you tidy in the morning, Moira.

MOIRA: I'll do it tonight.

PEG: I was never a housewife.

JACK: You're all right, Peg.

PEG: Won't you wish me a good night, Alex?

ALEX: Goodnight.

PEG: Put your lip back, darling. You look like a little boy, and that's not fair.

ALEX: Damn you!

PEG: [*curtsying*] Thank you, sir.

ALEX: And stop that squeaking cat-gut, if you can.

PEG: [*smiling*] It can be done.

> *She goes out.*

ALEX: [*shouting after her*] I can imagine how!

JACK: She's a good sort.

ALEX: They're all good for something.

MOIRA: [*cattily*] He's too young.

ALEX: Are you tired, Moira? Are you tired of the pack?

> MOIRA *tidies the room.*

Leave the room.

MOIRA: I like to wake up in the morning and know that there's nothing to be done.

ALEX: I wake up like that every morning.

MOIRA: I like things neat.

ALEX: 'Neat'. A mean little word. The music's stopped.

MOIRA: They get on very well. He's a nice boy, but shy, you know. And excitable.

> *She goes into the kitchen.*

ALEX: [*in a changed tone, very serious*] What are you going to do?

JACK: [*deceitfully*] What about? [*Smiling awkwardly, honestly*] Nothing. Wait.

ALEX: It's quiet, now. [*He looks up at the ceiling.*] Just waiting's a gamble.

JACK: 'Punters never gamble—

ALEX: —they imagine they know.'

>   *They smile.*

The old jokes! Not very funny. Friendly though. 'I'll wait, Marcia. My God, I'll wait!' We're getting on. There was a girl there tonight, at the studio. She asked me was I in the War. And when I said yes she was astounded.

>   JACK *laughs.*

No, not because we won. She just thought it meant that I was old. I've finished the drink. [*Pause.*] You want me to go.

JACK: Do what you like.

ALEX: [*hurt*] 'What you like.' [*He puts his glass down carefully.*] Neat. Moira's right. Things are easier neat. [*To* TANYA] Are you coming with me? Let's pretend that we're spies. I don't know what for.

>   *They go out,* ALEX *spectacularly.* MOIRA *returns.* JACK *is happy to the*
>   *verge of laughter.*

MOIRA: They've gone. I said they've gone.

JACK: Yes.

MOIRA: It's quieter now. It is quieter.

JACK: Yes.

MOIRA: I'm glad we're alone. I like just the two of us. [*Pause.*] I'm going to bed now. I'm—

>   *She goes into the bedroom.* JACK *smokes. He looks at the Turf Guide.*
>   *Then he laughs and throws it away.*

[*From the bedroom*] Jack. What was that about Fay Someone and Tristram and Isolda? I never know what Alex talks about. I never know when he's talking sense. What did it mean?

JACK: Some story. I'm not sure. They drink poison. It makes them fall in love. It's not poison. Then someone kills them.

MOIRA: [*from the bedroom*] What did Fay Morgan mean?

JACK: Some sort of witch, a fairy. Knows everything. Causes trouble. Magic stuff.

MOIRA: [*from the bedroom*] Oh. I thought for a while he meant a girl. Fay Someone. A real story. You know.

JACK: Yes.

>   MOIRA *comes in wearing her dressing-gown. She picks up the paper,*
>   *tidying.*

MOIRA: I'm going to bed, now. Are you coming?

>   JACK *doesn't answer. He is suddenly serious, surprised at himself.*

Don't be long, Jack; I might go to sleep. I must have drunk too much. I get tired of watching.

JACK: [*uncertainly*] Yes.

MOIRA: [*coaxing gently*] Come on… Come on, Jack.

> *She stands there smiling at him. He looks at her—for the first time—and sees her rights. He makes to speak, half-turns away, stands still. She stops smiling.*

[*Firmly*] Jack. Don't be long.

> *She goes into the bedroom.*

END OF ACT ONE

ACT TWO

SCENE ONE

The flat has been tidied. It is Sunday night. JACK *is smoking in the dark. There is a knock at the door. He goes to it, puts on the light and opens the door. He is wearing an old army shirt outside his trousers.* PEG *sweeps in.* SYLVIE *is behind her.*

PEG: Sitting in the dark is not good enough; I knew you were in, and Moira out, so I came to see the moon rise. I brought Sylvie with me. She didn't know the door. Last night is years away; it always is. Alex hasn't been here? Not all day?

SYLVIE: I left a glove.

    JACK *takes it from his shirt pocket and gives it to her.*

JACK: Here.

SYLVIE: Thanks.

    They stand looking at each other.

PEG: I'm very tired. Do I look old? No answer. Not one brave lie. Oh, dear, I mustn't let myself become arch; it's not becoming. And I don't need compliments. I've only to close my eyes and sleep or dream and there I am, here I am, not a want in the world, not a wish. And in the morning, when the sun comes in and I'm awake again, and there's the mirror—and there's the mirror… [*standing looking at one*] staring at me, every morning, in its catty way. It almost makes me think I'm old, and nothing that I want to be. Why then, then there's nothing for it but to go to it… [*doing so*] and look it in the face; put on my make-up and pretend that everything's all right. And by the time I've finished the last fingering of the rouge, it is all right; I'm not pretending, I know that even if my neck is giving me away, that even if I should wear gloves and hide the backs of my hands, that really it's true—I'm thirty-nine, twenty-seven, twenty, whatever I want to be. I feel the same as when I was twenty; I know more, that's all. The mirror tells me that I'm much the same. My eyes, for instance—they are twenty or twenty-seven, they are certainly quite young. And all my life seems nothing—I can think of it so quickly and get it over—and all my real life seems stretching out before me. It's not a pleasant prospect, I can tell you. Even a real life is never very nice. It's quite a nasty shock to face it, especially when you're tired. But you have to go on living, something has to happen, tired or not, because you're only twenty. What's your age?

SYLVIE: I'm twenty-five.

PEG: You're both such children… Look, here's the moon.

The moonlight rises over the stage.

JACK: A piece of it.

SYLVIE: Don't be greedy. We must take it as it comes.

PEG: I am—getting old. I never advise, you know. What do I know? I only wanted—I must not chatter.

She goes out.

JACK: [*taking her hand*] Hi.

SYLVIE: Hi.

Suddenly she pulls her hand away. They look at each other. They smile and laugh gently.

JACK: Have you ever been loved by a man?

SYLVIE: I will—be loved by you.

JACK: Are you—? Have you just begun?

SYLVIE: [*laughing*] You make everything seem new.

JACK: We're talking in rhyme.

SYLVIE: An accident—

JACK: —of time, that you and I—

SYLVIE: —should echo and reply.

They laugh.

The Greeks hated rhyme.

JACK: The Greeks loved men—

SYLVIE: It might have been simpler.

JACK: Simple's not easy.

They kiss and part.

SYLVIE: No! I know now.

He holds her.

ALEX: [*outside the door*] Jack.

JACK: [*without turning or glancing*] Busy.

ALEX: [*outside the door*] I've got to come in.

JACK: [*still indifferent*] Busy.

SYLVIE: [*to* ALEX, *urgently*] Come in.

JACK: [*letting her go*] Simple's not easy.

ALEX *enters. He looks from* JACK *to* SYLVIE.

ALEX: [*seriously*] I need to be inside. I can't be on my own. [*In a changed tone—the party line*] So I've bought some jazz-caps. Isn't that charming? And a bottle of beer.

He puts caps on their heads, giving his to SYLVIE.

One for you. One for me. And none for me. [*He snatches a hat from behind the door.*] I'll wear this one. [*Putting it on*] Do I look funny?

JACK: No.

SYLVIE: Somebody's birthday?

ALEX: There's always somebody being born.

> *The violin plays.*

Now he was born. With a silver violin in his mouth. What for? Will I open the bottle with my teeth? I'd have to take them out, and it's very disgusting.

> JACK *goes into the kitchen.*

SYLVIE: Last night, I left my glove—

ALEX: A glove in the jungle! No, not so much fun—the circus, the zoo, the zoocus. Love in the zoocus! A glove in the zoocus; you are respectable.

> *The room is bright with the moon. There is some light from the kitchen. The moon casts their shadows on the wall.*

You're a pretty girl, Sylvie—but you make me sad.

SYLVIE: Don't you like my cap?

ALEX: Leave it on. [*He roams onto the balcony.*] Let's enjoy the moon; the white moon's round of perfect love. You never see more than half of the moon.

SYLVIE: Peg brought me to watch for it—

ALEX: And it came. But only half! The other side—how will you see that? Spaceships, ecstasies, passion—potion, poison.

> JACK *returns with glasses and an opener.*

JACK: I found it.

ALEX: Such perfect faith! He's found it. He knew he would. He always believed that the War would end. I used to despair. [*He looks up at the ceiling.*] What a morbid, mournful, moonful, moocow bloody tune! Play a scale! Get somewhere!

> *The violin stops.* JACK *laughs and pours.*

He's stopped it all. He's got somewhere. Ah! Hemlock. [*He drains his glass.*] Not enough hemlock.

> JACK *pours the beer from his glass into* ALEX's.

Thank you. All you rich are generous. Have some money.

> *He pulls out his roll.* JACK *shrugs it away.*

[*To* SYLVIE] Then, you take it. Don't either of you want it? [*He throws it in the air.*] Don't worry. I'll pick it up. I won't untidy Moira's domestic domesticity. Neat, that!

> *The violin plays a czardas.*

I brought my violin, by an odd coincidence. Ask me to play. [*He grabs an imaginary violin and plays it desperately. He speaks partly with an Hungarian accent.*] Ah, my moonlight girl, my beauty, this is for you—

the czardas, the music of my country. You are like my music—all passion, all despair. Difficult bit, this! I could play to you forever— [*The damn thing bucks!*] I probably will.

The violin stops.

String broken. Interrupted music. Story of my life, my love. One moment.

He repairs the string. He is still working at it when, suddenly, the violin begins again. It repeats what we have heard, presto.

It was easy to fix. Story of my life. [*The music jolts him around the room. He puffs and pants.*] The secret of all playing is singing tone and shining spurs. Ah! Got you, you brute!

The music stops. He wrestles with the violin and strangles it.

Never defy me again. [*He puts it under his foot and beats his chest.*] Oistrakh is the Paderewsky of the violin. I am the Tarzan. [*He drinks his beer.*] My glass is empty.

JACK *pours* SYLVIE*'s drink into* ALEX*'s glass.*

Generous. The rich can always turn to generosity.

He puts off the lamp and sits by them, fixing his hat. He points to their shadows.

Look at us.

JACK *and* SYLVIE *laugh.*

Why are you laughing? They are perfectly serious shapes.

SYLVIE: I'm laughing.

JACK: Laughing.

JACK & SYLVIE: [*together*] Because I'm happy.

The violin plays scales softly.

ALEX: Happy. Scales! Up and down. We must live, I suppose, and let learn. Tanya's dead.

SYLVIE: Tanya?

ALEX: Tanya. The girl. The girl, Tanya. Tanya Tatyana with hair like night and arms to bite and yellow nicotine on her fingers. Tanya. Dead.

JACK & SYLVIE: [*together*] How?

ALEX: The usual way. Oh, I didn't do it! Nothing's important enough for me to kill. [*He takes a small bottle from his pocket and holds it up.*] Such a little bottle for such serious shadows. Up and down. Down and up.

They are watching the shadow he makes on the wall. He goes to the lamp and flicks at it.

On and off. Off and on. [*He leaves it on.*] I suppose she was pregnant. People take this for that. She couldn't have meant it; a spoonful too many. I don't know why she chose me or chose my place. I suppose there was no place else. I rushed her to hospital, and they asked me who she was. I told them: Tanya. They didn't seem to understand why she had to die.

The violin stops.

He's stopped. Just like that. The bow from the string. You can still hear it though, fainter and fainter. She moaned in the taxi. The cab-driver kept saying, 'Is she sick, mate? She'd better get out if she's sick.' And suddenly she stopped, was gone; the bow lifted from the string. He said, 'That'll be six bob, mate'. But the meter said four-and-six, so I argued with him. It was something I could do. I won. Four-and-six. I gave him five bob. He had let me win. When I lifted her up—I'm big and strong, you know—her mouth fell open. But she had nothing to say. What a lesson! That was years ago. The sun was shining. And I couldn't buy a drink—Sunday! I had to beg for this bottle—the landlord. I had to sit up like a dog and beg. He kept talking about the rent. I forgot I had money. Look at it. What can I buy?

He begins gathering the money.

JACK: It wasn't your fault.

ALEX: Fault? Where's the fault? She did it, didn't she? It was real. She made a choice. She did something that mattered, to her at any rate. 'She had her logic.' Why haven't I got mine? [*To* JACK] And you... [*including both of them, politely*] you two. What have you done?

SYLVIE: Nothing.

ALEX: You're in the cage, the zoo. You'll get a peanut now and then... There's only one way out, one thing real—

SYLVIE: Love...?

ALEX: [*surprised she does not know, softly*] Kill. Tanya's way. Yourself. Or someone... And nothing's important enough for me to kill. I said so, didn't I?

JACK: Well, don't mope about it.

ALEX: I'm always moping. It must be nice to admit you care enough to do anything real. And death looks real. Tanya looked more interesting dead. [*Holding up the bottle*] Drink this and don't look boring! I'll patent it. Have secrets and—

SYLVIE: Don't talk about it.

ALEX: Do you want me to tell you something—true? Why they'll never drop a bomb on us. [*He imitates a plane.*] Brrrr... bang! Flick! It's too easy for me. They'll just let me—let us—wait. And wait. And wait.

SYLVIE: You think she was pregnant. It was an accident.

ALEX: There aren't any accidents. The door opens and someone comes in. Unimportant, yes. But not an accident.

The door opens and MOIRA *comes in.*

You see! Moira. Tanya's dead.

MOIRA: Is she?

ALEX: Is she not!

A long pause. MOIRA *is staring at* SYLVIE.

All right, all right, I'll talk. I only meant to liven her up. Spanish Fly, an accident. Liven her up! Potion turned to poison. Headlines for the papers. Purple Passion. Potion Poison. Tristram and Isolda.

SYLVIE: [*to* MOIRA] I left my glove. I'm always losing them. One of them—I leave them everywhere.

MOIRA: I didn't see any glove.

SYLVIE: Jack found it. Jack. I'd better go now.

MOIRA: You've found what you came for?

SYLVIE: Yes.

ALEX: [*sharply*] Have you?

SYLVIE: Yes. I'm always losing things, incompetence.

ALEX: Accident.

JACK: [*to* SYLVIE] I'll walk with you to the lights.

SYLVIE: [*touching him for a moment*] No. I'll be all right.

MOIRA: It is a dark street.

SYLVIE: The moon—

JACK: Come on.

ALEX: [*astonished*] You won't let her go alone.

JACK: No.

ALEX: [*half-singing, schoolboy-mocking*] You're walking her home, you're being the gentleman, doing the decent—

SYLVIE: [*interrupting*] Goodbye.

ALEX: [*solemnly*] Farewell.

> JACK *and* SYLVIE *go out. A pause.* ALEX *is exhausted. His hysteria with its mania and depression is done. He stands and speaks listlessly, thinking of* JACK *and his* SYLVIE.

[*Sadly*] I didn't kill her, really.

MOIRA: Didn't you?

ALEX: [*looking at her, surprised by still speaking tiredly*] Are you surprised? Or disappointed?

MOIRA: No one cares if I'm surprised or disappointed.

ALEX: [*mechanically, softly, to himself*] I care.

MOIRA: None of you do! Jack's wife. That's the only reason you ever think about me at all. Because I'm Jack's wife. No one cares about me.

ALEX: No one cares about anyone—not for long.

MOIRA: [*interrupting*] I care. I care all the time. He'd go with her...

> ALEX *looks at her.*

He doesn't even know her; I haven't—?

ALEX: Go with her?

MOIRA: —got anyone else; I couldn't get anyone else. I'm different from your—girlfriends.

ALEX: He's had other girls.

MOIRA: This one is different. I'm different. And I can't float around like your girls—like you.

ALEX: [*in his party-voice, but quietly*] Me, float?

MOIRA: You're always joking. I don't know—

ALEX: Where would he go? To the end of the street?

MOIRA: [*over him*] —when you're joking. He'd go away. This girl'd make him; she'd cry.

ALEX: All girls cry. He'd never go away.

MOIRA: You're jealous—like me. It's been all right for you. You could have this one and that one; this could happen and that could happen. It didn't matter. You could come and talk to Jack. And even if he didn't listen… [*cruelly*] and he didn't—

ALEX: [*hurt*] That was a cruel thing to say.

MOIRA: Even if he didn't take any notice at all, you could think you were friends and you weren't on your own. I feel cruel. But I can't be really cruel. She's the kind that's cruel—

ALEX: [*fascinated, serious*] What will you do?

MOIRA: What will you do? You don't want to lose him. You love him too.

ALEX: I— [*A pause. He stammers.*] He—he's my best friend.

MOIRA: What sort of friend? Like Bert? Like the smart people you work with? You're in love with him—like her.

ALEX: [*trying to joke*] That's dramatic! That's… [*softly*] not true.

MOIRA: It's true. But I don't care. You're nothing. She's the one who'll get him.

ALEX: Don't you want him happy?

MOIRA: He'll never be happy.

ALEX: I—I don't see anything so clearly. You… you're a—

MOIRA: Why don't you tell him that you're just like me; you can't keep away from him, you hang round and watch, you want to hold him and change him—like me. Like me. You'd be frightened to tell him. You know he'd laugh—

ALEX: [*softly*] Sneer.

MOIRA: Like me.

She is laughing.

ALEX: You—I— [*attempting a 'party' tone*] write for the radio, I—don't know—much.

MOIRA: I don't know about your writing, your Fay Morgans and things. Are you laughing at me now? Feeling sorry for Jack? Well, that's good. Because he hates that and it makes him like me. It makes him tired of you. It'll make him drop you. He'll always need me. He'll never need you.

ALEX: [*speaking slowly and softly*] What if I could make him love you. What if I could make him see—you, and no one else? What if I could give you a—drink of love? I'm mad, of course; I'm Fay Morgana. I'm a wizard, a witch, a fairy—don't laugh! [*He is half-laughing himself, tensely. His voice is strained as though the words hurt.*] Don't laugh!

> How Alexander, that confusing artist,
> Arranged it all, that work of art, their love;
> How it should come between that white-skinned girl
> And him the least suspicious in the world;
> How they should drink the magic drink of love
> And go their destined and most perfect way.

I tell you that I have a way— Now listen. Listen. If I gave you poison, you might kill—him, her, the world. You might, mightn't you? You could kill. And if I gave you a magic drink... [*showing her* TANYA's *bottle*] a fairy-story drink; and if he drank it, then he'd love.

> *She puts out her hand. He holds the bottle away from her.*

[*Slowly and deliberately, for himself*] But this is poison. Magic's done. [*More quickly*] If there were two bottles, if I had two—the poison here, the love-drink here—which hand, which hand would you choose? Which hand?

> *She raises her hands.*

But it's all poison. It all kills. You get no choice. You choose.

> *He puts his hands behind his back. She points to one side. He holds that hand in front of her, then opens it slowly. The bottle is there. She takes it. He speaks guiltily, confused but with sudden clarity about his 'work of art'.*

I shouldn't let you have it. This is life. You might do something stupid, nothing. But it's no use to me. I'd have to throw it somewhere; it's too real for me, to keep. Give it to me.

> *She will not.*

A perfect work of art. They love and die. There's no confusion. [*Sharply, in a normal voice*] Give it to me.

MOIRA: No. It might be useful. They use it for medicine.

ALEX: Abortion's not medicine. Perhaps it is. Give it to me.

MOIRA: I've never been pregnant. Jack doesn't want—

ALEX: Perhaps she'll have his child.

MOIRA: You are—

ALEX: [*talking about himself*] Yes. But I'm truthful now. I see a way. You are going to try? Are you going to get old and hate him? Are you going to let him get old, and hate him? Let him die. Have that much done. Have something neat.

> JACK *returns.*

JACK: She's gone.

MOIRA: Has she?

> ALEX *stares at* JACK.

JACK: Yes. Gone. [*To* ALEX] Peg knows you're here.

ALEX: [*brightly*] She's like a spider in a web. You touch a strand; she knows you're here.

MOIRA: She's fond of you.

ALEX: Loves me! Whatever that means.

JACK: She said to ask you to see her.

ALEX: Should I? Should I, Jack? Or should I be rude and mean and goosestep past the door, and let her chase me through the street?

MOIRA: She would, too.

ALEX: Women are stronger than men. They do things, have babies, drink afternoon tea. [*He imitates.*] 'No one would dream that she's over forty. But, my dear, her feet! They give her away.' I suppose I like her conversation. Gentle creatures, women. Moths of peace. They eat everything.

MOIRA: You ought to go and see her.

ALEX: Ought? Ought I, Jack? Or stay here and talk?

JACK: You used to go once.

ALEX: Once the Anzacs were brave. They're older now. [*Seriously*] Come in and protect me.

JACK: What are you frightened of?

ALEX: I'm lonely.

JACK: You can always say no. That's the easy thing to say.

ALEX: Not for me. It's just as hard as yes, and much more definite. I'm too tired to fight, too old. I might give in, cry like a baby. What would become of me then, a baby my size? Peg's baby? Come in and protect me. You've done it before. [*He sounds like* MOIRA *at the end of Act One.*] Come on, Jack. Remember the old days. Pretend she's the Japs. Jack.

JACK: No.

ALEX: You won't. I need you.

JACK: I want to be on my own. I don't want anyone. If I have to talk, I'll break a clock. We haven't got many clocks.

MOIRA: I'll come in with you. You mustn't be cruel when she loves you.

JACK: Go and see her, Alex.

ALEX: [*appealing*] Jack.

JACK: Mind him, Moira.

> *Pause. The violin plays.*

ALEX: Ah, the music! Perhaps it's not so loud in the other flat. Anything to escape that blasted boy. He sounds so useful. Come, Moira. Neither of us is wanted here, not without clocks. Exit with music. Peg and that boy? I thought not.

> *They have gone.* JACK *smokes, walks around the room, lies on the sofa. He counts things.*

JACK: Six chairs, two tables, three French windows, four corners—Christ!

He throws the ashtray against the wall. He gets up and goes on to the balcony. He bangs his fist on the arch again.

Sylvie! Sylvie!

SYLVIE: [*from below*] I'm here, Jack. I'm here.

JACK: You came back, you came back.

SYLVIE: Yes. Yes.

JACK: Come up. Come here.

A little pause.

SYLVIE: Yes.

He looks down at her, turns and hurries to the door. The violin plays.

SCENE TWO

The same, an hour later. JACK *and* SYLVIE *are on the divan. She is lying on her back. He is sitting by her.*

SYLVIE: It isn't me. This isn't me, really it isn't. Don't laugh. It isn't me. I don't jump into beds, onto divans.

She bounces on the divan.

JACK: [*laughing*] Steady!

SYLVIE: Not that I'm virtuous or anything or—anything. I couldn't see the point.

JACK *gestures and grabs at her. She rolls away.*

Don't make me laugh. I just couldn't, if it meant you got up after, shook yourself, went away; nothing changed.

JACK: It isn't me, either. I feel shy.

SYLVIE: It's all—all changed. Like magic.

JACK: But nothing's changed. We changed, that's all. We changed a bit.

SYLVIE: Every bit—I could do anything. You left me at the corner—years ago—near the tram-stop, in the light; talking and talking. What was there to talk about? I was glad when you left me and we could stop talking because—because then I could watch you walk, back here. I was glad you were going, walking down the street away; I didn't have to think, I could just watch. You looked so small in the moonlight, going away. I thought I could hear your footsteps; it was my heart beating. It was so loud. That was all I could hear. I stood there at the corner, under the light, gawking like a fool. And a soldier brushed against me. I thought he was drunk. I suppose he was. He said, 'How about it for a fiver?'

JACK: [*laughing*] How about it for a fiver?

SYLVIE: And I said, 'I haven't any money'. He looked surprised.

JACK: I'll bet he did.

SYLVIE: I walked down the street, back here. Do you know what I thought when I saw you first?

> *He shakes his head happily.*

When the door opened and you stood up to see me? Oh, it pleased me, it pleased me, but I couldn't let myself be pleased. What if it had been Lorna you were looking at, and I'd made a mistake? What if it had been a line, something for every girl and not for me?

JACK: You can ask every woman you meet if you're game. You get ninety-nine percent knockbacks; but, oh!—that one percent!

SYLVIE: That one percent. That's not me. Is it? It doesn't matter if it is. Lorna had told me about you; your racing, your rages, your army with Alex. I saw you standing and I thought—I felt—everything about his life is different from mine, the way he thinks and what he wants, what he's done and what he is; I'll never touch him, never.

JACK: [*teasing*] So you decided to trap me.

SYLVIE: No. Lorna didn't say that you were married. But then, she never says when any man is married. She's a very clever girl. What's there to you and Moira?

JACK: Nothing. We're married.

SYLVIE: That's something. What sort of a person are you? You play the horses, play the field, girls. You said: 'God, how it happens, all the odds against!' Was that a clever thing to say? I am—I am a little bit frightened. What sort of a person are you?

JACK: I lose. All the time I lose. I hate it.

SYLVIE: Was it better in the army, when you weren't—?

JACK: It's always the same.

SYLVIE: There were girls. 'All the nice girls love a—'

JACK: There weren't any nice girls. You'd go on leave in your smart clean uniform—only I'd have some buttons undone, to show I'm a lout, see; that they couldn't tame me. You'd walk around the streets, a town you never knew. You'd go to the pub. You'd wake up somewhere; it was always the army. That's what the War was.

SYLVIE: You've had lots of girls. Did you go to places?

JACK: I never pay for it.

SYLVIE: [*nastily*] No! I'm sorry. I don't think I want to ask you questions.

JACK: [*lightly*] Let's run away.

SYLVIE: [*seriously*] Where to?

JACK: The beach. Into town. I've got the tram fare.

SYLVIE: Are you paying for me?

JACK: [*irritated*] I just want to go—

SYLVIE: And take me with you. I'm so happy! And that's silly. You said that nothing's changed. It's true. You're married, and I'm me.

JACK: [*laughing*] Do I look married?

SYLVIE: [*laughing*] Yes. Yes.

JACK: A ring through my nose?

SYLVIE: Yes. Nice nose! I—I feel like a child that's got a present—not for a birthday or Christmas, not for being good or wise; just a present. Look, I'm crying.

He goes to her and takes a tear from her cheek with his finger. He puts it in her hand.

JACK: My first present to you.

They cling together. He wants to kiss her.

SYLVIE: No. I'll drop my diamond. I don't get many diamonds. [*She moves around the room, delighted.*] I've dropped it!

He pretends to look for it.

[*Seriously*] Let it go. What about Moira? I wish I'd never seen her.

JACK: [*sulkily*] What about Moira?

SYLVIE: It's all right. Say it, say anything. But what about her? Tell me lies.

JACK: [*irritated*] She won't mind.

SYLVIE: Won't she?

JACK: There've been other girls.

SYLVIE: Other girls. They call them other women. Hold me. You see, I am frightened. I told you I was frightened. I'm cold.

JACK: You don't understand.

SYLVIE: I want to be little. I want to be explained to. I can't come here like this again.

JACK: There are other places.

SYLVIE: You've thought of that! Other places, other women. I can't. I can't sneak around. [*Stammering*] I can't meet you at parties and not say anything real. I can't wear a brave face. I can't talk to Moira.

JACK: You can if we have to, if you've got to. And we have got to. We can't stop now.

SYLVIE: Leave her.

JACK: No.

SYLVIE: That was quick! Have you said it before—'other places, other women'? I don't care. I won't. Only, only, let's run away. Really. A long way.

JACK: [*seriously*] I can't.

SYLVIE: Why not?

JACK: She—she needs me.

SYLVIE: Ah.

JACK: That's how we got married; there was nothing. It wasn't like this. She was just any girl; only we met. I went out with her twice. We slept together.

SYLVIE: It was quicker with me.

JACK: She stayed here some nights. This was my place. Her parents couldn't stand it, they wanted to know where she'd been. They asked me what were my intentions—as though they didn't know. Lies and lies, to themselves. She had nowhere. She might have been pregnant. She had no one. It's a long story.

SYLVIE: Life's a long time. I need you. I've got no one else.

JACK: You don't understand. She's not like you. Nothing's changed for her. Nothing's happened for her. The odds are all against; I can't just—I know that I can't. I'm not much of a bargain either way, am I?

SYLVIE: [*seriously*] No, but then... [*smiling*] there aren't any bargains after nine in the morning. [*Changing her tone*] She's strong. But you don't know that. You're only a man. I don't care. I'm just like Lorna—a wriggle, a shake; I'm ready to go now. Goodbye.

> *She has buttoned her dress.*

JACK: Don't go.

SYLVIE: You do want your cake and eat it too. [*She sits down on the divan.*] I'll never be ready to go. I was never ready for anything before. Nothing's changed. It doesn't matter. Nothing matters. What Alex says. We've got now. We've had now. Isn't it funny—don't you suddenly think it's funny, us? People like us, you and me, in a house or rooms without our parents— as though we were grown-up. Oh, I wish I could remember you. Why didn't we meet years ago? Before the other women. When I'd have hated you, loved you, or something. When it was different. It's not fair. It could have happened. If I'd walked down the right street, if you'd opened the right door—we were there.

JACK: I was a lout. Your mummy and daddy wouldn't have let you play with me.

SYLVIE: Why?

JACK: Come here.

> *She goes towards him.*

SYLVIE: [*coquettishly*] Why? Why? [*Suddenly changing her tone*] No. No, it's no good. Everything I do. It's no good when I've got it.

JACK: Wasn't it good? [*Grinning*] Wasn't it?

SYLVIE: Are you stupid? Don't you understand?

JACK: [*becoming angry*] I'm not stupid. But I can't help you. Someone else had doped the horses; they run for him and not for you. I can't do anything; can't give you everything. I didn't ask you here, didn't bribe you, didn't call out to you. I just said your name; you came. And wasn't that something?

SYLVIE: It was everything.

JACK: No. You're like the rest, not changed. You want more, and more, and more, longer and longer, promises, lies, wedding rings. Put one through my nose and—

SYLVIE: Nice nose.

JACK: You want to laugh. Well, don't laugh. Those things won't hold it; they can't hold it. Nothing lasts.

SYLVIE: It would, it could.

JACK: You're stupid. You're stupid.

> *He shakes her.*

You have to have what you have and then watch it go. It goes.

SYLVIE: What do you want?

JACK: Nothing. This— [*He flings a glass.*] A comforting smash. I want another— [*He kicks a small table over.*] And another. And another.

SYLVIE: Don't. Don't.

JACK: I will.

SYLVIE: You mustn't care. What you told me. Let things go—

JACK: It's easy to say. Sylvie—

> SYLVIE *is in his arms.* MOIRA *comes in and stands at the door.*

MOIRA: We heard the noise next door.

SYLVIE: I'm terribly sorry. I—I fell.

> SYLVIE *realises that part of her blouse is undone. She stops speaking.*

MOIRA: Are you better, Jack?

JACK: Yes.

MOIRA: [*to* SYLVIE] Did you find your glove?

SYLVIE: Yes, it—it was here. I—I left the—other one.

MOIRA: [*picking things up*] Jack's a bad boy. It's like having a baby in the house. He's the only one I've got. Though that's enough. You mustn't let him frighten you. He just breaks things.

JACK: It's true.

MOIRA: They're never things that he thinks much of, though.

SYLVIE: Is it true, that you never break things that you think much of?

JACK: I—don't know. I don't think. I suppose so.

> ALEX *comes in.*

ALEX: Have you calmed the beast? Sylvie, my pet! Moira's a traitor. She left me alone.

MOIRA: [*to* ALEX] You ought to be kinder to Peg. She loves you.

ALEX: Another clock? Ah, a glass! Sherlock! You missed this piece.

> *He hands a piece of glass to* MOIRA.

Moira tidies the wreck, rather like death.

JACK: You're brighter.

ALEX: Than before, yes. Improving conversation. Peg cheers me. Tanya's gone. Spring's begun. I'm living. I'll have fun. I'll see the police on Monday. They'll see me. They'll explain Tanya. New Australian, doesn't speak English, difficulty of adjustment, loneliness; inconvenience, sorry.

The usual story. I'll use them in my serial, a police inquiry scene—a mysterious death, a touch of life. The nice thing, you know, about a long soap opera is that it is like life. The listeners get confused. You can count on missed episodes; no one sure what's happened. They more or less know, and won't ask questions. None of the characters need be neat. You can forget one week which are men and which are women. Hardly anyone will notice, hardly anyone will care. And as long as you end with Jack— and his Jill...

    He hands SYLVIE *her bag and gloves.*

... then everyone's happy. The minor characters— Do you know I've just realised that I—me—I'm a major character in Peg's life; a minor one in my own.

SYLVIE: I have to go now.

ALEX: I promise to be quiet.

MOIRA: [*to* SYLVIE] Stay for a drink.

SYLVIE: No, thank you.

MOIRA: Stay for a drink. [*Moving*] I'll get you something.

SYLVIE: [*shaking her head slowly*] Goodnight. [*To* JACK] Don't come with me. Not this time.

MOIRA: Jack. We'll have something to drink.

JACK: [*at the door with* SYLVIE] Tomorrow night.

SYLVIE: No.

JACK: Tomorrow.

SYLVIE: No.

JACK: Sometime.

    She goes out. JACK *stands at the door.*

ALEX: [*to* MOIRA] Would you have? Would you have? [*A long pause.*] Like a perfect work of art, a criticism of life. Would you have? [*A pause.*] Give me the bottle. Go on.

MOIRA: What bottle?

JACK: The mob's coming.

    He goes from the door to the balcony and looks down. ALEX *goes to him.*

ALEX: Any luck? I kept her next door. You ought to tell me.

JACK: [*reluctantly*] Yes. Luck.

ALEX: [*softly*] Secrets. You used to be more graphic.

JACK: I— Moira.

ALEX: I suppose that's the reason.

JACK: She's going.

    He leans out to look.

ALEX: [*nastily*] She's not looking back. Who's the mob?

LORNA *bursts in, with* BERT.

LORNA: Alex, you're practically living here. I've heard the news. I know we're a terrible nuisance, Moira. You must have had a terrible time, Alex. Say hello to Bert.

ALEX: 'Hello to Bert.' [*To* LORNA] Actually, I enjoyed it.

LORNA: [*giggling*] I imagined you would, every gurgle. All notes for the masterpiece; coughing, blood—

ALEX: Lorna, have some delicacy. Have you been with Bert since last night?

LORNA: He's the divinest lover. Don't blush, Bert. He makes me feel normal.

MOIRA: [*to* BERT] Haven't you been home?

BERT: No.

LORNA: He rang, though. I insisted. The least he could do.

JACK: Did you tell her the truth, Bert?

BERT: She didn't ask me for the truth. She—

JACK: It doesn't matter.

ALEX: [*to* BERT] Have you had a good time?

BERT: Well—yes.

ALEX: What a recommendation. Lorna? Well—yes.

BERT: I'll have to go home tonight. The kids—they miss me.

LORNA: Sweet! Shall I tempt him? No, perhaps not. Sylvie was here?

MOIRA: [*to* BERT] Four children?

BERT: Yes. Four.

ALEX: [*counting on his fingers*] Four.

LORNA: [*to* ALEX] And poor Peg, I suppose, is next door all alone? You are a brute, Alex. Is there anything to drink?

JACK *starts towards the kitchen.*

MOIRA: No.

JACK *stops.*

LORNA: It doesn't matter. I don't need any. [*Sincerely*] Alex, you're not very upset? About this business? Tanya?

ALEX: She was Bert's Tanya.

BERT: I didn't know her.

LORNA: [*in a shocked tone*] Picked her up! Oh, dear!

BERT: She was just sitting there, there in the lounge. Her glass was empty. I'd finished work. I told them to fill it. She said her name was Tanya. Then Alex came to collect. He collected her, too. Just as well, I suppose, although she—

ALEX: [*after a little pause*]—although she mightn't have taken anything with you.

BERT: I'd better be going. Sometimes the youngest won't sleep—

MOIRA: [*to* BERT] Why didn't you go home last night?

BERT: Well...

ALEX: [*to* BERT] Well?

BERT: You know how it is. A bit of excitement. A bit of a drink. Work done. Something new.

ALEX: A new bit of schmoo. That's all we want. Wives are just mothers, Moira, habits—

LORNA: You haven't got a wife.

ALEX: I had a mother. And I've had proposals.

LORNA: Dishonourable, I imagine. Only a fool would take you. I suppose I will in the end.

ALEX: We've left it too late. When we're interestingly old, a hundred and thirty or forty… [*acting it*] we'll pass in the street like strangers. And suddenly, somehow, we'll remember—and it will be too late. I'll buy a rose or a carnation and hobble after you. I'll catch you up. I'll call your name. 'Lorna.' You'll turn. I'll offer you the rose. You'll cut me dead. Lorna, is it kind?

LORNA: Why should you get married? I don't blame you.

ALEX: Thank you.

LORNA: You're having fun.

ALEX: Fun?

JACK: Why should he be married?

ALEX: Bert's our prize husband. Why did he marry?

LORNA: [*to* BERT] Yes. Why? Talk. He hasn't had a chance to—he's been terribly busy. Why?

MOIRA: Why, Bert?

BERT: I forget. I wanted to.

MOIRA: Where do you live?

BERT: [*pointing*] It's on the calendar, the phone number. Jack rings up his bets when he doesn't go to the course. The wife works at home, see; answers the phone while I'm picking up the personals at the pub. I'll have all the checking to do when I get home. Tuesday's the pay-out.

    ALEX *holds out his hand.*

You've collected yours. [*To* MOIRA] Thanks very much for the party and—all. Goodbye, Lorna.

LORNA: Don't be shy.

    She kisses him.

Now, run along home. Ring me sometime.

BERT: What's the number?

LORNA: It doesn't matter. Off you go.

BERT: Goodnight.

    BERT *goes out.*

MOIRA: Goodbye. [*To* ALEX] You should get married.

ALEX: Why? Why? Why is everyone picking on me? I've had a most exhausting day.

LORNA: Don't mention Tanya's.

ALEX: It had nothing to do with me.

JACK: Women don't kill themselves over Alex.

LORNA: [*to* JACK] They don't need to; they've been through hell. [*To* ALEX] You should marry. You need a mother.

ALEX: The streets are full of little mothers.

LORNA: You need one with camouflage.

ALEX: Peg's my mother substitute.

LORNA: Peg will die.

ALEX: [*fascinated*] You are cruel.

LORNA: I'm what you need.

ALEX: You should never enter into relationships with women for what you need. You need a mother. She needs a father. One of you has to go under. Which one of us?

LORNA: Are you accepting me?

ALEX: No! No, I don't think so. Not this year. [*Primly*] Thank you for asking.

LORNA: I may as well go home. A wasted weekend! Perhaps not. I've got through it. Alex, it's a long way home by myself and I can't afford a taxi. I had to lend Bert the money for his. Aren't you coming?

MOIRA: [*to* ALEX] Say goodnight to Peg. Be nice.

ALEX: [*thinking*] Peg. [*Decided, to* LORNA] All right, I'll come. Just for tonight, mind.

LORNA: For the long ride home.

ALEX: And to pay for the taxi. [*He stops at the door.*] Moira. Moira— It doesn't matter. [*To* JACK] See you.

JACK: See you.

LORNA: 'Bye.

> LORNA *and* ALEX *leave.*

ALEX: [*offstage*] Don't push me. Don't run. Be patient.

JACK: You might have given them a drink.

MOIRA: I didn't want to. Bert shouldn't have left his wife like that. She wouldn't like it, no matter what she said.

JACK: She's got the kids.

MOIRA: Yes.

> *She takes Tanya's bottle from her pocket and puts it in her purse.*

JACK: What's that?

MOIRA: Nothing. Medicine. Did you want a drink?

JACK: No.

MOIRA: That girl…

JACK: She's gone, hasn't she? She won't come back.

MOIRA: She'll come back.

JACK: I don't know.

MOIRA: She's the kind.

JACK: Is she?

MOIRA: Aren't you interested?

JACK: I'm thinking.

MOIRA: [*after a pause, hastily and pathetically*] I wish you'd talk. [*Smiling*] I'm still here, you know.

   A pause. PEG *enters.*

PEG: May I come in? He's gone, I see. I heard, but I wanted to be sure. Lorna? He says he hates her, can't stand her. She's the only one he's interested in. I'll go. Or can I stay? I feel very lonely tonight. It all seems so quick when you're young. And so much quicker when you're old. But, at the same time, of course, so much slower; you think you can wait. I wonder if you can.

   The violin plays.

There's a lonely life. Poor boy! I suppose he's not a boy. He has a moustache. He sends money to his mother. That's really very old. He doesn't seem to have any life. He has work and classes and practice and reading and thinking. He writes to the papers, you know—'Dear sir'. And they won't print them. He does it to save the world—no wars. A lonely life. Still, he has his violin—as we all very well know. Often, he makes quite pleasant music. My life has been rather a jangle. I'm much older than you think I am. Or perhaps I'm not. You're both so quiet. Alex thinks it's 'grotesque', now; him, and me. What can anyone do? Things happen, they happen; you learn how to tolerate them. That's all you learn. I'm off to bed now. I like the way you break things, Jack. I get so bored with the flat next door. It's a bargain basement—ornaments, photographs, the past; junk. I should break something.

JACK: He's fond of you.

PEG: 'He's fond of you.' Fond's not enough. You tell yourself that it is, but it isn't. I'll dye my hair again. It'll pass away the time. Green, I think.

   PEG *goes out.*

JACK: [*to* PEG] Goodnight.

MOIRA: You wouldn't go away from me.

JACK: No.

MOIRA: I knew you wouldn't.

JACK: I haven't the guts.

MOIRA: I hate that girl. The others didn't matter.

JACK: Nothing unpleasant matters. You've said so often. You've told me, 'Don't worry, it doesn't matter'. It doesn't matter.

MOIRA: Oh, Jack. Jack.

She touches him.

JACK: No, I'm tired. I'm going to sleep.

MOIRA: Jack.

JACK: I'm tired.

MOIRA: Jack—

She tempts him, but suddenly he pushes her aside. She falls on the floor.

JACK: I don't want to. I don't want to.

He goes into the bedroom. She kneels on the floor. She rises and walks around the room. She pauses at the calendar. She starts towards the bedroom, changes her mind, takes her purse and goes out the front door.

[*Offstage, calling*] Moira.

JACK *re-enters.*

Moira, have you—? Moira?

END OF ACT TWO

ACT THREE

It is the big room in the 'flat next door'—Peg's flat—a 'bargain basement'. It is the same shape as the living room of Jack's place, but crowded with furniture and relics of the past: paintings, cheap ornaments, play posters, oriental souvenirs, a dressmaker's dummy, some outrageous hats. There is a bed with iron knobs on it and a dressing table crowded with make-up equipment.

ALEX *is on the bed.* PEG *is sitting at the dressing table, restoring her face. She is wearing a kimono. It is Monday night.*

ALEX: All right. I am jealous. Why shouldn't I be? You don't collect many friends. The number of real friends you have, you can count on the fingers of one hand; on one finger, friends like Jack. I am jealous. Well, it's a real feeling.

PEG: Is it?

ALEX: No, it isn't. I hate him a bit, too. You don't understand; can't, I suppose. It's that he's stronger than I am, like you. You all are, blast you! We're not friends who talk much or see much of each other or have lots of interests in common or anything like that. In the army we got interested in knotting. [*He ties a noose in a cord.*] I can tie a knot that won't slip. We have attitudes. We understand jokes. It gives me a sense of sense. I need to see him occasionally—to know I'm not on my own, someone else can see the joke. It's a bit of a blow to know, to know all the time, that he doesn't need me.

PEG: It is a bit of a blow. To know anything all the time.

ALEX: And this girl.

PEG: There have been other girls. He has a wife.

ALEX: This one's able to change him. It couldn't last, you know. It's too quick and intense. You can't live on one feeling.

PEG: That much is true.

ALEX: Either it changes or they do. This is a homosexual feeling, isn't it? So what? I don't want him to change. He wouldn't come here, to protect me, last night. It was only a joke, but he would have before; it would have been a joke. I need protecting. Don't I? You're making me change. It's no good. It couldn't last, that sort of thing. Suddenly it means everything! And that means nothing. You laugh at different jokes. The love-talk can't make up for the differences, not always. The love-stuff goes, and what have you got? Me. Reality. Marriage is unnatural. Men want mothers. Women want fathers.

PEG: What do you want?

ALEX: Nasty! I'm normal enough, aren't I, for you and Lorna and Helen and Sue and Tanya and—? Nothing was normal enough for Tanya. If they stayed together the way they came together, close; they'd end stupid and disgusting—like Moira and Jack. They'd be better to die; they'd have had something decent, and not had it spoilt. I'm disgusting, aren't I? Aren't I just a little bit disgusting? But you put up with me. Peg, you put up with me. Sometimes I wish to God you wouldn't! It's ten years, isn't it? Longer. I was young then, a kid, a boy, and you were younger, I suppose. I thought you were quite old then. You were the oldest I'd had. I was interested in that. Experience. You weren't the first, nor the best, not the— But you were the most useful; you listen to me, you teach me, you're grateful. How's that for a compliment? Are you crying? It'll spoil your face. I'm sorry. I'm sorry that it's so interesting to find out what will make you cry. They're healthy animals, aren't they—Jack and Sylvie? The kind you'd expect in a jungle. I don't belong in the animal world; it confuses me. I'm spoilt, overbred. I'm the horse that looks like a racehorse; I'm the kind only mug punters back. 'I'll wait, Marcia. My God, I'll wait!'—that's the race I win. I'd like to have done—wonderful things, great things. Shakespeare was only a man, you know. Not money things, or social things, but real things... Am I a good horse, Peg?

PEG: Splendid.

ALEX: I'm nasty tonight.

PEG: You always want to be told.

ALEX: Told what I know. You never married.

PEG: The 'Missus' was to impress the lodgers. The ring was to impress a lover. None of them were impressed. There was no one to marry. I couldn't have children. Those are the technical reasons.

ALEX: You don't want children. No one wants them. What would you do with them? Bring them up? Me and you, you and me...? What does that make me? Oedipus?

PEG: What does it make me?

ALEX: Wonderful. Life giving. Useful. They could have children. What for? To keep them together, when the love-muck finishes. Nature's way. Like Bert.

PEG: Like Bert.

ALEX: Do you know what comes out of nice little bourgeois homes? People like me.

PEG: Like others.

ALEX: So the race can survive. Is that important? I don't see the necessity.

PEG: It might produce Shakespeare.

ALEX: It might produce me.

PEG: That's a risk certainly. People take these chances.

ALEX: They don't want chances. They're certain, no. They've got something. I hope Moira kills them before they kill that. She's the type. It would be the artistic thing to do, neat. She could do it, I couldn't. They ought to die, 'in the flood-tide of their passion'. Romantic lovers always do. Tristram, Romeo—they all die, before the rot sets in.

PEG: The rot can be pleasant, in odd little moments.

ALEX: The only thing I'm certain of is this: none of it matters, nothing; not them, or me, or you, or all of this damned unreal city. Why don't they drop a bomb? A solution. The flats across the road—

He goes to the apron of the stage, the balcony, and looks at them.

PEG: I've seen them.

ALEX: [*looking from window to window*] The prisoners are eating, sleeping, knitting—knitting little garments doubtless. Reading. Watching. No one praying. I'm often like this after, aren't I? *Post coitum omne animal triste.* Latin's a dead language. We're a dead people. But it doesn't matter to me. I said so, didn't I? Should I marry Lorna?

PEG: She's been around a long time.

ALEX: Not as long as you have, if that's what you mean. I can't marry you.

PEG: 'Nobody asked you, sir, she said.'

She looks in the mirror. ALEX *plucks two flowers from the bowl. He presents one gallantly to* PEG. *He holds the other, then tosses it onto the bed.*

ALEX: Flowers for the dead. Everyone gets married. It looks so definitive. It looks like the point. [*He looks across the street again.*] Do you think they're happy? What's the password?

PEG: The boy upstairs is happy.

ALEX: He has a mother and a violin.

PEG: He has faith. He knows how to save the world. You don't.

ALEX: Pacifism! Saying no! Well, it's saying something. I envy him.

PEG: You should.

ALEX: What's he like, your fancy-boy upstairs?

PEG: He laughs. All the time, he laughs. But sad when he talks to you seriously, though never depressing, never like you. He suspects it's hopeless, but he believes in trying. It gives him purpose, point. His mother won't speak to him, you know. Because his brother was killed in the War. I don't see the reasoning. She takes his money and never speaks.

ALEX: [*with a German accent*] All women are prostitutes! A German told me so. But the real pros are honest; they give you something.

PEG: So I talk to him, or let him talk to me. The state of the world, what Christ would have done; how we have to choose. If you miss the choice now, you miss it forever. If you lose the choice here, then you lose it everywhere—he thinks he's converting me. Poor innocent boy!

ALEX: Does he have girls?

PEG: He has me.

ALEX: Has he asked you?

PEG: Not exactly. But when he's very tired, when we're both on our own and so very tired, he puts his head here. And he holds onto me.

ALEX: How very touching! When you least expect it, he'll up and grab you. That's the next move. Unless you grab him.

PEG: I think I find it very irritating when you pretend to be jealous.

ALEX: I am jealous.

PEG: Jealous of everyone, perhaps. It is pleasant when I can imagine you are jealous of me. But not now! Not here, looking in the mirror.

ALEX *goes behind her and points into the mirror.*

ALEX: Look. You see me.

He leans his cheek on hers.

I'm fond of you.

PEG: 'Fond' is an old word. [*Beginning to laugh*] What a pretty picture! Mother and juvenile delinquent. You'll spoil my face.

ALEX: Why bother? It doesn't deceive anyone.

PEG: It does deceive me.

ALEX: Am I very cruel to you?

PEG: Yes, but you, me, all of it—

ALEX: I can't love anyone. And I don't look like Narcissus.

PEG: You look what you are, amusing.

ALEX: Thanks.

PEG: And a little dull. Am I very cruel to you? No one would put up with you if it weren't that they grow fond of you before they find you out. You amuse them at first. You make them laugh, or you flatter them.

ALEX: I never flatter.

PEG: Your rudeness is flattering, and your bothering to perform; and your nasty, prying curiosity is flattering. And your jealousy. Then people get used to you, fond; that's what fond means. And then they're lost. They can't let go. Even though you do bore them and irritate them and hurt them a very great deal. I'm afraid I love you very much. It's very serious and silly. Not what I planned.

ALEX: I'm going to sleep.

He lies on the bed.

PEG: You should.

ALEX: Do you think I'll need my strength? No more tonight, Peg, please.

PEG: You don't rest enough. You don't sit still. You're too quick, acting and thinking acting all the time. I can flatter, too! You should just lie down, be still, the way I do, and let thoughts come. It makes things clearer, though just as impossible to control; less confusing confusion. When I was young, you know, I was very earnest and hopeful in some ways, very young. I thought for a while Communism, and psychological adjustment, and heavenly harmony, and oh-so-many important things were possible. I didn't understand then that people can know one thing and believe another, that you can feel so much more surely than you can think. Then I fell in love, the old story; just a little bit in love—just enough to feel sick if I met him unexpectedly. He could reason with me, and I could hear him saying things I knew were true, but we had rows all the same; hurtful, killing rows. I found that I could say yes and never believe it. The first time I saw him out with someone else—just a friend, not even another woman, just someone he preferred to be with for just a little time—I can still feel the pain when I remember. And people don't usually remember pain. Ten years ago. One day I'll die, or be very old; I'll look so old that not even make-up can show me the truth. One day, I'll die; be nothing here; be nowhere else. The room won't even know I'm gone; there'll be someone living in it, this—junk of mine thrown out, of no value at all. I can't believe it, of course. It's like you, blowing up the world. One can imagine it; one can't believe it, can't take it seriously; one day I'll die. You should marry Lorna. It's lonely and tiring to be old. Are you asleep? You're making piggish noises. You're not asleep. Alex. Alexander, stop it. Stop it. Stop it.

She goes to the bed to stop him pretending to snore. They scuffle, laughing.

ALEX: Don't wake me. Don't.

There is a knock on the door.

Damn!

PEG: Who's there?

SYLVIE: [*from outside*] Sylvie. Sylvie.

PEG: [*from the bed*] Come in, dear. We're respectable.

SYLVIE *enters.*

SYLVIE: I'm sorry.

PEG: Alex was sleeping.

ALEX: Come to the big, bad wolf.

PEG: He's awake now.

SYLVIE: Yes.

There is a pause while they wait for her to speak.

PEG: Well, you. Well, you—

SYLVIE: I was going to pretend I mistook the doors, my glove—I told those lies yesterday.

PEG: Jack's alone.

SYLVIE: That makes no difference.

ALEX: [*to* PEG] You miss nothing, do you? You and the boy upstairs.

PEG: It's my world, Alex, and welcome to it. [*To* SYLVIE] Moira's gone. She went away last night. Oh, don't be happy! Whatever's happened—whether she's left him or dead or just gone for a holiday—you won't be happy when you know.

SYLVIE: [*to* PEG] Is Jack—? What does Jack say?

PEG: [*to* SYLVIE] Yes, he's upset.

ALEX: [*to the world*] She's as weak as I am. I knew she was.

SYLVIE: [*to* PEG] I was going to ask you to bring him here.

PEG: [*to* SYLVIE] If you like—

ALEX: [*to* SYLVIE, *over* PEG] Go to him; Moira's gone. You can straighten the room again. As long as you leave her things tidy, Moira won't—

SYLVIE: [*to* ALEX] I can't. I've come to say goodbye. That's weak. I should have just gone.

PEG: Alex, go and get him.

SYLVIE: [*to* ALEX, *pleading*] Just for a minute, just for a minute—

PEG: [*to* SYLVIE] I'd forgotten how urgent these things are. You must be calmer when you see him. I do believe I was watching, watching you two and thinking, the way one watches the people across the road; not feeling anything at all—like Alex. [*To* ALEX] Alex. Alex, you're still here.

ALEX: Yes.

PEG: Well, don't be.

ALEX: [*definitely*] No.

> There is a pause. PEG *goes from the room.* ALEX *and* SYLVIE *look at each other.*

You're clever.

SYLVIE: I thought you liked me for a while, but I suppose you were only upset about the girl, the dead one.

ALEX: [*coldly*] I don't dislike you. It's just that win or lose, you lose. He can't get away from Moira, from what he is. You don't remember him. You'll fail.

SYLVIE: But I'm not sorry. That's something, isn't it? Something real. Real things never last—real flowers, real people.

ALEX: [*quite pleasantly, conversationally*] I went to the police about Tanya—

SYLVIE: [*interrupting*] Do you think he won't come?

ALEX: I bore you so terribly? Shall I do my imitations?

SYLVIE: No. Thank you. They make me laugh.

ALEX: And that's not necessary. Come and look from the balcony. This flat's the same—shape as next door. It has a balcony—not so enchanted, it's the one I stand on. You can see in the windows. It's like being God. It's the reason I come here—one of them. You get to know lives; it's good material, they tell me. The couple over there—the window above the door—no children. They both work, but different hours. She runs a sailor as well as him. He doesn't know, or at least we don't think so. She never lets them meet. We call the husband Hank the Yank. I believe he's Dutch. But he wears glasses like an American and he has a spectacular key-chain. [*He spins an imaginary key-chain, grabs the key and revets the door.*] There's a writer in that white block. His light stays on; all night he works or reads. It must be highbrow. He gets two pints of milk in the morning. The place under his has a dry-cleaner. He's got a truck and a daughter who can walk and call him daddy, so he doesn't seem to mind his wife. That flat is shared by two girls—air hostesses. They wear uniforms. I imagine their buttons hurt one's chest. They come home at all times, at all months, escorted by prosperous-looking beasts in Bentleys—

SYLVIE: [*interrupting*] There doesn't seem any point, does there? I think you're trying to be nice to me. Thanks.

ALEX: [*bowing*] Lady.

SYLVIE: I'll go now. I'm in control.

ALEX: It would be definite.

SYLVIE: [*laughing*] I wish I could love you!

ALEX: People get used to me, fond.

SYLVIE: Used to's not enough. Perhaps it's everything. [*Suddenly*] Moira. His wife. She wouldn't—wouldn't do anything silly? Like Tanya?

ALEX: Anything definite? No. I don't know. I don't think so. I did something— silly, yesterday. [*Touching her arm*] Don't go. I gave her the stuff that Tanya took. I—I thought—I think she thought of killing you, killing you both, someone. That's not the truth. I suppose it is the truth—but I made her think of it longer than she might have. Kill you both.

SYLVIE: There's no need.

ALEX: No. Habit wins all along the line. She's his wife.

SYLVIE: I did think, for a while, that— No I didn't think: it's just that you get used to—what's on at the pictures. You start to think like them, not what you really think at all. Close-ups and hundreds of violins— You don't expect friends—or ties—

> SYLVIE *falters to a stop.* PEG *and* JACK *have entered.* JACK *stands at the open door.*

PEG: If you've upset her, Alex— [*A pause.*] I'm sorry I was so long. I met the boy upstairs on his long, long way upstairs. He does touch earth, you see. I'm afraid before long he'll be giving us the music of the spheres again. [*A pause.*] But perhaps it will be something jolly. He's unnaturally bright. [*A pause.*] Quite like Alex! He's probably been called up for his National Service again. They're always calling him up and he's always conscientiously objecting. And then they call him up again. I wonder why they want him; he's not very fierce. I suppose it amuses the judge, or whatever it is, to see him again. It's the familiar jokes that are funny. [*A pause.*] Alex, the other room.

ALEX: Yes, Captain.

ALEX *salutes and marches into the other room behind* PEG.

SYLVIE: Hello.

JACK: Hi.

SYLVIE: Didn't you want to see me? Don't answer. I'm going away.

JACK: Moira's gone.

SYLVIE: I know.

JACK: I don't know where.

SYLVIE: She'll come back.

JACK: Will you?

SYLVIE: I've not the money to go to Europe. I almost went last year with Lorna. Not much money. There's a girl I know, she wants me to go with her, she's been pestering me. Dad might— Jack.

> JACK *embraces her. She falls on the bed, struggles free and holds him off.*

I suppose this is what I came for. What do you want?

> JACK *sits by her on the bed.*

JACK: I don't know. I told you that. Everything. You. That's greedy, isn't it?

SYLVIE: [*whispering*] Yes. [*Changing her tone*] What will Moira do?

JACK: Come back and want her own way. Make me lose my temper, do my block. Get her own way.

SYLVIE: Will she come back?

JACK: Why wouldn't she? She's got no one else. What else can she do?

SYLVIE: She hates me. She might kill herself.

JACK: It only sounds simple.

> *The violin plays.*

SYLVIE: That's not very appropriate, and I didn't ask for music. Perhaps he doesn't listen. Sensible boy. No burnt fingers. No burning ears. I've been thinking, remembering over and over; and just for a moment, I saw the pattern; I knew what to do. Do you love me?

JACK: Yes.

SYLVIE: Do you really love me?

JACK: Yes.

SYLVIE: Do you love Moira?

JACK: No. Yes. I don't want to tell you lies. In a kind of a way. I'm—

SYLVIE: Used to her, fond of her, married to her.

JACK: She's used to me.

SYLVIE: Yes. That's important. They weren't fair questions, were they? What's love? What am I? What does 'love someone' mean?

JACK: This.

> *He turns to her. They kiss.*

MOIRA: [*offstage*] Peg, Peg.

They break apart guiltily. JACK *stands.* SYLVIE *begins to smooth the bed. They stop.*

SYLVIE: It's disgusting. It's no good.

She picks up Alex's flower and plays with it. MOIRA *appears in the doorway.*

JACK: [*to* MOIRA] Where have you been?

BERT *comes into the room, passing* MOIRA. *He is surprised to see* JACK.

BERT: Hello, Jack. What are you doing here? I—I found your wife in the street. You shouldn't let her wander around. Blokes like me might find her.

MOIRA: He's telling lies. I rang him up.

JACK: [*to* MOIRA] Where have you been?

MOIRA: Somewhere.

BERT: [*hastily*] Peg here? This is Peg's room, isn't it? [*Admiringly*] Look at that bed.

SYLVIE: [*to* BERT] Hello.

BERT: Hi.

MOIRA *looks at* SYLVIE *and the bed.*

MOIRA: [*to* SYLVIE] Hello.

JACK: [*to* MOIRA] Have you been drinking?

MOIRA: No. I had a drink.

BERT: Just a short one.

JACK: [*to* MOIRA] Are you all right?

MOIRA: [*triumphantly*] Yes! Are you? Are you all right? [*To* SYLVIE] You look pretty. Playing with a flower. That's clever.

BERT: I'd better be going.

SYLVIE: I'll come with you; it's dark in the street. I was going now.

MOIRA: [*to* SYLVIE] Don't go. [*To* BERT] Why should you go, Bert? [*To* SYLVIE] And why should you go?

BERT: I thought I might be in the way.

MOIRA: Oh, no, you're the life of the party! That's what Alex says. Isn't that what Alex said? Where's Peg? Oh, it doesn't matter. She won't mind.

BERT: Are you having a party?

SYLVIE: I have to go.

MOIRA: [*to* SYLVIE] I want you to stay. Let's all have a drink. I haven't been very friendly. I haven't been well. I'm well, now. I needed some fresh air.

BERT *gives a guffaw.*

That's how I came to meet Bert. Oh, I forgot I told you the truth! There must be something to drink here. There must.

PEG *and* ALEX *return.* PEG *has dressed.*

PEG: [*to* MOIRA] I'm not as confirmed an alcoholic as that sounds, but there is. In the kitchen.

MOIRA *moves to go there, but* PEG *stops her.*

You've been away. We've all been worried.

MOIRA: Yes, I know.

PEG: [*a trifle amused*] Well, welcome home, dear.

> *A pause.* MOIRA *suddenly kisses her cheek.*

MOIRA: Thanks.

BERT: Hello, Alex. How are they biting?

ALEX: And here's Father of Four.

PEG: I'll get you something to drink now.

MOIRA: [*to* PEG] I'll get it.

ALEX: [*to* MOIRA] You.

> *A pause.*

SYLVIE: Let her, Alex.

> MOIRA *looks at her.*

MOIRA: What's it to do with him? Are you laughing at me?

> MOIRA *goes into the kitchen.*

ALEX: Sylvie—

> *A pause.*

PEG: Is there anything between you two? It's quite possible. I left them alone
for fully three minutes.

SYLVIE: Jack.

> *She puts his arm around her.*

JACK: You're shivering.

SYLVIE: Yes.

ALEX: [*to* SYLVIE] Are you frightened?

SYLVIE: Cold.

PEG: [*speaking over* ALEX *and* SYLVIE] You haven't said hello to me, Bert. Not
one word! No, don't speak now. What good's that? You might have said I
looked nice and I'd almost have believed you. But not now. Not now that
I've told you.

BERT: But you do look nice.

PEG: I do almost believe you.

ALEX: [*to* SYLVIE] Will you?

SYLVIE: [*while* PEG *is speaking*] Yes.

JACK: [*tightening his arm around her*] What's going on?

> ALEX *stands looking at her, watching her with* JACK.

BERT: [*to* ALEX] Are you propositioning her, too?

PEG: No one's safe, Bert; woman, dog or man.

BERT: Anything with hips, eh?

PEG: [*perhaps shocked*] Sometimes you are a little—quicker than I expect, Bert.

BERT: It's only Alex who thinks I'm dumb. But Moira said—Moira and I have been talking and—

ALEX: [*interrupting*] Sylvie. It's not right. It's not fair. It's not—proper—

PEG: Alex should have been a parson. He has exactly the drone and not a word that means anything—

ALEX: Not properly arranged. Not what I—meant. Jack wouldn't know... It's not—

SYLVIE: But I will.

> *She tightens* JACK's *arm around her.*

ALEX: [*finishing in a whisper*] —not real...

> MOIRA *brings in three glasses.* JACK *drops his arm quickly, hiding his action.* SYLVIE *looks at him, dismayed.*

MOIRA: [*serving*] Peg, Bert—you deserve a drink. Alex.

> ALEX *holds her glance, but she only smiles at him.*

ALEX: [*after a pause*] Thanks.

> MOIRA *returns to the kitchen.*

PEG: I don't know if I can wait until all of you have yours. I suddenly feel sad and thirty-nine; that means I'm thirsty. I know why it is! The music's stopped. He's better than the wireless, I know; he has no dreadful commercials. But you can't turn him on and off. Both would have their advantages. I know I couldn't wait. I tried.

> *She drinks.* BERT *drinks with her.*

BERT: Cheers.

> MOIRA *returns with three more glasses. She holds them out to* JACK *and* SYLVIE.

MOIRA: That one's mine. It's got lemonade in it.

> JACK *and* SYLVIE *take theirs.* SYLVIE *drinks from hers suddenly. She still holds the flower.*

SYLVIE: [*to* JACK] No, I do love you.

ALEX: [*to* SYLVIE, *then looking at* JACK] Poison is potion. Now, you are free.

SYLVIE: I can be anything now.

ALEX: Good Tristram and Isolda of the flowers; how it should come between that white-skinned girl? And him the least suspicious in the world—

MOIRA: [*to* ALEX, *interrupting*] Oh, stop talking. I don't understand your talking. Let her talk.

PEG: She's quite right, Alex. Let's have a toast. Not 'cheers', Bert.

BERT: What's wrong with 'cheers'?

ALEX: [*raising his glass, watching* JACK] Spring when everything is born again, and all the world is young.

PEG: No, no, I'm tired of that. And of love. And of wishes. And of flowers for the dead. Let us just drink to us.

They raise their glasses to drink.

ALEX: Jack, don't drink it!

SYLVIE: [*at the same time*] Jack, no! No!

She puts up her hand and stops him drinking. She and ALEX *look at each other, beaten.*

JACK: [*to* SYLVIE] What is going on? What are you two playing?

MOIRA: I want to drink to the spring when everything is born.

BERT: I just want to drink.

PEG: [*to* BERT] So young. [*To* ALEX] Is Jack drunk enough?

SYLVIE: Yes. Yes.

JACK: I've had nothing to drink.

SYLVIE: [*to* JACK] It's poisoned. [*Suddenly to* MOIRA] Isn't it? Isn't it?

MOIRA *laughs at her. She hands* ALEX *Tanya's bottle.*

ALEX: [*to* SYLVIE] No. We couldn't make the pattern. We could never do it.

MOIRA: [*to* SYLVIE] I couldn't be bothered.

MOIRA *goes on laughing.* SYLVIE *sits on the bed and plays with the flower, her head down.*

PEG: Would someone, some kind person, tell me where we are, what's going on?

ALEX: [*to* PEG] Something real—almost happened.

JACK: [*to* MOIRA] Are you all right?

MOIRA: [*laughing*] Look at her.

She points to SYLVIE.

SYLVIE: [*to* JACK] If you'd thought the drink was poisoned, poisoned for both of us, would you have?

MOIRA: [*to* JACK] She thought I'd try. Well, I thought of it.

SYLVIE: [*to* JACK] Would you have?

JACK: [*to* SYLVIE] I don't know.

ALEX: [*to* JACK, *triumphantly*] You wouldn't have, would you?

JACK: [*to* ALEX] No. But—

PEG: I think we should all have another drink. The conversation is far too uninhibited. Alex, the kitchen, the beer.

ALEX *goes into the kitchen.*

I don't approve of this modern passion for sincerity in other people's presence. Do you, Bert? Bert agrees. We like a little decency, and insincerity is a great help.

ALEX *returns with an open bottle or two.*

Alex, pour.

ALEX: [*acting*] 'Ganymede sells drinks!'

BERT *laughs at him.*

MOIRA: You all talk and sometimes I understand you and sometimes I don't. And it always sounds clever and you all keep laughing, so I have to listen. But it doesn't say anything; it doesn't go anywhere. It's only your talk. Not your life. It's not real life.

ALEX: What's real life?

MOIRA: I am. I'm going to have a baby.

ALEX: [*facetiously*] Whose?

MOIRA: Mine.

JACK: Moira—

SYLVIE: It's not Jack's.

MOIRA: No.

BERT: You shouldn't talk like that, Moira—

ALEX: [*laughing*] It's Bert! Good old Bert.

JACK: [*to* MOIRA] When?

MOIRA: Today.

PEG: [*to* MOIRA] But you can't know, dearie.

MOIRA: [*to* PEG] I do know. And if I'm wrong I don't care; I'll get someone else. I'm not pretty anymore, but I'm not old like you. I thought I couldn't, that I wasn't like her. But I can now. I know what I want. I've a right to have it. [*She puts a hand to her abdomen.*] And he'll be mine.

PEG: [*to* MOIRA] Oh, dear girl—

ALEX: [*nastily*] Bert's.

MOIRA: Mine.

BERT: You don't understand, Alex, it—

PEG: Shut up, Alex.

BERT: I'm sorry, Jack, I didn't mean—

PEG: We all know you couldn't help it, Bert. Now, for heaven's sake, be quiet.

MOIRA: [*to* JACK] You can go with her now. You can go with Alex. Or any of them. This is something you can't break. I'm free of you. Everything's changed. Well, go on. She's waiting.

JACK: [*to* MOIRA] You didn't— It was an accident. Bert— You met him. Bert—

MOIRA: Bert! I had to ring him four times. I had to make him drink. I had to flirt. Like her. I had to get a room; it was lucky I had money. Bert! It was me. Me.

The violin plays.

And the next time, if I need a next time, I'll use him again, or anyone, and the baby'll be mine.

JACK *falls on his knees by her chair, his back to the door.*

JACK: Moira. Moira.

ALEX *kneels spectacularly at her other side.*

ALEX: Mary. Irish Mary.

PEG: Well, we must be philosophical. Perhaps he'll be Shakespeare.

BERT: Not from me.

PEG: Who else? You see it is spring, just as I told you; and something is to be born, has been born. Moira. I said all along it was spring.

SYLVIE *has gone to the door, but* LORNA *appears at it, barring her way.* MOIRA *watches* SYLVIE.

SYLVIE: [*softly*] Give him this.

She gives LORNA *the flower.*

But not now, not now.

LORNA: [*taking it*] This. Everyone! What a surprise! The whole gang, the old gang, like the last scene in a vaudeville. Hello, Peg. [*To* JACK *and* ALEX] Are you praying?

ALEX: Yes.

He gets up. SYLVIE *goes out of the door while he is talking.* MOIRA *smiles.*

LORNA: And my darling Bert, the perfect gentleman. Have you been a good boy, Bert? Shall we dance? No. The music's not appropriate. Are you picking other people up? Hello, Alex. Alex. Now, speak nicely to me.

ALEX *notices the flower in her hand.*

ALEX: My flower for the dead.

LORNA: You don't look dead. I don't believe it's yours. Sylvie gave it to me. For him. Him, I suppose—Jack. [*She puts the flower between her teeth.*] Do I look like Carmen?

ALEX: No.

LORNA *gives the flower to* JACK.

JACK: [*to* LORNA] Where has she gone?

MOIRA: Jack.

PEG: She's gone, that's all.

MOIRA: Jack.

JACK: [*to* MOIRA] Yes? Yes. Yes.

He leans back with his head in MOIRA*'s lap. She strokes his hair.*

PEG: They all go, Bert. Only the wives or the old ones hang on.

JACK: [*softly*] Yes.

The *flower drops from his hand.*

LORNA: [*to* PEG, *while* JACK *is speaking*] Or me, of course.

PEG: [*to* LORNA] Of course.

ALEX: [*to* LORNA] I ought to marry you.

> BERT *points to* JACK.

BERT: [*softly, to* ALEX] You don't think he minds—
PEG: [*to* BERT] Why should he mind?

> BERT *is embarrassed.*

You've given him a new wife, and he's going to sleep. It's quieter. The music's stopped!

> *She drinks.*

MOIRA: [*to* JACK, *very softly*] Sleep. Sleep, bubba, sleep.
ALEX: [*singing*]

> Lully, lully, lully, lully;
> The falcon hath borne my mate away...

PEG: Enough, Alex. Alex, enough.
MOIRA: [*singing softly*]

> I found my bonny baby a nest
> On slumber tree,
> I hold him warm upon my breast,
> Lullay, lullee... [et cetera]

LORNA: My god, you're all drunk.
PEG: [*to* LORNA] Living.
ALEX: [*to* PEG] And partly living.
BERT: [*to* PEG] It must be the spring.

> *He drinks.*

ALEX: [*to* LORNA] We'll get married. I feel old.
LORNA: [*to* ALEX] I'm not sure that I want an old husband.
ALEX: I'll buy you a ring. Doesn't that tempt you? I've got enough money. [*He produces his inevitable roll.*] Not as much as yesterday.
LORNA: No.
ALEX: Let me buy you... Let me buy something.
LORNA: What about Peg?
PEG: [*to* LORNA] What about Peg? Peg's had her fun and now she's done with him, for a great part of the time.

> BERT *drinks, delighted.*

LORNA: [*to* ALEX] No.
BERT: Everyone ought to be married. It's the natural thing.
LORNA: He's a fool!
ALEX: What about it, Lorna? We could have fun. I'd come home in the evening from sweating all over a hot microphone. You'd bring me my slippers. I'd throw them at you. It'd be fun.
LORNA: I'm tired of fun. Why not stay here?
PEG: Tonight I'm engaged. Isn't that true, Bert?

BERT: I've got to get home.

PEG: The natural answer.

BERT: And—no offence meant—but you're not really my type. Everyone sticks to their type.

LORNA: [*sincerely*] Yes. It's a kind of fate.

BERT: Well, I have got to be going. The drink was good. [*He avoids* LORNA.] Goodnight, people, and— Jack, I'm—I'm—nothing. Bye.

> *He goes out.*

ALEX: How about it, Lorna? For ninety-six pounds. Not a bad bid.

LORNA: More than I'd get in a brothel. But then the work might be pleasanter there. Why have you changed? What do you want? Are you making fun of me? You've made me cry. Have a flower.

> *She picks up the flower from the floor.* PEG *takes it.*

PEG: He gave it to me.

ALEX: No. That's my flower for the dead—Sylvie's flower, Jack's, mine.

PEG: Mine.

> ALEX *clicks his heels and bows to her. He turns to* LORNA.

ALEX: [*with a French accent*] *Mademoiselle*, may I have the honour of asking your papa for the hand in marriage? Is not that correct? A bachelor's life is terrible hard. I'm lonely.

LORNA: She's lonely. I'm lonely. Everyone's lonely. It's not a good bid.

PEG: [*to* LORNA] You don't think I'd ever bring him his slippers, do you? Why, I'm old enough to spank him with them. It would be—why, for us to be together, for a great part of the time; that would be—grotesque. It would make Bert laugh. Not the natural thing at all. And I'd find it very boring.

MOIRA: [*while* PEG *is speaking, to* JACK] Lie there, lie there, and one day you'll hear him…

ALEX: You know me too well, Peg. There's nothing to find out. That's what marriage is for: to find each other out.

LORNA: All right, I will. Tomorrow. Tomorrow, understand. Not the next day. Oh, it'll have to be the next day. I'll have to buy things. Give me that money.

> *She snatches it from him.*

And I'll invite Mother. If you won't agree to Mother at the wedding, then I won't go through with it. She's waited long enough; she deserves some pleasure. Do you agree or don't you?

> *He has had no chance to speak.*

No. The whole thing's ridiculous. It wouldn't be any good. I love you.

ALEX: I need someone.

LORNA: Anyone. You're used to me and I've put the idea in your head; you never think for yourself. Except when you're hurt. And then you're mean. I couldn't stand it, not all of the time.

PEG: She knows you, too.

ALEX: [*appealing*] Jack?

JACK: [*not looking up, without expression*] You're all right, Alex.

   A pause.

ALEX: Yes. I am all right. Look at me! My own head. My own legs. My own teeth; I've paid for them. And I don't care if you marry me or not. It would probably be inconvenient; your mother, at any rate, sounds so. And if we are to be married, I won't have her there. I want you. I want you there. And I want you at home, for when I'm tired, when I want to sleep or throw my slippers. So will you kindly stop this nonsense and come with me, now or never.

LORNA: Yes.

   MARINA *enters. She is dressed in fresh clothes. Her hair is neater than before, more conventionally done. She is happy.*

ALEX: Ah! I'm saved!

PEG: You could call it that.

   LORNA *stops herself from calling to* ALEX, *who grabs* MARINA.

MARINA: Alex. Alex.

ALEX: My dear. My darling dear, don't, don't explain. I needed a miracle, and you came.

MARINA: Oh, Alex, Alex, I'm engaged.

   She waves her left hand. ALEX *silences* LORNA *with a glance.*

ALEX: Break it!

MARINA: He works in the accounts office. I'm not going to break it. I'm going to be married. But I just had to see you because—just because. I've been thinking hard and I know what I want. I want to be still. I want someone who likes me. I want a nice house. I don't want thin walls and lives mixed up. I don't want to be clever. I don't want to be drunk. I—I came looking for you, though, because I'm in love with you.

ALEX: Well, then?

MARINA: If I'd found you alone, by yourself, lonely, then I'm not sure. I might have thought— But I'm not taken in. It was worth chasing round to find him, to see him. I was afraid— But it turns out I'm over you, or nearly over you. I'll be a good wife.

ALEX: 'You'll never be free. Trilby, look into my eyes.'

MARINA: Don't joke about it, Alex; it's so serious to me, even though I keep wanting to laugh. He's awfully nice, but he's got a moustache. There was someone with a moustache outside on the landing! I've always liked him, confided in him sometimes— But I never once thought of him, not in this way; I never imagined— [*Laughing outright*] His moustache tickles.

ALEX: You do seem to have been busy. None of you waste time.

JACK: [*lazily*] They win and they win...

MARINA: Oh, Alex, I love you. I love you and I'm free.

> *She gives* ALEX *a hug.*

ALEX: Unhand me, madam! Lorna! Peg, make Lorna have me.

PEG: Oh, you're impossible. Lorna, just listen to him. Never a thought for—No one means anything. Only his vanity. If you love him, run. Run far away. It's too shameful to love. It's nothing but shame. Do you want him?

LORNA: [*to* PEG] I won't be happy.

ALEX: [*to* LORNA] What's happy to do with it? Lorna, my love, my lady, my life—in a sense—I'm not asking for a comfortable wife with moustaches for my declining years. Leave that to Marina. I need a friend who'll believe me. Who remembers me. You can come, you can go. You can sorrow, you can joy. I mightn't be interested. I mightn't help. But I'll be there. We'll be like friends.

LORNA: I am shameless. Peg, I'm shameless. On any terms, I'll take him.

MOIRA: I knew she would.

LORNA: I would have all along, on any terms.

MARINA: We could have a double wedding—

> ALEX *glares at her.*

—but Rupie—his name's Rupert; he mightn't approve.

ALEX: [*delighted, crowing*] Rupert the Rooster, the Rhode Island Red!

MARINA: It's funny, isn't it? Not you, Alex. It's funny how everything's settled. I used to despise the idea that girls should end in marriage; that all of them wanted the *Woman's Weekly* stuff.

LORNA: You should kiss me, Alex. It's my right. I've got witnesses.

ALEX: It's all of it beginning.

> *He kisses her cheek.*

PEG: Let me kiss the bride.

> *She holds* LORNA.

Yes... yes.

LORNA: Thank you, Peg.

ALEX: [*to* PEG, *cheerfully*]
> You, an old turtle,
> Will wing you to some wither'd bough, and there
> Your mate, that's never to be found again,
> Lament till you are lost.

Sorry. I wasn't thinking, just the tune—I am a brute.

PEG: There's no need to boast. You might make me cry.

ALEX: And marriage isn't so definite.

LORNA: [*firmly*] You know nothing about marriage, yet.

ALEX: You see, it is beginning.

PEG: Such a sentimental scene!

LORNA: I'm a sentimental person.

MARINA: We're sentimental people. But isn't it nice? What I mean is— Well, isn't it nice?

There is a shot from upstairs. A pause.

PEG: A car. In the street. Backfiring. It must be.

ALEX: [*certain, joyful*] It was a gun. A rifle.

A pause. JACK *goes from the room.*

MOIRA: [*worried*] Jack—

PEG: Melodramatic people.

MARINA: It must have been a car—

PEG: Upstairs.

ALEX: It was a rifle.

PEG: I remember I had a friend who collected guns. He was showing them to Jimmy Henderson. Jim only had two fingers on his left hand—something messy to do with farms; a combine, I think. Jim was looking at a prize piece, a French pistol it was. Yes, it must have been French; it looked terribly wicked. A car backfired. Jim fainted. When he came to, he swore that he'd had three fingers on his hand. He still swears so; but it was only a car. It *was* only a car?

JACK has returned. He carries a violin.

JACK: It's the kid upstairs.

PEG: Ah.

JACK: He shot himself. With a rifle. In the mouth.

PEG: [*wearily*] Why? Why? Why?

ALEX: No answer.

PEG: It's too cruel.

MOIRA: He was all alone. He didn't have anyone.

ALEX: [*to* MOIRA] Don't cheapen it. He didn't need anyone.

JACK holds out the violin.

JACK: [*to* PEG] This was outside your door. I nearly fell over it. I suppose it's a present. There's no note or anything. Not that I could see. There's a paper in his room, the news. Perhaps it was the state of the world.

MARINA: Perhaps it was love.

JACK: [*to* MARINA, *seriously*] No.

ALEX takes the violin.

ALEX: The violin. His violin. The instrument of torture. No one plays?

He plucks the strings.

LORNA: Don't!

MOIRA: Leave it alone.

PEG: It's mine.

> *She takes it from him.*

MARINA: I never knew him.

JACK: He's messy now.

MARINA: [*quickly*] But I'm sure he played very nicely. Not always correctly, not very well—but very nicely.

PEG: You had better go, Alex. We can't have our star involved in two accidents. That's like real life. Jack. Ring the police. I'll go up and wash him.

JACK: [*to* PEG] It's not very pretty.

ALEX: [*to* PEG] They won't want him touched.

PEG: [*determined*] Pretty doesn't matter. What they want doesn't matter.

JACK: [*brutally*] There's nothing left of his face to wash. [*A pause.*] I'm sorry. [*To* MOIRA] Are you all right?

PEG: Then I'm—then we're all of us quite useless. Alive, and quite useless. I used to be useful. I'm sure I was useful once. Life giving. Wasn't that your word, Alex? Wasn't that the word?

JACK: [*before* PEG *has finished, to* MOIRA] Are you all right?

MOIRA: Yes. Yes.

JACK: Because I'm going now. I'm going to the phone. And I'm not coming back. I'm going away from you. Away from this house and its talking, away from Alex and his friends. I don't want any of you. I can't change you, and I can't commit suicide. I'm not coming back.

MOIRA: [*to* JACK] You're going to that girl.

LORNA: [*surprised*] Sylvie?

JACK: Sylvie! Yes. Yes—Sylvie.

MOIRA: [*to* JACK] All right. Go. I've got what I want. I don't mind waiting. Nine months isn't forever. But you won't like it, you know. You'll have to work, get a job. To keep her and to keep me, to keep me and my baby. I'll see that you do. I've got my rights, and any baby I have could be yours. The law's on my side. I'll make you pay. You can work nine-to-five, like everyone else. I'll be all right. Go if you want to, but one day you'll come back.

JACK: [*seriously questioning*] Will I?

MOIRA: Yes, she's not strong enough for you. She'll get in your way, more than I do. She'll make you mad. She won't remember. Then you'll come back.

> JACK *looks at her for a long time.*

JACK: Perhaps you're right. We'll see.

> *He goes out.*

MOIRA: Yes, we'll see… I'll see. I'm not crying.

ALEX: Moira, you're a woman.

LORNA: Alex. Come here.

MOIRA: A week. A month. That's all.

PEG: Life giving. Wasn't that the word? [*She holds the violin.*] He didn't have a week, a month. It makes it seem urgent. The police will be here soon, Alex. Take Lorna away. No, there's no sense in your staying. There's no reason why everyone should be mixed up in a catastrophe; such an insignificant death really. I wonder if his mother will cry? Alex, when they come, what am I to say?

ALEX: What I said about Tanya. Learn from my experience. Nothing. There's nothing to say.

PEG: There never is, is there? We'll do what we have to do.

ALEX: Be like Moira. Wait.

> *He goes to the door.*

LORNA: That's what I did.

ALEX: It's what all women do.

MARINA: Yes, it is, isn't it?

MOIRA: And you win in the end.

> ALEX *goes off.*

PEG: I wonder if I do.

LORNA: [*sighing*] Probably.

> *She follows* ALEX.

MOIRA: I know that I will.

THE END